Organizational Careers:
Some New Perspectives

Theories of Group Processes
Edited by Cary Cooper,
University of Manchester Institute of Science & Technology

Task and Organization
Edited by Eric J. Miller,
The Tavistock Institute of Human Relations

**Creating a Community of Inquiry: Conflict,
Collaboration, Transformation**
William R. Torbert,
Graduate School of Education,
Harvard University

**Organizational Careers: Some
New Perspectives**
Edited by John Van Maanen,
Sloan School of Management
Massachusetts Institute of Technology

Organizational Careers: Some New Perspectives

Edited by

John Van Maanen

Sloan School of Management
Massachusetts Institute of Technology

JOHN WILEY & SONS

London · New York · Sydney · Toronto

Library of Congress Cataloging in Publication Data:
Main entry under title:

Organizational careers.

  (Wiley series on individuals, groups, and organizations)
    1. Executives—Addresses, essays, lectures.
2. Organization—Addresses, essays, lectures.   3. Industrial sociology—Addresses, essays, lectures.   I. Van
Maanen, John,
HF5500.084   658.4 0023   76–13537

ISBN 0 471 99409 ×

Photosetting by Thomson Press (India) Limited, New Delhi,
and printed at Unwin Brothers Limited, The Gresham Press, Old Woking, Surrey.

Editorial Foreword to the Series

Over the last decade, there has been an emormous growth of interest in the social and psychological aspects of institutional and organizational life. This has been reflected in a substantial upsurge in research and training in the field of organizational behaviour particularly in Institutes of Higher Education and Research throughout the Western World. Attention in this development has focused on the interrelationship between the individual, the variety of groups to which he belongs and the organizational environment within which he and his group operate.

The purpose of this series is to examine the social and psychological processes of these interrelationships, that is the nexus of individual/personal development, group processes and organizational behaviour and change. Within this context, a wide range of topics will be covered. These will include: the individual, his role and the organization; multiple roles and role conflict; the impact of group processes on personal and organizational development; strategies for 'humanizing' the organizational environment to meet individual and group needs; and the influence of technical and economic factors on organizational life.

The series will attempt to draw together the main schools of organizational behaviour including, for example, the American behavioural science tradition as reflected by Harvard, UCLA and National Training Laboratories, and the British socio-technical and open systems approaches of the Tavistock Institute of Human Relations. It is hoped that this will add significantly to understanding the distinctive characteristics of the various approaches and also provide a link between them through which individual, group and organizational behaviour can be seen in fuller perspective.

CARY COOPER
ERIC MILLER

Preface

This book is about lives in progress. The work presented here represents, we think, important new directions leading toward a richer understanding of the relationship between the individual and the organization. It is our hope that this book will be of use to students and laymen alike interested in the nature of organizational careers. More importantly, we hope that our work will provide members of organizations some insight into the dynamics associated with their own careers, creating perhaps a deeper sensitivity to the issues raised by participation in the work world. Such a sensitivity is indeed a prerequisite for the perceptive choice and design of career paths which amplify human capabilities rather than diminish them. At the time these chapters were written, all authors were members of the Organization Studies faculty of the Sloan School of Management at the Massachusetts Institute of Technology. The idea for this book grew from an Industrial Liaison Program Symposium on Career Development held at M.I.T. in May, 1974. To some degree, we viewed the Symposium as an excellent opportunity to come together before a questioning audience to reflect upon and assess our collective work. Aside from the manifest purpose of sharing our research concerns with interested representatives of public and private organizations, we also wanted to see to what extent our individual conceptual and empirical work was or was not convergent. Certainly there existed a sort of dim awareness among us that we were indeed overlapping in some areas, but questions concerning where and in what manner were just beginning to be asked. In no way were we—nor are we—part of an integrated and focused research effort. To the contrary, we have all worked largely on our own, linked intellectually only by a common interest in the varieties of work experience. Consequently, it was something of a surprise to discover that given the career as a sort of leitmotif, our separate work could be put together usefully and that it in fact made sense to do so.

I do not want to leave the impression, however, that we see no conceptual problems with the merging of our work. This is not the case. There are a number of issues on which we are at odds with one another. While some of these points can be answered empirically, others cannot, for they represent—as the chapters themselves best demonstrate—different philosophical and epistemological viewpoints. Also, we work in very different research styles—some of us prefer to use social surveys, others personal observations, some in-depth interviews to gather data. Yet, I suspect that we would all readily agree that we can and have learned from one another and that in the long-run, it is perhaps best—not to mention that it is also more exciting—to follow several research paths for there is no singularly ideal way to study careers.

Two points should be kept in mind when reading the following chapters. First, as implied above, we have not tried to consciously coordinate our efforts. Each chapter presents a set of variables that provide a more or less unique way of looking at careers. For most of us, this was our initial attempt to speak directly to career oriented issues. And, as of now, we have only the vaguest of notions about how these variables might be combined. Second, with a few significant exceptions, we do not try to draw out practical implications — managerial or otherwise — from our work. This is not a collection of 'how-to-' papers. To make applied suggestions would be in most cases premature. While we have some normative views on the processes of development and socialization during the early phases of an individual's organizational or occupational career, we know considerably less about such matters during the middle and late phases of the career. In general then, these papers show that the world is infinitely more complex than any one of our models and much work remains to be accomplished before practical implications will become apparent.

Finally, I wish to convey the gratitude of the authors represented here to all those involved in one way or another with the publication of this book. In particular, Colleen McCallion deserves special recognition for interrupting her 'Realwork' to provide able technical assistance in the preparation of the manuscript. She proofread much of the copy, designed the graphics, and helped in that thankless task of index construction. Much credit as well is due Dilip Mathur, director of the Industrial Liason Program at MIT. He contributed an enormous amount of time and energy to organizing and running the career symposium which provoked the writing of these chapters in the first place. Perhaps it is also safe to say that without the gentle urgings and support of those who attended the symposium this collection would not have appeared. Their enthusiastic response was, in fact, unexpected, but it served to signify to us that we were indeed working on something of value. Since our own careers have taken on a new dimension through this effort, we extend our appreciation.

JOHN VAN MAANEN
Cambridge, Massachusetts
January, 1976

About the Authors

RICHARD BECKHARD is an active consultant concerned with the application of behavioral science knowledge and technology to the management of organizations and institutions. In addition to MIT, he has taught at Columbia, UCLA and the London School of Economics. He is the author of numerous articles and several books, the most widely read of which is *Organizational Development: Strategies and Models*. Currently, he is concerned with the management of health care systems and the strategies appropriate for large-system change.

LOTTE BAILYN has written extensively on various career problems experienced by professional men and women as well as the implications certain careers have upon family and work adjustment. She has taught both at Harvard University and MIT. Her special interests include dual career families, research methodology, and the patterns of work involvement. She is currently completing a book (along with Edgar H. Schein) concerned with technically-based careers.

RALPH KATZ is interested in leadership processes, quantitative methods, and the organizational properties of state and local governments. He has published several articles concerned with job satisfaction and role redesign and is currently working on a manuscript (along with John Van Maanen) dealing with the nature of work in the public sector.

PETER KEEN is concerned with the implications that differences in cognitive style have upon individual and group problem solving and more particularly the impact such differences have upon the effective use of computers and analytic techniques. He has taught at Harvard University, MIT, and is currently teaching at Stanford University. His published work includes several articles dealing with the design of computer-based aids to support managerial decision-making. Most recently, he organized and chaired an international conference on the implementation of computer systems and models.

DAVID KOLB is concerned primarily with individual learning styles and the influence such styles may have upon behavior. He has taught, in addition to MIT, at Harvard University, the London School of Business, and is currently the director of the Institute for Developmental Research in Cambridge, Massachusetts. He has written numerous research articles and coauthored several books including *Organizational Psychology: an Experiential Approach* and *Changing Human Behavior: Principles of Planned Intervention*.

MARK PLOVNICK is interested primarily in learning styles, the delivery of health care, and the management of organizational change. He has written several articles concerned with the education and training of health care professionals and is currently involved in a large-scale project seeking to improve the quality of medical services in the greater Boston area.

EDGAR SCHEIN is the Chairman of the Organizational Studies group at MIT. He has written extensively on the topics of individual change in adult life and behavior in organizations. Several of his better known books include: *Coercive Persuasion, Organizational Psychology,* and *Process Consultation.* He is presently at work on a manuscript concerned with issues in career development.

JOHN VAN MAANEN has contributed to several books and journals on topics concerning urban policing, public bureaucracies, and socialization processes in large organizations. He is the author of a short book on *The Process of Program Evaluation.* His research interests include ethnographic studies and the sociology of occupations. Currently he is at work on a manuscript concerned with the forms, functions, and content of organizational socialization processes.

Contents

PART I. TOWARD A THEORY OF THE CAREER IN EVERYDAY LIFE

PART II. UNDERSTANDING ORGANIZATIONAL CAREERS AND INDIVIDUAL DIFFERENCES

PART III. THE INDIVIDUAL'S ORIENTATION TOWARD WORK ACROSS THE CAREER

Introduction:
The Promise of Career Studies

John Van Maanen

AN OVERVIEW

A career, like a culture, is something we all have but often fail to recognize. Although it represents a familiar concept we almost automatically employ in our society, the commonsensical use of the term is somewhat peculiar. In fact, most people, when pressed, would find it difficult perhaps to define the word 'career' outside a given context.

To the ancient Greeks, the term career referred to a fast paced running of a course—some sort of race. And today a vestige of the original use remains in the verb form of the word, as in 'to career' a horse. But conventional usage is considerably more slippery. At times, the term career is used to convey upward occupational mobility—e.g. the route taken by a person to the executive suite as in the 'business career'. Other times, it is used to imply occupational stability—e.g. the lifetime occupation of a person as in the 'career soldier'. Both usages have in common, however, the notion of continuity or consistency. Whether stable or mobile, the career represents an organized or patterned path taken by an individual across time and space.

The career then is simply a series of separate but related experiences and adventures through which a person passes during a lifetime. It can be long or short and, of course, an individual can pursue multiple careers either in rough sequence or at the same time. In this sense, the concept is descriptive not normative. It is shorthand notation for a particular set of activities with a natural, unfolding history—involvement over time in a given role or across a series of roles. A career can be either brilliant or disappointing, a success or a failure. In the work world, therefore, prostitutes, plumbers, doctors, factory workers, managers, housewives, bartenders, waitresses, lawyers, criminals, and cops all have careers. What is most significant about a person's career is, however, the degree to which it serves as the principle around which the individual organizes his or her life. And this depends not only upon the status, direction, tempo, and length of the career, but upon the meaning the individual ascribes to the career as well.[1]

Perhaps in simpler times, the notion of an individual choosing to pursue a particular line of work was irrelevant. One's career was by and large a perfectly predictable outcome of one's position in the traditional order of things—taken for granted as an irrevocable feature of everyday life. Whether peasant, artisan, or aristocrat, a person's life work was determined at birth. An individual imposed little separation among various pursuits because one's station in life was the fundamental reality around which family, work, and social activities were organized—the many roles played by the person being, as it were, fused together. A career in such a context is redundant to one's more or less fixed location in society, an issue therefore of little concern to the individual.

The concept of *Gemeinschaft* as utilized by the early sociologists captures this non-problematic sense of career nicely.[2] In *Gemeinschaft* society, the individual is fully incorporated or integrated within a social network which by and large defines who he is, what he is to do, and how he is to do it. The development of individualism is minimal. Relationships among people, whether based upon neighborhood, kinship, or friendship, are characterized by shared sentiments, values, and beliefs. Experiences in the work sphere of a person's life cannot easily be split from experiences in nonwork spheres for there is an absence of an institutional differentiation between the two. The community embraces its members such that all activity rests upon convention and agreement. Thus the notion of an individual choosing certain work is essentially alien to the *Gemeinschaft* world. The person simply orients his or her activity to the community at large—a social order based upon consensual folkways, mores, and religion. Indeed, children in such a society can see in their parents and grandparents a fairly precise image of themselves grown older— thereby achieving a sure sense of the future that awaits them.

It is only with the coming of relationships based on individual exchange and calculation rather than mutual trust and knowledge that work itself becomes problematic to a person. This shift in social relationships is associated with the momentous historical transition of nineteenth century Western society from its communal and medieval character to its present competitive and industrial form. In place of the old *Gemeinschaft* orientation of the workman to his work, upon which Nisbet (1967) remarked 'the person gives himself limitlessly to his job without calculation of its time or compensation', there arises the *Gesellschaft* orientation in which the workman strives primarily for his own advantage. Individualism is highly developed and work, in modern society, can be approached in an instrumental manner for it is separable in theory and practice from other spheres of a person's life.

This transformation of perspective from the *Gemeinschaft* to the *Gesellschaft* represents, as numerous writers have observed, an impressive victory for philosophies based on rationalism. No longer is the world a place where the present is indistinguishable from the past. Volunteeristic beliefs replace deterministic ones and we see ourselves making choices that affect the course of our lives. In the world of work, for example, the ever expanding list of job titles suggests to the individual that career possibilities abound. Indeed, nowadays, few children enter the occupations of their parents. In a world thus disenchanted, the person in theory can master all things. A planned career is therefore possible for the choices we make in the present can be seen to have recognizable, if probabilistic, consequences in the future.

From the eyes of the beholder, a career can provide order and meaning to the events and relationships in which the person is involved. Certainly, in this society, these experiences are closely tied to the institutional context in which the person moves. Hence the suggestion by Hughes (1958) that 'a man's work is as good a clue as any to the course of his life and his social being and identity' has been taken quite seriously by social scientists. This concern for individuals and their work has led to an enormous amount of study regarding, for example, the association between occupations and personality types, or the connection between the division of labor and individual work attitudes, or the process by which occupations and organizations are included within a person's self-image.

One recent byproduct of this somewhat eclectic concern for the individual in the workplace is the realization that change must be central to any account of the person's relationship to a job. To understand this relationship at any one point in time requires knowledge of the changes that typically occur in a person's life and psychology as a result of passage through the life cycle. Career lines are not to be forged absolutely through the process of simply joining an organization or selecting an occupation. Rather the nuances of membership, participation, and progression are always in various stages of revision and negotiation. People change, as do organizations. In short, to study careers is to study change itself.

WHY STUDY CAREERS?

There are at least as many reasons to try to understand careers as there are careers. Let me suggest here, however, that there are two major or pivotal concerns that provide a sort of scientific pedigree for career-related research. First—and perhaps of most importance—the career concept is central to a concern for individual identity. As recent work has made abundantly clear, any account of adult personality must allow for perpetual change within the individual of either subtle or dramatic character. Experiences provide the raw material from which a sense of the self grows and experience is unceasing. To paraphrase Erickson's (1950) now classic statement, identity is never gained once and for all but is achieved continuously over a lifetime. Thus, while we cannot fail to recognize that each moment of life possesses its own inherent value, personal identity is built on the dimension of time and emphasizes both the continuity and discontinuity of experience.

Time and identity are what the notion of a career so nicely conveys. To develop an empathetic understanding of the individual, we must have some idea of the person's experienced past and anticipated future. More specifically, to grasp certain situationally denoted constructs such as 'work involvement' or 'job satisfaction', we must view people within their careers—a context that explicitly directs attention toward the changing patterns of involvement or satisfaction. And even the most casual concern for these patterns suggests that they cannot be studied apart from personal experiences occurring within the individual's nonwork spheres of life—notably those which take place in the person's immediate family. To highlight this point, the interest expressed of late in what has been called the 'mid-career crisis' suggests that a growing number of people, at certain points in time, critically reassess and significantly rearrange their work role, personal career, and total life situation. Certainly we cannot begin to understand these Protean turning points unless we study career processes which promote such alterations.

In important ways, the study of careers forces the analyst to tie together the interrelated and interdependent concepts of role, reference group, expectation, motivation, and identity. When examining work careers, for example, stress must necessarily be placed upon the manner in which selected others are crucial in supporting one's valued self-image as well as the manner in which the self-image itself is shaped. Career studies fundamentally involve an examination of the successive minor and major changes in a person's life—changes such that persons may find themselves at some point in time quite different from what they were before. Consequently, career research entails a consideration of both the process and structure involved in identity-bestowing and identity-changing situations.

The second and, for the most part, complimentary theoretical interest that is served by the study of work careers revolves around the research into the nature and workings of complex organizations. In large measure, organizations cannot be understood unless we first have at least a rudimentary conception of the values, beliefs, and behavior styles of the people located in various positions within the organization. And these values, beliefs, and behavior styles are related most clearly to the training and subsequent careers of individuals. Unfortunately, a concern for the careers of people—particularly power holders—is a key missing feature in all but a few organizational studies.[3]

Within this context, an emerging trend in large, bureaucratic organizations seems to be decreasing reliance on control through the fixed chain of command and an increasing tendency to rely more on indirect or remote kinds of control. Some prevailing indirect mechanisms are based on various incentive systems that have explicit career implications—e.g. bonus plans, retirement packages, automatic pay increases, and so on. Even more significant is the emphasis upon control through recruitment, promotion, and transfer. Using the career as an unobtrusive form of control has the advantage of seeming more legitimate than a system based on fist or fiat. Not only is such a system likely to excite less resistance from organizational members, it may work more smoothly.[4] As Blau and Schoenherr (1971) suggest, 'slave drivers have gone out of fashion not because they were so cruel but because they were so inefficient.'

Relatedly, in many organizations, the criteria for selection and advancement can be seen to set the premises and define the parameters within which the decision-making of organizational members is confined. Indeed, organizations are relying more and more upon the judgements of those presumed to have 'professional expertise'. This is based not only on the increased complexity of the environments in which organizations operate, but also upon the growing awareness that the efforts of people are channelled more effectively by mobilizing a person's expressive commitment to the work than by coercion or instrumental exchange. This opens the door for an insidious form of control over the organization itself, as well as over the participants. The form is insidious because it arises out of the background, training, and assumptions carried by the organizational experts and is not easily identified or counteracted. One result of this growing dependence upon professional judgement is that decisions such as laying off workers or investing corporate funds are made on the normative grounds of technical efficiency absorbed by experts during their lengthy professional, occupational, and/or organizational socialization (Salaman and Thompson, 1973). Hence, many decisions are often only rational in the most local sense—serving the organization but not the society.

The promise of career studies lies in learning substantially more about why both individuals and organizations act as they do. On the one hand, the career represents to the person an opportunity and a constraint. The ability to look ahead in terms of a career perspective may be a real source of inspiration and value for some people, for others, it may be a curse, a source of discontent, and even dispair. But, on the other hand, organizational problems are not necessarily the same as those faced by the individual. As Weberian bureaucratic theory details, things are accomplished by organizations in part because people are concerned about their careers.[5] Consequently, the career must also be seen as a significant feature of the regularity imposed by organizations.

THEORETICAL FOUNDATIONS

Work careers have become a topic of considerable scholarly attention. Not insignificantly, they are also a subject of increasing popular concern.[6] Yet, research into the various aspects of careers has not simply appeared overnight, omnipresent and unannounced. There is a long standing, if not distinguished, tradition in the social sciences that has provided at least the embryonic framework for this emerging area of study.

A theory of occupational choice, one which would be equally useful for guidance and counseling as well as selection and placement, has long been the concern of many psychologists and social psychologists. Although specific models have taken sundry forms, there are, according to Lancashire (1971), two classes of occupational choice theories. One such class can be called the differentialist view. This perspective places primary concentration upon the diversity of talents, abilities, and psychological endowments existing among people. Choice is seen as a kind of matching process. The differentialist aim is to build a theory which will allow jobs and people to be described by use of the same sorts of terms. Satisfaction and stability of occupational choice is judged then by the congruence between the two sets of terms for any one individual. Such theories usually rely heavily upon biological and psychoanalytic concepts for elaboration and explanation. Thus, patterns of ability, interest, style, and disposition are seen to be shaped early in life and although modifications can occur, they are slight. The work of Roe (1957) and Holland (1966) are excellent examples of this perspective.

In contrast, some psychologists have attempted to redress what they feel to be the static unyielding quality of the classifying and matching model. These theorists employ what has been labeled a developmental perspective. The view implies that occupational choice is not something which occurs at one point in time, but rather represents an evolving sequence of individual decisions. Choice, from this standpoint, is a more or less irreversible process of limiting decisions beginning with a person's first childish fantasies about work and ending with reflections or retirement. Occupational identity is seen as part of the individual's wider development or what could be called 'the confrontation of work in living'. Examples of this view can best be seen in the work of Ginzberg and coworkers (1951) and Super and coworkers (1963).

Differentialists have concentrated by and large upon searching for personality correlates of occupations. Their studies tend to reflect not only the psychoanalytic bent, but a psychometric one as well. And indeed a whole industry has been founding on the advising, selecting, testing, recruiting, and assessing of individuals in the workplace—an industry deeply indebted to the various diagnostic devices for vocational interest and ability. The sources for developmentalist theory and practice, however, have been the writings of educational, child, and cognitive psychologists concerned with general identity formation. Lifestages such as growth exploration, establishment, maintenance, and decline, are used as the starting point by many theorists interested in a development approach to the work career (Super, 1957). The main aim here seems to be the construction of a theory which establishes norms for thought and behavior at various chronological ages. While developmentalists have been less devoted to the narrow scientific approach of the differentialists, their theories have been looser, almost metaphoric, less subject to empirical test.

A third strain of psychological theorizing—organizational psychology—can also be distinguished. Organizational psychologists have devoted substantial attention to the problems which stem from a person's involvement in the work milieu. For example, issues such as supervisor-subordinate relationships, work motivation and satisfaction, performance measurement and evaluation, and communications and decision-making patterns have been central concerns of this field (see Schein, 1970; Leavitt, 1972; Porter, Lawler, and Hackman, 1974). However, all too often, organizational psychologists focus on areas of study that are oriented solely towards managerial problems and priorities— such as efficiency and effectiveness. By concentrating on the official objectives of the organization, organizational psychologists tend to emphasize implicitly, if not explicitly, the point of view of people working *for* the organization rather than the point of view of people worked *on* by organizations. Career studies, by their very nature, must be about people who are exposed—as we all are—to actual organizational treatment in their everyday lives, people who constitute the raw materials of the organization and are its customers, workers, clients, inmates, managers, beneficiaries, and sometimes victims.

More generally, psychologists, by focusing most of their attention upon mental processes, have tended to neglect the considerable limitations of economic and social factors on the individual—although they sometimes apologize for doing so during those times in which people are less concerned with the problem of choosing appropriate work than they are with that of simply finding any work at all. Sociologists, from their beginnings, have taken a completely different track. In fact, sociologists as a rule give slight attention to the question of occupational choice because they feel that by the time race, class, sex, religion, nationality, education, family, and area of residence have played out their respective parts, not only has the range of individual choice been severely restricted, but so also have individual expectations. Consequently, rather than concentrating upon the person, sociologists focus upon the setting in which the person carves out a career.

There are essentially three distinct, although overlapping, sociological approaches to the study of work careers. The three approaches resemble subdisciplines and can be labeled industrial sociology, the sociology of occupations, and organization theory. Each approach typically asks different questions, employs different models, and is concerned for the most part with different groups of people—industrial sociology with workers, occupational sociology with all members of a particular occupation, and organization theory with managers and professionals (Salaman and Thompson, 1973). Each area tends to consider its subject matter (workers, managers, or whatever) as a relatively homogeneous group whose most significant characteristic is that covered by the sociological specialty. Thus, organization theorists consider membership in the organization as crucial while industrial sociologists typically consider membership in a task-specific category as most salient. And, of course, occupational sociologists deem membership in a particular occupation and its associated subculture as the primary determinant of behavior. Although this academic division of labor is a source of strength, broadening our perspective on work careers, it is also a weakness. The fact is that people are usually members of all three categories at once. To restrict one's attention to just one of the categories is unnecessarily limiting.

Yet sociologists have contributed in critical ways to the study of careers. Each subdiscipline, in its own manner, emphasizes the individual's discovery of common elements in a particular role through the process by which one learns the norms and values of participation in a specified work world. Whereas psychologists often have a very unrealistic perspective on the actual requirements of certain careers, sociologists have developed rich descriptions of what it is like to be on the inside of certain occupations. Certainly sociologists have compelled us to recognize that what is claimed as the essence or critical function of a particular career is sometimes little more than rhetorical justification for occupational status and prestige, an ideology bearing little relationship to what people do within the career (e.g. Wilensky, 1964; Goode, 1957, 1969; Vollmer and Mills (Ed.), 1966). But perhaps the greatest contribution of the sociological approach concerns the ellusive nature of reality—it does not, as

Marx reportedly said, 'stalk about with a label'. Indeed, there are multiple realities available for personal use and choosing one depends upon the complex interaction of the individual and a concrete situation. A career therefore is a relative phenomenon, one which must be viewed from a variety of perspectives or frames of reference.

Historically, the two career frames of reference—psychological and sociological—have remained remarkably independent. One comes away from reviewing the career-related literature with a sense of frustration at the dearth of cross-referencing. Although there are undoubtedly good institutional reasons for such a limited theoretical accounting of the career, the situation is just short of appalling. While psychologists have been busy developing conceptual measurement tools like the Strong Vocational Interest test or the Kuder Occupational Preference blank, sociologists have been busy infiltrating occupations and organizations trying to discover general properties of the work experiences of people. There exists, therefore, a curious contrast between the two approaches—on the one hand, we have psychologists saying essentially that 'people make careers' and, on the other hand, sociologists claiming that 'careers make people'.

What is required of course is a focus which shifts from an inordinate concentration on occupational roles or personality characteristics, to one that emphasizes the career itself as an object of inquiry. Researchers must begin to study both sides of the coin—the detailed study of the individual and individual differences with the detailed study of the occupational setting and the issues that participation in the setting raise for the people who are in it. Fundamentally, to seriously study careers requires a profound respect for the dialectic quality of human experience. Man is both the creator and the determined. An excessive commitment to either a position emphasizing an ordered world of constraint, manipulation, and conformity, or a position accentuating man's capacity for growth, vision, and originality, would be a mistake.[7] What is needed, indeed demanded, is the recognition of the unfolding character of social life viewed from within a framework that explicitly includes the many roles a person is called upon to play.[8]

Perhaps the best direction in which to proceed at this moment is to begin constructing a framework upon which an interdisciplinary study of careers can rest. Certainly we must continue exploring the processes and settings in which people discover careers as well as building learning theories which relate experience to cognition. But we also must cast our methodological and conceptual nets such that they capture the meaning people attach to actual situations and not simply catch the meaning of those of us employed to carry out research on such situations. Theoretical abstraction and statistical elegance are not the goals, but rather the means by which we can better understand the various shapes, properties, and meanings a career can have.

A PREVIEW

The chapters to follow represent at least a tentative start toward building a comprehensive perspective on careers. This is not to say that each particular work does not reflect the disciplinary base and problem interest of its author—for certainly each chapter is bounded by such considerations. Yet, there is a welcome recognition on the part of the authors of the complexity of the situation surrounding individuals. No claims are made for instance regarding the 'one-best-way' to study careers, nor do any of the authors argue for the bedrock utility of using a particular set of variables to describe the contingencies upon which careers depend. Rather, running throughout, is an appreciation for the limitations in both scope and practicality of particular frameworks—each writer realizing that his or her approach addresses only a small fraction of the issue involved in a fully rounded view of careers.

When the chapters are taken as a whole, several themes are apparent. First, there is explicit acknowledgement of the necessity to view careers from at least two basic perspectives—the *internal* perspective which refers to the individual's subjective apprehension and evaluation of his or her career, and the *external* perspective which delineates the more or less tangible indicators of a career (occupation, family state, mobility, task attributes, job level, and the like). One is subjective, the other is relatively objective and there is little reason to assume the two coincide on any dimension. This distinction is perhaps the most crucial for future research because in the past the two perspectives have often been confused.

Second, the chapters suggest that work careers can be clarified analytically only by understanding the person within the total life space, including the many roles the individual plays in that life space. Knowledge about careers must be therefore personally and situationally specific, keyed to the unfolding complexity and dymanics of career progression. In fact, whatever personal, occupational, and family features eventually prove most interesting, they must not be seen as fixed. But, rather, they must always be scanned for the longitudinal evolution affecting the relationships among career variables.

The third theme growing out of the following chapters is that causal, linear models, emphasizing stimulus-and-response explanations, may be a too restricting, if not inappropriate, way to think about work careers. The century-old strategy of varying one factor and then observing the results upon another factor is suitable only when the phenomenon in question is unamiguous, controlled, and simple, something careers most assuredly are not. Patterns and relationships are what the authors here highlight, not deterministic equations of cause and effect. Career outcomes are seen as a result of interaction among a fairly large set of variables existing within a complex career domain. From this standpoint, rules and principles of interaction may eventually be constructed leading to what some might call a grammar of situations instead of the separate and competing propositions of individual motives or external demands presently in vogue. Indeed, the metaphors and analogies that inform and frame our empirical and deductive work should be drawn from ecological, not mechanical, etiologies.

These themes, as pointed out in the summary, are not stressed evenly across the following eight chapters. They are apparent only by stepping away from the specific concerns of the authors and viewing the work in its entirety. The chapters, when examined individually, address different problems, stress different temporal stages, employ different theoretical as well as methodological models, and, more generally, provide different sorts of contributions to the developing career framework.

With this said, let me comment on the organization of the chapters to follow. I have somewhat arbitrarily divided the contributions into three sections— reflective perhaps of my particular biases rather than any natural ordering. Part I—Toward a Theory of the Career in Everyday Life—represents a suggestive commonsensical framework for the study of careers. Concerned primarily with organizational meaning systems and an individual's definition of his particular work situation, this chapter attempts to illustrate by example the interplay between external and internal career considerations. Part II— Understanding Organizational Careers and Individual Differences—focuses upon the person and contains three research reports each addressing in effect the question of individual differences and the impact such differences may have upon the person's career. Edgar H. Schein's chapter suggests a new way to characterize managerial careers such that certain careers can be seen as expressive of an individual's underlying needs and values. The next two selections in Part II explore the concept of cognitive organization as a means of capturing perceptual and behavioral differences among people. David A. Kolb and Mark S. Plovnick submit that there exists a strong correspondence between what they call a person's 'learning style' and the individual's career choice. In a similar vein, Peter G. W. Keen suggests that cognitive orientations influence the problem-solving strategies—and by implication the career strategies— adopted by persons in the workplace.

Part III—The Individual's Orientation Toward Work Across the Career— directs attention to certain external features associated with work careers. Looking at technical occupations, Lotte Bailyn investigates the role-based patterns of work involvement and family accommodation in several engineering-based career paths and then relates these patterns to the attitudes and values persons hold toward their job, family, and self. Using state and local governments as a data base, Ralph Katz argues in the following chapter that time on a particular job is perhaps more crucial in evaluating an individual's response to certain varieties of the work situation than are the more commonly used variables of individual age and tenure—at least when it comes to estimating the probable affects of job enrichment schemes. And, in the concluding chapter of this section, Richard Beckhard draws upon his considerable consulting experience to describe a recent phenomenon in large organizations: the so-called high-potential manager who decides not to pursue the road to the top. Various alternatives to traditional career paths are discussed from the standpoint of what an organization might do to retain and nurture managerial personnel.

Finally, the major concepts introduced in this book are summarized and reviewed in the concluding selection. More critically, this last chapter considers several analytic frameworks capable perhaps of integrating the seemingly diverse interests of each author. Although far from definitive, this chapter demonstrates the real theoretical and practical necessity of using career variables if we are to both understand and respect the meaning people attach to their work-a-day lives.

NOTES

1. I must note that occupational concerns do not constitute the *sui generus* for the term career. Indeed, one can speak of family careers, deviant careers, leisure careers, aesthetic careers, and even moral careers. But, in the main, interest here is with work careers existing inside not outside of what the economists so appropriately call the labor market.
2. The *Gemeinschaft* and *Gelleschaft* conception of historical process is attributable to Tönnies (1955). Unlike Marx, Tönnies saw changes in the form of economic production as a result, not a cause, of the move in social relationships—although otherwise their views are quite similar. For the most part, Tonnies, typology is very close to Durkheim's (1933) subsequent notion of an evolutionary transformation involving movement from the 'mechanical solidarity' of medieval society to the 'organic solidarity' of present day society. Weber's (1947) theory on the bureaucratization and related rationalization process is also closely associated to Tönnies work. More recently, Berger's (1964) discussion of the meaning of work in sacred (traditional) and secular (modern) societies conveys many of the same points. Even Riesman's (1950) inner- and other-directed man and Merton's (1957) local and cosmopolitan types have much the same flavor as Tönnies, masterful twin concepts. For a good discussion of these concepts, see Salaman (1974), pp. 5–41.
3. The career as a variable useful in exploring and defining the relationship of an individual to his or her work can be seen primarily in the ethnographic studies of anthropologically inclined sociologists. See, for example, the illuminating work of Becker and coworkers (1961), Crozier (1964), Dalton (1959), Glaser (1964, 1968), Chinoy (1955), and, especially, Hughes (1958). Two very recent studies exemplify this perspective quite nicely—Faulkner (1974) and Platt and Pollock (1974).
4. The arguments supporting this point are subtle but essentially boil down to propositions which suggest that certain management policies regarding recruitment, promotion, and transfer promote a conformity of thought and behavior among participants at various levels in an organization. In other words, the factors or contingencies upon which mobility from one position to another depend, insures the stability of a particular, organizationally-defined, outlook. While the consequences of selection and advancement in organizations have been reasonably well-established, the transfer policies of large national or multinational corporations represent an interesting, case-in-point regarding unobtrusive control. To take one example, several writers have suggested that as more and more moves are made by an employee in response to the company's request, the more likely that the employee-in-transit will develop an almost fierce loyalty to that organization (Seidenberg, 1975; Whyte, 1968). In summary form, the reasoning goes as follows: as community bonds weaken, corporate bonds tighten and the company becomes, to the dependent employee, *in loco parentis*. In extreme cases, an individual's roots become so shallow and transitory that moves for the company are viewed as patriotically as moves for the Mother Country. Needless to say, when the allegiance of people to their employing organization transcends their allegiance to a community or society, their actions on behalf of that particular firm may well reflect a most narrow conception of the public good.
5. Even for members employed at the lower strata in the organizational hierarchy, career considerations may provide a sort of membrane within which work-related decisions are limited. For example, many patrolmen working city streets tend to adopt a 'lay low, avoid trouble' outlook toward their occupation lest they jeopardize their potential

movement into other aspects of policing—detective work, radio communications, or up the hierarchical ranks (Van Maanen, 1973; Walsh, 1975).

6. Several recent best sellers have been deeply concerned with work and its consequences. Stud Terkel's *Working* (1974) and *Division Street: America* (1968) are perhaps the best known. But consider also Jack Olson's *Sweet Street* (1974) and the *Girls in the Office* (1972) as well as Kenneth Larson's *The Workers* (1971), Gail Sheehy's *Hustling* (1974a) and Martin Mayer's *The Bankers* (1974). Indeed, the thinly disguised fiction of Joseph Heller's *Something Happened* (1974) is most appropriate to a concern with corporate careers. And no list of writings in the popular culture would be complete of course without mentioning the HEW Report, *Work in America* (1973) or Sheppard and Herrick's *Where Have All the Robots Gone?* (1972).

7. These two contrary views on the career are worth exploring in slightly more detail. For example, Slater's (1970) influential perspective on careers is developed within the context of a stern, Calvinistic world. He remarked that a career orientation 'connotes a demanding, rigorous, preordained life pattern to whose goals everything else is ruthlessly subordinated'. However, an equally influential but considerably more optimistic perspective on careers is provided by Tiedman and O'Hara (1963) who suggest that through a career orientation, a person is 'able to accommodate the environment to suit himself'. The point here is simply that both views underemphasize the dialectic process taking place continually between the individual and the environment. As in so many other controversial areas within the social sciences, the 'seeing-is-believing' empirical paradigm has been converted to a 'believing-is-seeing' ideological paradigm.

8. A simple example will suffice in this regard. Consider the number of studies carried out on job satisfaction which characterize man's turning away from the world of work as aberrant, an alienated, if not destructive response. Very little positive worth has been attributed to the family or other nonwork spheres as potential wellsprings of support, self-esteem, and growth. Such studies which depict the partial involvement of individuals in the workplace in disparaging terms barely conceal their managerial bias. Indeed, they represent little more ideological pronouncements—on the 'sacred' worth of a hard days work—and as such fall outside the realm of scientific endeavor.

PART I

Toward a Theory of the Career in Everyday Life

When we label a problem as psychological or sociological, practical or philosophical, factual or intuitive, we display a tenacious unwillingness to allow the problem itself to guide us in our study. From this standpoint, it is important that we study the problems careers raise for the people who follow them. Such problems are perhaps most apparent when individuals begin their respective careers, for it is at this point that uncertainties regarding the applicability of the past, the demands of the present, and the prospects for the future are most likely to be at a peak. In particular, when persons enter organizations for the first time, they are immediately faced with the problem of constructing a definition for the situation they find themselves in. And, without relevant organizational experience to guide them, the period of building a suitable definition will be a disconcerting, time consuming, and difficult one.

The following chapter attempts to provide a general theoretical framework for the study of socialization and careers. As such, it addresses the fundamental question: 'How do people make sense out of their experiences in an organization?' The theory presented here is, however, an actor's theory. That is, the focus is upon what the individual must learn in order to act knowledgeably within an organization. Although the focus is upon a person's early career experiences, the problems faced by a newcomer are not unlike the problems faced by anyone in an organization whenever a transition from one career stage to another is made. Indeed, in a very real sense, this chapter is about how people convert strange and puzzling surroundings into a familiar and ordered environment. The point is simply that unless we understand how those who are our subjects of inquiry construct their social worlds, we cannot possibly develop meaningful explanations for their careers.

Chapter 1

Experiencing Organization: Notes on the Meaning of Careers and Socialization[1]

John Van Maanen

> '*An experience must run counter to expectation if it is to deserve the name experience.*' Hegel

THEORETICAL GROUNDINGS

People will not accept uncertainty. Regardless of how rich or poor the material at hand, people make an effort to structure, interpret, and define the magnificently commonplace world of their experience. By and large, they succeed. What it means to succeed is the underlying theme of this essay.

The specific focus is upon an ordinary phenomenon or process labeled here and elsewhere, organizational socialization (Van Maanen, 1976; Manning, 1970; Schein, 1968).[2] The phrase concerns the manner in which individuals become members and continue as members of an organization—both from the standpoint of the individual and from the standpoint of others in the organization. Thus, one's work career—from beginning to end—can be used to represent a socialization sequence.[3] While socialization occurring during an individual's early career in one organization is the primary focus of this writing, I occasionally make use of the full career as a socialization process of interest. Ideally, a theoretical scheme useful at one level should be equally useful at another level as well.

The notion of actors learning to play social roles on social stages is crucial to the analysis presented here. This Shakespearian metaphor suggests that in the drama of life, as in the drama of theater, there are parts, props, coplayers, and audiences to whom one must direct and orient a performance. Until one is able to construct guidelines regarding what is expected in a given role, the performance acted out will be incomplete, inauthentic, and detached from all other parts being played simultaneously. When one moves to a new stage, a dramaturgic interpretation must be made by the individual as to the meaning of the plot, cast of character, backdrop, and one's own role in the sequence of acts (Messinger, Sampson and Towne, 1962).

The social stage considered in this paper is the workplace. My main concern is with how individuals locate (and relocate) themselves within organizational boundaries. I have argued elsewhere that the 'breaking-in' phenomenon (i.e. occurring when individuals first join an organization) represents a prototypical crisis period which occurs regularly throughout an individual's career (Van

Maanen, 1973, 1976). It is a *breakpoint* in which established relationships are severed and new one's forged, old behavior patterns forgotten and new ones learned, former responsibilities abandoned and new ones taken on. In short, breakpoints require the individual to discover or reformulate certain everyday assumptions about their working life.

Central to the underpinnings of this essay is the philosophical maxim that objects and events have no meaning in and of themselves. In other words, men create, sustain, and refine reality everyday through symbolic interaction with other men. Thus there can be no one-to-one correspondence between situation and action. An interpretation process whether conscious or unconscious mediates all personal encounters.[4]

Schutz (1962) in a critical work on the sociology of knowledge presents a social world comprised of 'multiple realities' within which any particular 'reality' utilized by a person to organize, direct and ultimately justify their actions in the world is dependent upon their socio-temporal location. For any given event, multiple meanings are therefore possible.[5] Depending upon such intertwined variables as one's past experiences, reference groups, roles, future expectations, and so on, the individual actively constructs a reality within which present events are assigned commonsensical interpretations. Take, for example, the idea of occupational achievement. A man may, at 21 years of age, make $10,000 a year as an accountant. He may, at 35, make $100,000 as President of the firm. If at 21 he has reason to expect that in the future he will be President of the company, his $10,000 a year job will hold an entirely different meaning for him than if he expects to remain at the same job forever. If upwardly mobile, he may see his work as 'good preparation' or as 'learning the discipline of work'. If his future is viewed with a more dismal prospect in mind, the person may interpret the exact same job as 'dull' or 'tedious'. Similarly, after he has become President, the past accounting job may have different meaning for him (e.g. 'starting at the bottom with basics') than if he had not become President (e.g. 'stuck in the bureaucratic mud'). There are chronological times (age) and spatial points of reference (jobs) in this example, but their influence upon one another transforms the meaning attached to the external world as the course of events unfolds.[6]

The view subscribed to here suggests that when novel organizational settings are encountered the individual must construct a definition of the situation suitable for day-to-day use. To the newly recruited, the organization is alien territory, full of unforeseen surprise. As James (1892) observed long ago, 'knowledge about' and 'experience of' a phenomenon imply quite different levels of understanding. Entrance into an organization upsets one's everyday order. Matters concerning self, friendship, privacy, time, competence, demeanor, and the future are suddenly made problematic. The individual—if for no other reason than simple epistemic curiosity—searches for commonsense theories to explain and make meaningful the myriad of activities going on in the workplace. Indeed, such diverse features as the specialized argot, conventional boundaries of discourse, attire, how to deal with the boss, and even the appropriate length of a coffee break are likely to occupy a prominent position in a person's initial agenda of matters to be attended to. In short, to come to know a situation and act within it, implies that a person has developed a way to interpret the experiences associated with participation in a given social world.

The critical nature of an individual's early organizational experience can be related to the developing theory of adult socialization as presented by Schein, (1968, 1971), Brim, (1966), and Becker and Strauss (1956). Essentially this theory suggests that when a person first enters an organizations, a portion of his life space is blank. Regardless of the neophyte's generalized values, motives, and abilities, he will feel a strong desire to define the expectations of others—clients, colleagues, supervisors, and so forth. The person must learn what is customary and desirable in the setting, as well as what is not. According to Meadian social psychology, the construction of such definitions are necessary if the person is to create a perspective on himself and build certain situationally-contingent understandings necessary to continue in the organization.

An insightful illustrative analysis of adult socialization is provided by Lyman and Scott (1970). They view initiation settings in terms of the manner in which the novice experiences and manages 'stagefright'. Such stagefright occurs precisely because one's claimed identity becomes open to public scrutiny. Like stage actors, individuals in novel organizational settings may well experience apprehension regarding their competence to perform adequately in the called-for role and are therefore overly receptive to clues originating from others in the environment. From this angle, a newcomer is *invited* by others to accept certain definitions of organizational activities and of one's own role in the organization. These definitions provide the individual with the conceptual machinery to build and maintain certain perspectives which provide plausible explanations and justifications for one's actions and experiences within—and sometimes outside—the organization.

The perspective adopted by an individual is, in essence, a means of legitimizing various choices to be made in the setting—beginning of course with the initial decision to join. Perspectives inform the individual as to why certain actions are to be preferred over others and as to why things are as they are. Shibutani (1962: p. 130) writes: 'a perspective is an ordered view of one's world—what is taken for granted about the attributes of various objects, events and human nature'. Certainly perspectives are not adopted overnight. They evolve continuously over time and are dependent upon one's past experiences. But, at no other time during a person's organizational experiences is, as Hughes (1958: p. 17) suggests, the development of a perspective likely to be 'more important and lively—more exciting and uncomfortable, more self-conscious yet perhaps more deeply unconscious—than in the period of learning and initiation.'

Perspectives are not provided, however, by environmental fiat. They are not somehow 'out there'—tied inextricably to the so-called objective characteristics of organizations—waiting to be claimed by an individual. Nor are they simply the result of some unseen but pervasive social forces acting upon the individual independently of the person's perception of the organization. To argue along these lines is a little like comparing the relations between a social institution and human behavior to the relations between a magnet and iron filings. People are not mere puppets responding to the firm tug of social strings. Indeed, socialization settings do not have unambiguous, natural properties beyond those which individuals attribute to them. Individuals must actively construct definitions to describe features of their organizational situation. This recalls W. I. Thomas's (1931) justly famous dicta: 'If people define situations as real, they are real in their consequences'. Put another way, identical situations may surround people, but the meaning of the situation may vary substantially from person to person.

What follows is a consideration of the individual's search for meaning and relevance in organizational settings. I am interested primarily in what people must first discover in order to find their bearings in an organization and to come to terms with it. In other words, I ask the question: 'what must people know to be able to locate themselves within an organization such that they can operate in a manner that is viewed as appropriate, if not desirable, by other members.' The focus is therefore upon the underlying patterns of meaning individuals assign to the appearances, actions, and situational features of their social settings.

DECIPHERING ORGANIZATIONS

'Toto, I have a feeling we're not in Kansas anymore ...'
Dorothy, on entering Oz

Locating One's Self in Social Space and Time

When an individual steps into an unfamiliar region for the first time, he is faced with the problem of creating order from at best vague surroundings. The stage may be vacant, quiet, and without clues as to the role the newcomer is expected to play. Or it may be raucous, chaotic, and full of conflicting clues as to the role the newcomer is expected to play. In either case, the person must actively construct an interpretative scheme if the situation is to be made meaningful. Standing at the entrance point of an organizational career, the individual is essentially a stranger, and his position within the organization is premised upon this very fact that he is an outsider—one who has not belonged.

Simmel (1950) suggests that only during the orientation period is the individual categorically free, for his criteria for evaluating organizational activities are most objective and general since he is not yet tied down by habit, piety, or precedent. However, no matter how free or objective the novice may be, his practical problem—that of making sense out of the progression of new faces he encounters, the complexities of the new demands made of him, and the ordering of others' activities relative to his own—will be paramount.

Habit, piety, and precedent may be restricting, but once learned, they provide comfort for the individual enabling him to discover and maintain a fix on his location within the constellation of organizational activities.

Human actions are not undertaken randomly. Following Mead (1930; 1932), Garfinkel (1967), and especially McHugh (1968), I argue here that a person cannot make sense of his work situation and hence act within it unless certain phenomenological questions have been at least partially answered. Indeed, I will suggest that little can be accomplished that is of organizational interest unless organizational members can locate themselves along the meta-phoric axes of space and time. Only by converting continuous, chronological time and contiguous, physical space to internally relevant coordinants re-presenting discrete, social time and partitioned, social space can the individual meaningfully develop a situational identity capable of sustaining the perform-ance of work activity.[7]

These twin dimensions can be separated analytically only. Spatial and tem-poral framworks play off each other in a variety of ways. A young ball player may be, for example, on the 'fast track' to the major leagues, but moving relatively slowly compared to some historical reference group comprised of bonafide baseball stars who moved on an even faster track. In other words, the social comparison space used by an individual acts as a yardstick for an inter-pretation of temporal position. Time is necessary to the calculus of motion, but motion itself requires a frame-of-reference. Thus while I conveniently consider the two in isolation, they are by no means empirically distinct.

By use of the phrase social time, I am implying that persons make meaningful their organizational present only through their understanding of the past and their expectations of the future. As St. Augustine observed in *Confessions*, 'there are only three times. A present of things past; a present of things present; and a present of things future'. In this sense, the past and future fold back on one another to determine one's interpretation of the present. The college graduate, for instance, who can only find work digging ditches is likely to experience an incongruity between his past and foreseeable future, leaving him perhaps embittered with his present 'in the hole' status.

The temporal framework adopted by the person following entrance into an organization is, in essence, a means of routinizing and making tolerable—or at least predictable—the future. As Mead (1932) remarked poignantly, the environment in which men live is based on things remembered and things anticipated. We do not experience a neat Newtonian time which is continuous, without lacunae. Rather, one's experiences render quantitatively equal amounts of time, qualitatively unequal.[8]

To the newcomer in an organization, time is problematic. One must discover: when to take a break; have lunch; or quit work; when to read the paper; how long one must stay at a certain pay grade; when to press for a promotion; and so on. The individual must develop certain short-range timetables (which assist him in dividing up the days and weeks into manageable components); as well as certain long-range timetables (which provide notions of how his career will unfold). Only by constructing such timetables can the past be linked to the future, making the present meaningful.[9]

Social space, which is also discussed at length, refers to the problem of 'fit' facing individuals who find themselves in novel surroundings. One's spatial location revolves in part upon one's choice of comparative or reference group(s). More importantly, however, spatial location concerns the assumptions a person makes regarding how others in the organization view him. The influence others have over the newcomer is not so much deliberate or coerced, but rather results from the fact that each person must take into account others' expectations when deciding on a course of action.[10] For consciously or unconsciously, each person performs for some sort of audience. In addition when a person enters an organization, he must not only orient his performance toward various audiences, but select those audience whose judgements he will attach most importance.[11]

Critical to the study of both social space and time is a concern for the nature of interaction occurring between people within the organization. In line with Schutz (1970), Cicourel (1970), and Silverman (1972), I argue here that all social interaction and understanding is *presumptuous*. In other words, interaction is possible only because of a tacit but loose psychological contact among person to 'agree to agree on what transpires'. As a feature present in all encounters, it suggests that individuals, unless shown otherwise, will assume that others' understandings are the same as their own and that there is agreement as to what is real and what is fancied. Such presumptions are required because of the infinite variety of potential viewpoints others could take in any particular setting. Without assuming or presupposing where others stand relative to one's self, communication would be impossible. Yet, these *a priori* assumptions are not without problems to an individual for they are continuously liable to subtle or dramatic falsification.

An example from the organizational context will illustrate this important interactional point. Suppose we take the neophyte: under normal conditions, a newcomer assumes that he knows what the organization is about, assumes others in the setting have the same idea, and practically never bothers to check out these two assumptions. What occurs upon experience is that the neophyte receives a surprise of sorts (i.e. what Hughes (1958) calls a 'reality shock') in which he discovers that significant others in the organization, perhaps his boss, do not share his assumptions. The newcomer must then reorient himself relative to others in space and time through a cognitive revision of his previously taken-for-granted assumptions. The individual knows where he is and what is expected of him only through the assumptions he makes—particularly those regarding how others in the setting view him. A critical violation of these assumptions leads to what could be called dislocation, forcing the person to reconsider his organizational position.

Locating one's self within an organization, therefore, can never be accomplished completely.[12] Due to the complexities of experience, an occasion of surprise or dislocation is always a possibility—assumptions may be ruptured or suspended at any moment throughout one's career. In this light, a person's position in social space and time is best thought of as a negotiated one. It arises out of bargaining and expediency in which the individual seeks to create, document, and enforce a favorable interpretation of where he stands in the organization. For example, newcomers usually try to quickly shed the more or less stigmatized 'rookie' label by attempting to broaden, redefine, or transcend their assigned portion. Tactics vary, but some common ones involve: taking on more responsibility than permissible, ingratiating one's self with superiors, making somewhat pretentious use of local argot, or even behaving vituperatively toward other newcomers—all of which are designed to convey the impression to those in authority that the newcomer has learned the ropes and should be taken seriously as a contributor to the organization.

Such negotiation need not be implicit or *sub rosa*. Certainly, in most work organizations, status negotiation over one's functional and hierarchical position is, to a degree, open. More importantly, hierarchical and functional location can be evaluated by the person according to *prima facie* circumstance. However, individuals must also position themselves relative to what Schein (1971) calls the 'permeable boundary of inclusion'. This boundary corresponds roughly to the person's centrality in an organization—that is, his notion of being more or less 'on the inside'. For the individual to locate himself along this dimension necessarily entails knowledge about such things as organizational secrets, task-related shortcuts, and the sometimes surreptitious power relationships. Rarely can such knowledge be gained without the individual first demonstrating a degree of trustworthiness and commitment to others in the setting—the *quid pro quo* for being 'in on the action'.

In general, the person's concern for either the spatial or temporal aspects of organizational location can be expected to vary over the course of their career. Since developing an idea of where one stands in social time depends inherently upon the social space one uses for comparative purposes, it is perhaps more important initially for a newcomer to position himself relative to others in the organization than it is for the newcomer to locate himself in the temporal order of things. The immediate need of a neophyte is to create a social field upon which the implied contrasts and similarities between himself and others will be readily apparent. Only later, after his spatial position is reasonably clear and established, does the individual attend to temporal matters (McHugh, 1968). Like the observer in a railway car who is unsure whether it is his train that is moving or the train on the adjoining track, without a frame-of-reference, the person in the organization cannot know where he is headed.

I suggest in the remainder of this essay that there is a commonsense structure regarding the individual's organization of experience. When people locate themselves in space and time, they are essentially resolving the confusion arising from an imposed sensory environment. Confusion is handled through the individual's development of perspectives which: (*a*) regularize experiences occurring in the spatial sphere; and (*b*) run ahead and guide experiences in the temporal sphere. These perspectives are usually firm and specific enough such that people can attach notions of variability or predictability to them—thus providing something of an operational test for their adequacy and accuracy. Furthermore, these perspectives also embody notions of causality in the everyday world—thus providing an explanation of why things happen as they do.

In the following two sections, I discuss the process by which people develop these two perspectives. The first section, Social Space, considers the manner by which individuals *normalize the setting* in which they find themselves. The second section, Social Time, examines the way individuals *discover a theme* to order their work life. In addition, within each section, I direct some attention to: (a) the variability of space and time perspectives—discussed under the headings of *range* and *explicitness*, respectively; and (b) the causality underlying space and time perspectives—discussed under the headings of *accounts* and *ownership*, respectively.

Social Space: A Map for the Career Unfolding

Cognitive anthropologists, social geographers, and experimental psychologists among others have made use of the concept of mental maps. Kaplan (1972) suggests, for example, that an enormous amount of information is stored by person in the form of cognitive maps with distinct spatial properties such as location, distance, and direction. These cognitive representations consist of major nodes or reference points joined by linkages and networks between them. Tolman (1948), Lewin (1938), Kelley (1963), Lynch (1960) and, most recently, Gould and White (1974) have explored this concept in extremely imaginative and thought-provoking ways. As utilized by these writers, a person's mental map is simply a model—the abstraction, simplification, and compression of a complex but unique social and geographic reality.

In some manner, we make and use mental maps all the time. For as human beings, we desperately need an ordering system to process all the information we receive through our senses. We classify, simplify, connect, and distill many observations into a few for the sake of clarity and comprehension (i.e. what McHugh (1968) calls homomorphic mapping). Indeed, day-to-day dealings would be virtually impossible if we did not have some sort of device to categorize and render comprehensible the environment in which we live.

Like laymen visiting the laboratory of a nuclear physicist, newcomers to an organization are blind to many of the defining characteristics of their immediate setting. Novices must learn, therefore, how and what to see and hear. In particular, they must determine where they stand relative to the objects, events, relationships, and types of people they encounter. By constructing what I will call here a social map, individuals are able to depict the invisible landscape upon which organizational activities take place. A map provides the person with a representation capable of linking, standardizing, and abbreviating the various characteristics of his environment. Colloquially, the social map enables a person to tell 'where he is at and where others are coming from'.

To fail to make meaningful links with others in a particular setting implies that the reactions of others to one's self are unpredictable. A person cannot anticipate how he will be treated nor how he should treat others. To act out a role in an organization demands that the perspectives of others are taken into account. Thus, Cooley's (1922) 'looking glass self' deliberately, intuitively, or unconsciously performs for an audience to whom some rather specific perspective is attributed. To map any particular social setting requires that the actor be able to put himself in the position of another and see the world as if he were the other.

I turn now to consider the problems people face when constructing a social map of their environment. Emphasis is placed upon the kinds of fundamental understandings individuals must eventually come to possess if they are to locate themselves within organizational space. I call the process by which these understandings are developed 'Normalizing the Setting' because such a label seems to best capture the active and creative character of the transformation— that is, newcomers must actually do something, rules and guidelines are not simply handed down from above but must be constructed and tested by the individual who is to use them. Furthermore, the label suggests that conformity to organizational standards is perhaps best pictured as a dimension which is a continuous and distributed more-or-less normally around a mean. Hence, slight to moderate deviations from this almost ideal–typical mean are unlikely to cause repercussions, although significant departures from the mean are almost sure to provoke some response from others in the organization.

Normalizing the Setting

Individual interpretations and perspectives grow microscopically from continuous interaction with others in the setting—in particular, interaction with those whom the person considers significant. But communication itself must be premised upon what Glaser and Strauss (1964) call a 'shared awareness'. In their thoughtful analysis, Glaser and Strauss suggest that for a social relationship to develop that is capable of mutual influence and one in which each party will understand what the other party is saying or doing depends on: (*a*) the degree to which subjective meaning is imputed to the other; and (*b*) the degree to which the subjective imputation is accurate. In other words, an awareness context involves 'the total combination of what each interactant in a situation knows about the other and his own identity in the eyes of the other' (Scheff, 1967). Hence, when a person enters a novel setting populated by others of whom he can know little about beforehand, he must immediately begin to denote just who the significant others are, what they want, and how his own self is viewed by them. Until such a scheme of things is arrived at, understanding is all but impossible for there will be no ground upon which to interpret what another is expressing.[13]

Normality refers to the judgements persons make regarding the typicality of both their own and others behavior. It is a means by which people classify their environment. In organizational settings, individuals must quickly learn the actions that are representative of persons in the locale and the enforced limits of such actions. For instance, when one interacts with another, both interactants must infer whether or not each others responses are typical of a group or category with which each has had some sort of experience, whether real or vicarious. For, once classified, a collection of appropriate responses can be marshalled out by the interactants to order the transaction (see McHugh, 1968).

Emerson (1970b) suggests that newcomers must develop certain orientations or stances to guide their behavior in organizations. These stances reflect the the 'normality of the situation' and are of two simple varieties—a 'Something Unusual' stance and a 'Nothing Unusual' stance. Both orientations are subtle and expressed largely through appearance and demeanor. At times, for example, middle management personnel can detect the coming of a major policy shift by virtue of the 'Something Unusual' clues to be found in the alertness or guardedness stance exhibited by top-level managers. Or, to illustrate the other possibility, workers may disregard rumors of an imminent plant layoff after noting the casual, relaxed 'Nothing Unusual' stance assummed by foremen and first-line supervisors. Although things are not always as they appear, the day-in and day-out experiences of members of an organization cannot be discounted when it comes to discerning subtle shifts in the organizational normality. While people may not always be let in on the reasons behind the 'Something Unusual' stance, it is to their credit that such stances are most often perceived. The ruse may continue, of course, but the individual is to a degree forewarned and suspicious. To normalize the setting, then, requires a person to be able to recognize such stances as well as to assume them at appropriate moments.[14]

Individuals enter organizations with notions of propriety and normality gleaned only from other situations of which they have had experience. The The accuracy of these *a priori* assumptions is almost never checked without some sort of reality shock first prompting the individual to reconsider what he takes for granted. Not surprisingly, however, persons often allow bizarre or incredulous behavior to pass without notice because they are uncertain as to what the behavior in question means. Since they do not have a ready explanation at hand and do not want to appear ignorant, individuals many times prefer to 'not make a fuss' over such occurrences and continue on as if nothing had happened. In such cases, the 'Nothing Unusual' stance is invoked as a sort of order-maintaining device (Emerson, 1970b). Thus, the normality of organizational life can be stretched to include many *de trop* or out-of-kilter events. Only in those dramatic cases in which the person is involved or challenged directly and unavoidably does the individual alter or recast his assumptions regarding what is normal in the organization.

Importantly, values are inherent in any normalization process. Standards designating normal behavior suggest that judgements of correctness, appropriateness, and/or morality can be accomplished. What is right or wrong in the situation depends upon what one considers to be normal. To label another's behavior as abnormal is to ascribe a motivational scheme to that person—that the other is unlike oneself. And unless an organization (or for that matter, a society) is so completely demoralized and without shame, certain behaviors, be they symptomatic or ordinary, will be grounds for barring or amputating persons from the organization. Indeed, Garfinkel (1956) notes that the boundaries of any community are maintained through 'degradation ceremonies' by which the identity of a moral offender is transformed from a normal, 'like us' status, to an alien, 'unlike us' status. Such transformations do not add new dimensions to the person's identity, but rather reconstitute the person. The former identity becomes accidental, the new one real. To know what is normal implies then that one knows why people act as they do.

In the everyday world there are times when 'we could drop through the floor' or 'run and hide' or 'wish that the earth would open and swallow us'. Such events signal the crossing of the boundaries of normality, for the embarrassed individual fears the creation of a non-flattering or negative image of himself. Of course, within work organizations, as with other areas of life, what is normal in one context may not be in another. Thus, individuals upon entering an organization must go about the creation of a normal order, one which is at least nominally shared by others in the particular situation.

One illustrative feature of organizational normality is found generally in the expression of authority relationships and in one's responses to them. In organizations, one must learn, therefore, what the boss expects and how to negotiate such expectations. One must discover, for example, when to be deferential or argumentative, when to be patient or to press ahead, and even when to be seen or not seen. In other words, from a subordinate's point of view, it is important, perhaps vital, to be able to typify the boss's normal behavior in various contexts and also develop notions as to how one acts accordingly in such contexts. Mistakes will be made no doubt, but such mistakes typically represent a crucial socialization experience.

Under most conditions, when individuals interact with others of whom they have had little first-hand experience, they must infer whether or not the utterances and actions of these others are representative of a group or category. The sociologist who claims, for instance, that veteran police officers are role models for recruits is saying simply that recruits classify the behavior of veterans as typically relevant to themselves. Similarly, the behavior of others who are not role models to an actor may be classified as irrelevant, but nonetheless the behavior will be classified as to its normality. Thus, the behavior of a bellicose shop steward may be seen by management as tempestuous perhaps but nonetheless typical—'isn't that just like a union man' (McHugh, 1968).

It follows from this argument that a major task in normalizing a setting is learning the labels person in the organization apply to one another. These labels allow individuals to 'type' one another such that any particular type is seen as a bearer of normal or alien attributes. For example, the college 'bookworm' is often seen by fellow students as a 'hack' or as a 'nurd'—a socially incompetent sort, who exists at the margin of campus normality. Similarly, the rate-busting operator on the factory floor may be seen by others performing the same task as a 'threat' or as 'management's boy'. In service organizations, clients too are labeled as to their fit within behavioral guidelines (Mannerick, 1974). Indeed, medical doctors reserve special treatment for those clients who are seen as 'crocks' as do policemen for certain categories of citizens who are viewed as 'assholes' (Van Maanen, 1974b). If a novice is to develop even a rudimentary linguistic competence in the organization, he must be attentive to and come to understand the 'people categories' utilized by the more experienced organizational members. And, of course, negative categories must be discovered relatively quickly lest the attributions others attach to certain stigmatized members be applied to the newcomer himself.[15]

A further example is useful in this regard. The distinction between locals and cosmopolitans made by Merton (1957) and Gouldner (1957) bears on those situations in which the reference groups held by various participants in a setting are incompatible. Locals are those persons rooted in the immediate organization. They are committed to the success of the organization and derive their perspective on normality from what they take to be the organization's interest. On the other hand, cosmopolitans derive their perspective from a wider audience reflected perhaps by a professional association cutting across organizations. Locals are sometimes suspected by the cosmopolitans of being 'mere company men'; whereas cosmopolitans are sometimes suspected by the locals of being 'disloyal'. Each to the other is at odds with the appropriate or normal motivational base. Normality in any situation is at least partially defined for the person by his reference group.[16]

Another critical feature involved in the normalizing process concerns what I call here the 'Realwork' perspective of organizational participants. Realwork is what is considered by the members to be their own, if not the organization's, mission—the *raison de être* of their role.[17] Tasks which interfere with the performance of Realwork are likely to be disdained, viewed as a frivolous waste of time. Merton (1957) suggests, for example, that scientists, by virtue of their training, internalize a 'Real Science' definition which prescribes what they 'ought to be working on. University professors in some institutions classify 'Teaching' as their Realwork, while professors in other institutions make 'Researching' their prime area of concentration. Policemen, as well, have firm notions concerning what police work is about—'crook catching, not social work'. The Realwork of any organizational role is the crucial justification used by a member to legitimize his position. When positions are held in common, a collective definition is sure to be present, and new members must soon learn the proper perspective *they are expected to hold* toward the many tasks they are asked to perform—a perspective which emphasizes some tasks and depreciates others—lest they jeopardize the 'what-everybody-knows-to-be-true' definitional fabric encapsulating the Realwork for which they were hired.

Relatedly, members in any organizational setting have standard ways for accomplishing what they take to be their Realwork. These procedures are, for all intents and purposes, rule-based, although such rules are rarely articulated. A good illustration of such procedural understandings is found in Sudnow's (1965) excellent study of a public defenders office. In brief, Sudnow demonstrates how the presumably well prescribed and delimited legal actions of attorneys working in the public defender's office—PDs—rests upon a knowledge of normal, typical clients and, more importantly, how such knowledge is used in attending to the treatment of the clients. In other words, the everyday problems of PDs are not derived from the available statutes and rules, but rather stem from the situational demands and exigencies which involve practitioners achieving what they take to be their main tasks in light of what they know about their clients. Once a crime has been classified 'normal' by a public defender (i.e. involving usual defendants, victims, and scenes), a set of prescribed and routinized activities are available to dispose of the matter.[18] Clearly, the new deputy PD must soon learn to recognize the attributes of 'normal crimes' and, crucially, to come to do so naturally.

Less obvious perhaps but also a key element in the normality of organizational life are the appearances assumed by actors in the setting in order to 'bring off' certain performances. We all understand, for example, the importance of 'looking busy' when the boss is observing, or the nuances that are involved in 'paying attention' to one another. Turner (1972) has described brilliantly the appearance required of individuals in group therapy situations to signal to others in the setting that they are now ready to begin 'doing therapy' as opposed to 'doing waiting'. Certainly in the workplace, the newcomer must soon learn the appropriate demeanor and appearances that are attached to the various tasks he is invited to perform. Thus, the salesman with a client learns how to appear 'sincere', the doctor with a patient learns how to be seen as 'serious', the magistrate in court learns how to produce an aura of 'dignity', and the director of funerals learns how to publically portray 'solemnity'.

In essence, what I have called here 'normalizing the setting' is a prerequisite for determining where one is socially located. Hence, once located, the person knows what to do within an organization and how he is to do it. Standards differ in subtle ways from place to place, but, before the individual can settle down to a work-a-day pattern, he must discover just what the work-a-day pattern means to others in the setting. Of course, a particular reality may be supported by a chorus of coworkers and subordinates, but it is usually defined for one by those in authority. Thus, significant others—such as the proverbial boss—can upset reality more so than others, creating havoc for the individual.

Range When persons normalize settings, they must do so in such a way that variations in their day-to-day experiences can be accommodated. There is, however, a thin line to be drawn around such variations. So long as the deviations from the expected order are of short duration and of only slight magnitude, the person has few problems in adjusting. Yet, deviations, to a large extent, must be predictable if the normality surrounding the individual is not to be threatened.

McHugh (1968) points out that persons assess the probability of an event as a way of determining its normality. Thus, the behavior of others can be atypical but still likely. For example, to paraphrase McHugh, 'a man crying may be atypical but perfectly predictable nonetheless as a result, for example, of bereavement or drunkenness'. Newcomers to organizational settings, if they are to make meaningful their situation, must develop a sort of commonsense statistical curve to assess the probability of behavior observed in the organization.

The range of probable events informs and specifies what is to be taken by the actor as normal within an organization. It allows particular evaluations to be assigned within a universal framework. Indeed, individuals must often orient their behavior toward certain others—both inside and outside the organization—as special persons and not as members of a particular category. The patrolman on the city street may know, for example, that all hippies are 'assholes'. Yet he also knows that such a label may. be misleading if not dysfunctional in certain cases—as in the case when a particularly disheveled young man turns out to be a detective's prized informant. Clearly, the police officer must have some probabilistic idea regarding the range of his normal world.

To some degree, the notion of range deals with the handling of 'mistakes' or 'screw-ups'—where the normal is not normal. Organizationally directed socialization such as that which might be taught in a training classroom or might be read in a manual of operations, specifies to the novice what is customary and desirable. But such learning rarely specifies how often there are deviations from the customary and desirable (nor what is to be done in the case of deviation). To insure a condition of normality on a day-to-day basis, one must know both how to predict and restore disorder. In Blau's (1955) bureaucracy, certain universal rules are applied only in certain contexts. Rules are also used to mask as well as prevent errors. The personal learning involved in such cases is necessary for the practical achievement of normality. Individuals, to some extent, build a dossier of precedents to follow when certain aspects of day-to-day life breakdown. Such breakdowns and their remedies become, to a degree, routine. Thus, when the boss incorrectly adds a column of figures on an outgoing report, a subordinate discretely fixes the mistake. Or the fireman who runs over and ruins an expensive firehose writes a false report attributing his error to some careless, but anonymous, motorist. In such cases, the event itself is not normal, although it occurs frequently enough such that there are precedents to follow.

The notion of range is also helpful when dealing with the social types encountered in the workplace. Indeed, a newcomer discovering what is typical of others in the setting cannot deal in a categorical manner with those of whom he associates with on a day-to-day basis. Uniqueness must enforce both its allowance and recognition. Hence, the considerate 'System's 4' manager idealized by Likert (1961) may be ignored when he temporarily turns sour and vindictive after a particularly busy day. The actors in the situation allow probabilistic detours form the acknowledged ideal–typical behavior pattern.

Relatedly, participants in any organizational setting have respective roles to play. But the roles people are asked to play provide only a normative definition for what a person is to do. Roles therefore entitle but do not coerce individuals to act in a certain fashion. What it is that the individual actually does is, of course, an entirely different matter. Even in traditional bureaucratic institutions where the attempt has been made over the years to lay out a whole fabric of prescribed interaction, role expansion (or shrinkage) occurs via bargaining over the sequences and contents of behavior that are to be recognized as applicable to a particular incumbent (Goffman, 1959, 1967; Homans, 1950). Persons do indeed transcend their assigned roles in organizations, although 'how much' and 'how often' they transcend their roles is perhaps best thought of, from the individual's point of view, as a probabilistic question. Thus, a person when discovering the various perspectives used by others to view his roles in the organization also makes judgements as to the range or flexibility of these perspectives.

To summarize, when one remarks, 'that's what I thought you'd say', the person is expressing a commonsensical probability. Socialization fails when a probability range associated with the normal order cannot be created and more or less agreed upon by individuals within the setting. In such cases, the world of probability recedes to a world where anything can happen. And, where anything is possible, the social actor is lost.

Accounts   To have a workable picture of what goes on in an organized setting, the newcomer must develop some idea of the 'why' which lies behind observed patterns of activity. Accounts refer to an actor's theoretical, but distinctly nonscientific, determination for why things happen as they do.[19] In other words, accounts represent the person's perception of the cause–effect mechanism operating in the environment. To the plant manager, for example, the erratic behavior of the operation's supervisor may be due simply to the pressure arising from a critical but complex and time-consuming production run. Or the perplexed file clerk in a city government may attribute the disarray of administrative records to the conflicting procedural demands made by department heads. In both cases, an observed pattern has been assigned a cause—an account has been constructed.[20]

Motivational schemes ascribed to persons in an organization are popular accounting devices used to explain why certain people behave as they do. Rightly or wrongly, they allow a person to make meaningful that which surrounds him. To most prisoners, the treatment they receive inside their steel and concrete homes, is a result of the dull, lumpish and sadistic character of prison guards. In the workplace, managers must contend with those persons who are seen as 'troublemakers' or 'attitude problems', contaminating the otherwise good workers. Slowdowns, horseplay, absenteeism, and sometimes walkouts can be therefore understood, assigned causal roots through characterological accounting.

Of course causality does not always rest upon the stereotypic categorizing of others. Situational accounts are not unknown. The underling who sees his superior's smile turn into a frown when the workload increases has a ready-made explanation for the cooling of the relationship. The jazz musician who feels he cannot 'cook' unless the audience is deferential also has developed a causal structure. In fact, in settings where role failures commonly appear (i.e. persons who are fired, 'don't make it' or, in nomenclature developed elsewhere, 'ineffectuously socialized'—Van Maanen, 1976), rich explanatory paradigms are developed by those remaining in the setting to provide guidelines to a newcomer as well as denote the reasons for observed failures.

Individuals may occassionally or frequently utilize perceived causality mechanisms for their own advantage. An assistant professor, knowing that the Dean dislikes certain kinds of research, may contrive to withhold information about his research that the Dean might otherwise see. On the other hand, a person may 'blow his own horn' when the opportunity to curry favor arises. Indeed attempting to use the perceived causality mechanisms to better one's situational location is a grounded folkway in all organizations. It is, in fact, consensually approved, often a matter of formal policy (e.g. promotions the result of achievement). It is when individuals perceive some variance between official standards and observed events that the causal texture of organizational life becomes problematic.

To conclude this section on the Normalization process, it is safe to assume that until a social map of one's spatial location is at least partially constructed, little work will be accomplished by a newcomer. Before the mapping can be said to be accomplished, the person must normalize the setting by determining the behavioral terrain in the setting considered *normal*. This involves (*a*) knowledge of the detail and probability associated with the normal terrain, (*Range*), and (*b*) the everyday theories of why the normal terrain is shaped as it is (*Accounts*). The map provides therefore a situationally specific definition of just who one is and what one is doing (or supposed to be doing) in the organization. Perhaps accurate maps can be constructed prior to joining an organization. But certainly experience will be required before the map can be verified.

Social Time: A Clock for the Career Unfolding

Social time refers to the manner an individual ties together the discrete events in which he participates into a more or less chronological order. It refers not to the simple running of sand through the hourglass, but to the marking of interludes or benchmarks in one's life. Calendars arise and are perpetuated not by the physical movements of the planets, but by the social arrangements and requirements of the societies to whom the calendar divisions are meaningful. Sorokin and Merton (1937) suggest that calendars both express the rhythm of collective activities and assure their regularity.

Organizations have calendars. They divide long periods of time into shorter ones and denote ritualized rounds of activity. Designated holidays, founders' days, paydays, and budget days all break up the even distribution of clock time.

Individuals too develop calendars to mark the passage of time. Anniversaries, birthdays, religious occasions, patriotic observances, and vacations all serve to divide the year, making lengthy amounts of time psychologically manageable. And, as Roy (1960) so painstakingly demonstrated, even minute time divisions in the workday of factory stamping machine operators, such as coke time, banana time, and quitting time, serve to provide respites from and meaning to the long, dreary, punch-in and punch-out day. This then is the material of which social time is constructed.

Time, in Mead's (1932) view, is emergent. He suggests that events are never achieved continuously. One's past is forever being rewritten as the future is experienced. For example, when the aspiring doctors described so well by Becker and coworkers (1961) discovered that much of their learning was inappropriate in the real world of doctoring, their past experiences in medical school began to take on an entirely new meaning. In fact, McHugh (1968) suggests that sociologist's emphasis on feedback explicitly recognizes that situational definitions are regularly revised—just as the jilted suitor may recognize that his definition of love was really lust.

I am suggesting that one is able to understand the present only in terms of where one has been and where one wants to go. The individual is able to function effectively in the present to the degree that he can provide continuity between the past and the future. Thus, the environment is made intelligible by assuming that future events will occur as past events have occurred. The hard working, upwardly mobile student of business must believe, for example, that something is 'out there' and that it is worth looking toward and preparing for. Indeed, for one to be 'going places', there must have been places where the person has been. Or, as H. G. Wells put it so well, 'a novel future demands a novel past'.

The image of a rewarding personal future generates, under most conditions, a pleasant emotional state that intrudes upon the person's current experience and motivates present behavior.[21] Just as folktales prepare people in most cultures to see visions of the future in the present, being told that one will 'go far' can provide a person with an immediate sense of accomplishment and satisfaction. On the other hand, there is growing clinical evidence to indicate that when a person's image of the future is impoverished, cloudy, or dismal, the individual's sense of the present is dulled (Klineberg and Cottle, 1973). In extreme cases, temporal discontinuity arising from a dissolved image of the future leads to a senseless present—the person being unable to say just who he is or what he is to do. To the analyst, this is depersonalization; to the man-in-the-street, this is a breakdown.

I now consider the process by which individuals build a temporal framework. Using the organization as a general frame-of-reference, I label this process 'Discovering a Theme'. My contention here is simply that, once discovered, a theme enables a newcomer to construct a stable set of expectations concerning the possibility of an orderly organizational career.

Discovering a Theme

McHugh (1968) points out that people assume before the fact that a pattern of meaning will be discovered in the occurrences they observe. In other words, individuals take for granted that they will be able to make something of what is yet to occur. Indeed, people assume that what has already occurred will not only inform the present, but inform the future as well.

The term *theme* is used here to denote a discovered pattern by which people link the activities in their experienced past and expected future together. A theme generates therefore an evaluation of present activity, not by describing the immediate moment itself, but by describing the immediate moment's relation to the past and future. In the workplace, a theme refers to an actor's notion of where he is going regarding his organizational career. A theme might be, for example, that one has an 'interesting, challenging job with good prospects'. Or, conversely, that one has a 'dull, routine job with no prospects'. Both themes postulate a pattern to one's activities in the work world—a pattern to which subjective meaning is attached. As such, the theme explains, provides context, and guides one in the workplace. Themes can, of course, be realistic (in the sense that they are continuously being experienced and documented) or fantastic (in the sense that they are never being experienced and documented). But the critical point is simply that themes are necessary components of the individual's present work definitions, tying together his past and future.

In general, when a person enters a work organization, he assumes that regularities in the relationships and activities surrounding him will soon be discovered and that the observed regularities will include his own activities. The young account executive assumes, for example, that only a few, unimportant clients will be assigned to him initially. But the aspiring executive expects also that if his performance is acceptable, more clients with larger accounts will be forthcoming, as will promotions, pay raises, and the like. In this case, the theme embodies a notion of increasing responsibility and is therefore subject to a commonsense empirical test, it can be, as McHugh (1968) would say, documented or not documented.[22]

The theme serves to place the present within a stream of work life events. What occurs when one fails to document as expected a given theme is surprise. And surprise entails at least a momentary unhinging of the person from his constructed reality—necessitating reappraisal and reconstruction of the theme. A neat example is provided by Kopelman, Dalton, and Thompson (1971). In a study of the work careers of engineers, the authors note that their early occupational experiences are marked by highly challenging tasks, a number of pay raises, and for many, promotions into managerial slots. It is a time of interesting work, excitement, and high aspiration. This work situation clearly embodies a most optimistic 'getting ahead' theme. Temporal continuity is achieved by connecting a perceived difficult but worthwhile college pre-paratory experience to a perceived rapid rise in the corporate engineering structure. However, the likelihood of this advancement theme being documented throughout the length of one's career is low, for as one moves out in the career, plateaus are reached and promotions become infrequent. Hence, in this example, as career lines flatten out, work themes must undergo what for some are no doubt, painful transformations.

Chinoy's (1955) auto workers or Blauner's (1964) factory hands may not see their jobs as part of a career that channels aspirations and sustains dreams, but they do construct themes based on the difficulty of their work, nature of their supervision, and the monotony of the job.[23] Certainly work themes stressing security are discoverable in many occupations (Walker and Guest, 1952; Dubin, 1956). For some workers, simply being able to retire free of an occupationally-induced disease is a major theme that an individual seeks to document (HEW Task Force, 1973; Shepard and Herrick, 1972). In the short run, Roy's (1960) research makes salient the difficulty some people have just building a daily theme to convert chronological time into social time—the nature of the task being inherently meaningless. In this regard, Frazier's (1968) comments are perceptive:

'Time is what the factory worker sells, not labor, not skill, but time, dreary time. Desolute factory time that passes so slowly compared with the fleeting seconds of the weekend.' (Frazier, 1968, p. 12)

It is perhaps little wonder that 'marking time' is a significant work theme. Many workers use in fact a sort of 'backwards calendar' which marks the days, weeks, months, or years that are left until retirement benefits may be claimed. Similar themes characterize life in other institutions as well—students in educational settings, draftees in peace-time armies, and patients in hospitals. And for prisoners 'doing time' in jail, a day is considered over when one wakes up in the morning (Cohen and Taylor, 1972).

A predominant theme has a number of implications. For example, the career of a US business executive—where the theme of advancement is not only available but central to the occupation—seems to carry with it what Henry (1963) calls a 'permanent sense of the unobtained'. Thus, the executive who at 30 years of age considers himself successful only if he is head of the department at age 40, will, at age 40 consider himself successful only if he is head of the division at age 50, and so on. A consumer theme revolving around the accumulation of material goods has much the same character as does an artistic theme stressing the achievement of excellence (Roth, 1963). These themes not only have a Sisyphus-like nature as the individual seeks to reach the unreachable, but also become progressively more difficult to document as the individual travels through the career.

Some themes require more correction over time than others. Such thematic revision is necessitated perhaps more often out of failure than out of success.[24] Indeed, it is not so much the discovery of a theme that is so difficult or mysterious, but rather it is the continued documentation of a theme that is most problematic to an individual. For instance, the plateaued and aging executive who hopes to rise to the head of the corporation must eventually recognize his folly and construct a new theme if possible to provide meaning to his organizational role. Or, for many workers who hold the attainment of 'independence from the company' as a revered work theme, the time will come when they must realize that such a theme is not to be. Chinoy (1955) writes evocatively:

'The worker faces the day of reckoning when he is called upon to admit that he is trapped— that his American dream of being his own boss is not to be fulfilled.' (Chinoy, 1955, p. 112)

Realistically, the theme one selects to emphasize in the work career will be restricted to areas of life that seem most promising. To utilize Piaget's (1969) seminal insights, if past and present experiences give one reason to trust the promise of future reward, the individual can construct a developmental theme emphasizing control, planning, and growth. Work themes can be expected to reflect these features. To wit, the middle classes have 'careers' built on future reference, while the working classes have 'work' built on a day-to-day reference. And, for the pariah classes, this sphere of life is usually empty, thus, there may be little point in working at all since there is empirically nowhere to go.

In brief, the concept of theme is critical to a person's definition of his work situation. It must be discovered and carved from experience. To the degree that the individual's past experiences, daily pattern of activities, and longer run vision of future events are perceived to be homologous, temporal continuity results (McHugh, 1968). Discontinuities or the critical violation of the homology can be expected to lead to a problematic sense of the present. Indeed, if the results of one's actions are indeterminable or indistinguishable from all other possible actions, the construction of a satisfying theme will be impossible for the future is empty, lacking in design.

Explicitness As implied above, themes can be seen to vary along several dimensions. One of these dimensions is the explicitness built into a work theme. Explicitness deals with what could be called the practical achievement of a theme (McHugh, 1968). It is roughly equivalent to the degree of 'fit' between theme and experience—a set of benchmarks to handle and compound the theme by categorizing expectations and specifying probabilities. To illustrate, if a theme of upward mobility were present, the explicitness of such a theme would refer to the timetable that *tests* the theme. But, such a timetable would refer to a range of time surrounding certain benchmarks of an upwardly mobile career rather than a precise time. Take, for example, the aspiring university professor who makes explicit his anticipated rise in the scholar's hierarchy by planning to acquire his Ph.D. before turning 25, publish his first book before 27, receive university tenure before 30, and make full professor by 35. The failure to achieve any one of these particular benchmarks precisely on time is not likely to cause a revision in overall career theme, rather the failure would probably be excused as an institutional failure, not a personal one.

Thus, timetable inaccuracies are often errors of range, not theme—to the person, a misplaced concreteness in the flow of time.[25]

Themes, therefore, have their occasions. To varying degrees, they are made explicit by locating thematic particulars over a series of chronologically-given discrete events (McHugh, 1968). But, as illustrated, events do not always correspond precisely to a theme. In everyday life, such occurrences require the invention of an excuse. Thus, a writer whose theme is writing quality books permits himself a bad book—both in anticipation and in retrospect—because of his 'crass materialism'. Or, a manager with a good 'track record' knows occasionally he will make a poor decision—because of a 'time crunch'. As McHugh (1968) notes: 'phenotypic contradictions need not recommend genotypic transformations'.

In some organizations, however, the maintenance of a theme through the creation of an excuse will be difficult, if not impossible, for the timetable that tests the theme is handed down by fiat and is therefore structurally explicit. The professorial careers in some academic organizations carry the so-called 'up or out' proviso—one must look elsewhere for employment if promotion does not come within five years or before one turns 35. The timetable of officers in military organizations often fall under a similar rubric. And, in such careers, there are few euphemisms to protect the losers. On the other hand, some career timetables are open-ended, without structural texture. Timetables for business careers can vary a great deal from organization to organization. Thus a failure to be promoted within a two-year stretch in one organization may lead a person to what some have called a 'status panic' (taken as a signal that one's upward thrust has been halted). Whereas, in another organization, such a failure is not a failure at all, representing to the person simply a taken-for-granted organizational policy.

In most work organizations, norms regarding success grow around promotional timetables. These passage-governing norms usually represent a social consensus around expectations of when career events should occur. To the individual, such norms are the yardsticks by which progress can be measured (Roth, 1963). Yet, upon entrance to an organization, these yardsticks need be discovered (at least those pertinent to the novice-to-member transition) if the individual is to make meaningful the events of the early career.

Explicitness also refers to the detailed occurrences of the work-a-day situation. If one has little idea of what tomorrow will bring, understanding of today's activities will be difficult. In project organizations, for example, Pert charts or Gnatt charts rigorously detail the short-run and provide much explicitness to the temporal meaning of work activity. On the other hand, in typing pools where day-to-day activity patterns are unpredictable and vary considerably, explicitness is clearly lacking and therefore little thematic structure is likely to grow around the work itself. In such situations, themes will often grow around the cycle of events occurring in the organization. In fact, in most organizations, regardless of one's actual work, there exists a predictable cycle in which some days are dull, others tumultuous—the 'red-letter days', 'blue mondays', 'dog days', and the perennial 'thank-god-its-fridays'.

To those in positions of authority within the organization, time is an important resource by which control over others can be exercised. Unclear timetables governing career progression provide an administrator with a most powerful tool by which to influence subordinate behavior. And differences are bound to arise between superior and subordinate regarding certain explicit features of the subordinate's work theme (e.g. when one should be promoted, granted full membership, change tasks, or receive a pay hike). Yet no matter how much structure is embedded in the situation nor the degree to which those in authority try to discourage people, an attempt on the part of the subordinate will be undertaken to bargain for a 'better' timetable (Roth, 1963). Even in prisons, where the warden or parole officer unequivocally declares that he will not bargain, a prisoner will always attempt to negotiate (or at least try to discover ways around the limits) an easier and/or shorter career (Sykes, 1958; Irwin, 1970). Certainly, in less coercive settings, 'making a deal' regarding timetables is a part of the texture of everyday life. Again, however, timetables are flexible and misunderstandings occur. Themes are hence subject to sudden twists of benevolent or malevolent fate.

Ownership The relation between the individual's past and future is not self-evident. To locate oneself temporally requires effort—an active search for patterns that underlie movement across social time. Even if the result of this search could be said, in another context, to be determined by a person's role, biography, or surrounding environment, the person must still *do* something. Suppose, for example, a police recruit is unsure as to whether or not he will make it through the ordeal of the training academy. But, even if he does not make it through, he cannot answer his original question unless he participates consciously through personalized effort in the academy. Individual actions are required for temporal location even though it could be said that the results are determined historically.[26]

Ownership refers then to the individual's control over his fate—whether it be real or imagined. It represents another dimension along which themes can be expected to vary. Organizations differ as to the degree through which a person, by his own efforts, can create and sustain a temporal theme. Under some work conditions, themes may be based entirely upon what, to the individual, are structural characteristics of the organization, leaving the person, therefore, little room in which to maneuver and strike upon an owned theme. Civil service based bureaucracies exert almost monopolistic control over the themes of employees. Similarly, contacts and agreements provide narrow limits within which the members of some unions can create an individualized occupational theme. In such cases, temporal homologies are most certainly present (i.e. the future will look like the past) and are perhaps quite explicit (i.e. career steps are documented). But the individual is unlikely to have had much to do with the authoring of his present circumstance. Nor is he likely to be able—other than by changing settings—to author his work future. Career timetables, while they need be discovered, are not always owned by the individual. And while thematic revisions occur, they are attributable less to individual effort than to environmental conditions—the person being simply a miniscule cog of some Kaffkaesque machine. Even in the higher circles of managerial and professional position, a person's career may be determined largely by events not of his making. For instance, demands for service may shift, the economy may fluctuate, or one's superior may act capriciously, seemingly without rhyme or reason. Hence, there are many occurrences possible which may wrench temporal control from out of the individual's hands.

Persons may also come to possess, however, a great deal of ownership over their career travels. This seems particularly true in Western industrialized societies where the individualistic philosophy reigns supreme. Proverbs, for example, exhort one to assume personal responsibility—'where there's a will there's a way'. Such old saws often proffer direct tips on how to deal with time—'the early bird catches the worm'. All the while of course 'time marches on'. Ownership, not fickle fate, typifies the homiletic but ever-popular autobiography of the 'self-made' man. And such organizational development activities as 'open-systems planning', 'goal setting', and 'management-by-objectives' encourage the individual to act, not react. Indeed, even therapeutic techniques such as transactional analysis are quite direct insofar as they exhort the individual to take control of his own destiny—e.g. 'pack your own chute'.

Ownership reflects then the attribution of causality by the person to himself regarding his temporal situation. In other words, ownership is akin to personal responsibility—the degree to which the individual feels responsible for the shape and documentation of his theme. When the theme is owned, questions concerning 'how I got here and where am I going' are answered by the person in individual terms. Temporal control is individualized. Furthermore, there is evidence from the psychological laboratory attesting to the impact self-set expectations have on future accomplishments. For example, Locke (1965) demonstrated experimentally the powerful effects of individual goal setting when attending to certain tasks. To be successful, goal setting must rest on the individual's presumption that certain acts will be followed invariably by certain consequences. Indeed, the so-called 'self-fulfilling prophecy' makes explicit the idea of predictability of theme since what occurs is simply what one expects to occur (Rosenthal, 1967). The ownership of a theme is therefore ironic—the future is, as it were, already accomplished.

If one looks to the past, ownership is documented by what information processing researchers call selective recall. Events are emphasized, annulled, transformed, and forgotten depending upon their fit within one's adopted temporal frame. Indeed, personal histories are rewritten continuously and serve as a base for the retrospective learning of new self-conceptions. This sort of revisionist mode of recall is the stock in trade of the psychotherapist. To punctuate this point, note the self-serving reinterpretations of the past as revealed in the memoirs of famous generals, business tycoons, movie stars, prime ministers, and even notorious crooks. Some events, notably positive achievements, are decorated with personal nobility or acumen, while other events are attributed to sinister outside forces that could not be controlled. Thus, to the individual, if things are going well, the temporal theme is more likely to be owned than if things are not going so well. Although the theme connects temporal events, ownership of that theme reflects subterranean values and evaluative schemes the person ties to such a theme.

To summarize, themes include varying degrees of explicitness and ownership. Themes allow chronological time to become conceptually social, hence, meaningful. Greenwich time notwithstanding, individuals must make disparate slices of life continuous enough to maintain activities. And, as I have suggested, it is not so much the discovery of a temporal theme that is most problematic to the individual, but rather it is the persistent and enduring documentation of the theme that is most difficult.

ON ANOMIE AND ALIENATION: AN INCONCLUSIVE END

> *'What is needed is a continued readiness to recognize that every point of view is particular to certain definite situations.'*
> Wittgenstein (1965)

Socialization deals with the practical question of how people learn what is required of them within a particular environment. However, most models of socialization ignore or gloss over the specific content that is said to be transferred in the setting and concentrate instead upon detailing the process by which individuals are taught a generalized 'such and such' about 'this or that'. In this paper, I have tried to rectify this situation somewhat by focusing attention directly to the content side of the socialization issue—in other words, the 'such and such' and 'this and that'.

Summarily, I have suggested that a newcomer to an organization cannot participate in the organization unless he first locates himself in space and time. Thus, the individual must both 'normalize the setting' and 'discover a theme' if he is to define and make meaningful his organizational situation. The question now arises as to what occurs if these conditions are not fulfilled?

Durkheim (1933, 1964) suggested initially that the antithesis of order was anomie. To Durkheim, anomie was a state of experience marked by individual feelings of despair, hopelessness, helplessness, and confusion. More specifically, Seeman (1959) argues persuasively that anomie is best characterized as a state of *normlessness*. For my purposes here, this state can be said to exist when the person is unable to determine what is going on about him. This condition occurs therefore when the individual is unable to 'normalize the setting' in which he finds himself. The situation will be viewed by the person as senseless, without *purpose*, and, hence, the actor cannot, in any meaningful way, connect and commit himself to the social network and activities observed to be going on.

Yet, even given that the individual can more or less normalize the surroundings, the person must still develop a notion of where he fits into the temporal scheme of things. That is, he must discover a theme which can guide his actions in the organization such that the experienced past and anticipated future provide a *means* for accomplishing present activities. Such a theme can of course be personally significant or insignificant. Themes reflect a part of the individual's self-identification—or lack thereof—with the work situation. Thus, they can be either engaging or alienating in character.[27]

Within this framework, the interplay between these two analytically separable features can be detailed. Taken together, the individual's assessments on normality and assumptions regarding a theme provide a set of background expectancies that allow the individual to organize experience such that spatial and temporal meanings can be attached to one's experiences in the work place.[28] Hence, space and time coexist and coalesce insofar as the individual is concerned. Certainly, a person's background expectancies can be at odds with the expectancies of others in the setting. But it is unlikely that a serious gap between what the individual takes to be true and what significant others in the setting take to be true will persist for extended periods of time without some sort of surprise prompting either the person in question or his colleagues to reconsider and revise certain definitions.

Thematic development is preceded usually by the normalization process since the discovery of a purpose to one's involvement should take place, at least logically, prior to the discovery of a means to achieve such an end. Sometimes, however, the assumptions an individual makes regarding his organizational theme will obviate accurate assessments of the setting itself. Thus, themes can predecide what will be perceived in the environment. To illustrate, take the case of the highly sought after recruit for a college football squad. Believing beforehand perhaps that he 'can't miss' and is certain to be a 'big star', the young man may well fail to read the signs in early practice sessions that he is not measuring up to his preseason assumptions. In such cases, we can speak meaningfully of the 'prima donna', the 'out-of-touch', or the 'swelled head'—the person seen by others on the scene as 'living a lie' or 'caught in a world of fantasy'. When—or, in rare instances, if—the individual eventually recognizes his error of self-exaggeration, a new theme must be built upon freshly normalized grounds.

Under more typical circumstances, themes are constructed upon firmer foundations. Yet normalization is not always possible. Anomie arises out of those situations in which the social actor cannot assign an intelligible purpose to what is observed. Thus, an individual who finds himself in such a situation can be said to be without a social framework from which to make understandable the actions of others. Suppose, for example, the well-prepared and confident MBA asks his supervisor on his first job what it is he is to do, and the supervisor answers in unequivocal terms, 'Nothing!' Suppose also that the aspiring young manager is surprised, or, as he might well be, shocked. Without probing further, the individual's idea of the normal shape of things has been shattered. He can no longer continue in the situation matter-of-factly. Such an interaction may leave the young man in a state of anomie—his work situation having become suddenly meaningless.

Now consider the case of a young female professor who teaches her assigned classes, pursues her specific research interests, and takes an active role in the affairs of the academic community. She has, in short, normalized her setting and has begun, no doubt, to develop a notion of just how her professorial career should unfold. Consider also that our eager young scholar approaches the Dean at some early point in her career and asks whether or not it is possible for her to be granted tenure in the institution and the Dean answers without blinking an eye, 'No!'. Again, surprise and shock is the likely response. The individual's career expectations have been fractured prematurely. In such a case, she may perceive few means available to her within the organization to rectify the situation. Indeed, her self-image as a competent and promotable woman may be in severe jeopardy. Other than waiting it out, she is powerless for the environment is not responsive to her means. Consequently, she will be unable to build a theme around her involvement in the workplace that is not conflicting with her own desires. Under these circumstances, we could say that she is alienated, for her perceived organizational destiny is altogether bleak and uninviting.

If the individual does not leave the organization, does the anomie or alienation manufactured in the above cases persist forever? Or does the person go on to reconstruct the situation in such a way as to restore or regain a sense of normality and theme? According to McHugh (1968) and Garfinkel (1967), the answer would be a qualified yes. In the instance of the superior's vacuous job assignment, the newcomer may turn to others for a role definition and discover to his relief that the boss is a 'card' or a 'kidder', never to be taken seriously. In the case of the Dean's negative promotional forecast, the woman in question may also turn to others in the setting and discover that the Dean is merely an organizational 'curmudgeon', an adherent perhaps of out-of-date tenure policies and the wielder of little power over the actual situation.

What these grossly overstated and unadorned examples are meant to suggest is simply that neither anomie nor alienation is an absolute condition from which there can be no return. Indeed, individuals will search far and wide for clues to help establish a favorable organizational location. As long as there are socially navigable alternatives to replace anomie or alienation, individuals can and usually will find them. Although the relationship between the person and organization may of course change, it does not disappear. The analytic possibility arises that a sort of intermittent anomie or alienation characterize individual careers. Theorists must allow therefore for temporary not terminal states.[29]

This conception of temporary states of alienation and anomie is quite similar to the Lewinian notion of 'unfreezing' events which serves to prepare an individual to change. Thus, through occurrences which create states of anomie or alienation, the person is literally forced to reconsider his or her situated identity or self-concept vis-à-vis the organization. Normality assessments and thematic assumptions are precarious, if not delicate, cognitive states. While disconfirmation of these states can run from what is merely annoying to what is totally devastating, such occurrences nearly always result in some changes on the person's part.

To conclude, role taking fails when people are unable to discover where they are located in space and time. Unless persons can deduce what is normal in the setting from what is not, they are incapable of entering into the concerted action patterns of a given social order. Indeed, without such understandings, people cannot construct realistic themes to guide their participation in the organization. Anomie and alienation are therefore always present to some degree whenever persons enter novel surroundings. What is extraordinary, however, is that most transformations are accomplished with relative ease. Individual bewilderment is, with few exceptions, only rare and fleeting. Indeed, the observed ability to convert the strange to the familiar is a tribute to individual ingenuity and adaptability—homage perhaps to human capacity.

NOTES

1. I would like to thank Professors Edgar H. Schein, Peter Keen, Donald Schon, Chris Argyris, and, especially, Lotte Bailyn for their patient and rigorous criticisms of the original draft of this paper. While they all may not agree with what is said here, this version was written with their comments in mind.
2. The term organizational socialization is preferred to occupational socialization primarily because it directs attention to the dominant setting in which the process occurs. Although the two socialization processes are often interdependent, the position taken here is that the characteristics of the setting are far more crucial to the eventual outcomes of the process than are the specific occupational attributes to be inculcated.
3. To study work socialization apart from the study of careers seems an unfortunate reminder of the slow development of the study of human behavior in social systems. Indeed, to speak of one without the other is artificial and limiting—both from the everyday actor's perspective and from the theorist's perspective. A career is therefore part and parcel of a continuous socialization process, representing to the person a result of the encapsulated past and a historical reference for an exposed future.
4. Whatever the epistomological status of the symbolic interactionist approach, it is impossible to deny the importance of unravelling the actor's perspective for organizational theory. The orthodox approach to the study of organizations tends to adopt theories of organizational functioning that are oriented towards a managerial concern for practical outcomes (Mouzelis, 1967; Perrow, 1972). This perspective has been, in my view, misleading and unduly restrictive. This paper represents an effort to view organizations in terms of the ways in which they are problematic to persons which comprise them. This position is argued well by Silverman (1971), Salaman and Thompson (Ed.) (1973), Albrow (1968), and Bittner (1965).
5. As McHugh (1968) points out, if the character of an object were self-evident, the idea of meaning would be redundant to reality. Thus there could be no misunderstanding because the character of an object and hence its treatment would be universal and always correct. Ergo, in a real sense, objects are social artifacts for they require

the ascription of social meaning before they can be said to exist at all. This philosophical position is made most forceably by phenomenologists. See, for example, Schutz (1970), Husserl (1946), and Ichheiser (1949).

6. This point is indeed a cornerstone of critical sociological thought. The world, from any perspective, must be seen as a result of continuous reciprocal interaction between subject and object, between social substructure and organizational superstructure. Such a view rejects the hypostatization of any one particular finding or moment of reality to the exclusion of others. Indeed, what is missing in so many otherwise excellent organizational studies is the consideration of the historical dimension and the notion of subjective mediation.

7. In a series of laboratory experiments tailored along the lines of Garfinkel's (1967) pioneering studies, McHugh (1968) demonstrated graphically the viability (indeed, the advisability) of regarding emergent (i.e. temporal) and referent (i.e. social) definitions as preconditions for the actor's assignment of meaning to his situation. Although in this essay I collapse and reinterpret certain locational dimensions and extend the conceptual framework beyond the dyadic interactional encounter to that of general perspectives taken by an actor, my intellectual reliance throughout this chapter on McHugh's work is substantial.

8. Sorokin and Merton (1937) make this point well. To James (1950) time represents a 'useful fiction' quite unaffected, from the individual's point of view, by astronomy. Psychologically, time is directly influenced by the number and importance of concrete events occurring in a particular period under study. As James indicated, 'a time filled with varied and interesting experiences seems short in passing, but long as we look back. On the other hand, a tract of time empty of experience seems long in passing, but in retrospect short' (James, 1950, p. 624).

9. The concept of social time, while not necessarily esoteric, has seldom been examined by social scientists. Yet all conceptualizations of process make implicit use of time. The only systematic works with which I am familiar that gives time its due are Doob's (1971) admirable broad brushed canvas on time patterning, and Klineberg and Cottle's (1973) speculative but thoroughly enjoyable and enlightening investigation of time perception. Perhaps, these two recent works will prompt others to begin serious and sustained study in this area. To everything there is a season.

10. Mead's (1913) observations on empathy are pertinent in this regard. He states:

   '... the very sounds, gestures, especially vocal gestures, which man makes in addressing others, call out or tend to call out responses from himself. He cannot hear himself speak without assuming in a measure the attitude which he would have assumed if he had been addressed in the same words by others.' (Mead, 1913, pp. 376–377)

11. This recalls Thoreau's famous lines, 'if a man does not keep pace with his companions perhaps it is because he hears a different drummer'. Thus, an individual's choice of audience to whom he orients his performance may not necessarily come from among those present in the workplace. Indeed, some persons, believing they are 'ahead of their time', may perform for future generations or for posterity. Others with similar grandiose visions may perform for 'humanity' or 'for-the-country'. While complete estrangement from those immediately around the individual is rare, in pluralistic organizations, it is not unheard of for persons to pursue goals incomprehensible to colleagues. Perhaps, by a similar logic, the acts of the daydreamer, loafer, or even saboteur can be understood and assigned meaning, see Shibutani (1962).

12. I am not denying here the relevance of one's biography, role requirements, reference group, level of aspiration, and so forth. But simply recognizing the existence of these factors does not absolve the analyst from exploring how the person goes about fashioning a specific definition for a given situation. Thus, I emphasize in this paper an *interpretive* perspective in which the meanings an actor attaches to his situation evolve

and change over time rather than the more commonly applied *normative* perspective in which the meanings attached to the situation are seen as governed by the role expectations of actors in respective states. For an excellent introduction to this interpretive, see Filmer and coworkers (1972).

13. Mead (1930) goes so far as to suggest:

'The human individual is a self only in so far as he takes the attitude of another toward himself. In so far as this attitude is that of a number of others, and in so far as he can assume the organized attitudes that are cooperating in a common activity, he takes the attitudes of the group toward himself, and in taking this or these attitudes he is defining the object of the group, that which defines and controls the response.' (Mead, 1930, p. 192)

14. The importance of taking an appropriate stance is highlighted in many situations by the elaborate attention given to enforcing the casual, 'Nothing Unusual' definition. Some offbeat examples are useful in this regard. Consider the nudist camp where participants artfully strive to suggest that the situation is no different than it would be if everyone were fully clothed (Weinberg, 1968). Or, for instance, note the reassuring nonchalance and matter-of-factness of the medical staff attending gynecological examinations which serve to insinuate to the patient that the probing of private parts of the body is no different than the probing of, say, the elbow (Emerson, 1970a). Consider also how swiftly a sort of forced conviviality replaces the awkward silence in party situations. The point here is simply that a great deal of attention in any social situation goes into maintaining the smooth flow of interaction by constructing 'situation as normal' rules prohibiting interruption (Glaser and Strauss, 1964).

15. More generally, labels usually reflect local organizational argot. Indeed, for an individual to accurately map his position in the organization, requires at least a working knowledge of the linguistic terrain. Polsky (1967) suggests that argot serves both to separate insiders from outsiders and to approximate methods and tools of the trade. Thus, for example, the rookie policeman in some departments must learn to 'shake doors', 'do the paper', and 'handle a 220' before others who are experienced in the occupation will treat him as a colleague (Van Maanen, 1974a).

16. While few argue the well-established point that the reference group provides a person with an intellectual strategy for coping with the environment, there is considerable debate over the basis upon which one chooses a particular reference group. Some claim that individual aspirations are determinative (Merton, 1957). Others suggest that choice is made on the grounds of social comparability (Katz and Lazardsfeld, 1955). Still other writers contend that both are influential (Kelley, 1952). My point here is simply that all are correct and incorrect at the same time for they fail to spell out the situational contingencies of individual choice.

17. Realwork definitions are usually upheld by the wisdom of tradition. They are then somewhat tautological in nature. Thus, the rationale for Realwork takes the form, 'we-do-things-this-way-around-here-because-that-is-the-way-they-are-done'. To a newcomer, Realwork is often defined via the 'don't-ask-me-why-just-do-it' format — the reasons for a certain procedure apparently lost to history.

18. As Sudnow (1965) points out, for any series of offense type, a PD can provide a characterization by adage. For example, 'normal' burglary is seen by PDs as involving regular violators, no weapons, low-priced items, little property damage, lower class residences, largely black offenders operating independently with a distincly nonprofessional orientation toward crime. When situations significantly deviate from this typification, the actions of a PD do not follow a regularized recipe (i.e. typical burglaries are reduced to petty theft in which a guilty plea is obtained from the defendant and the matter handled without trial). In the idiosyncratic case, outcomes are unpredictable for the normal order upon which the organization rests has temporarily been suspended.

19. I use the term 'nonscientific' here to suggest that the theories developed by an actor

to inform himself as to the 'why' of his everyday life have no necessary and/or sufficiency requirements. They may be logically consistent or inconsistent, explaining the general or specific. The point is simply that a 'cause' for certain events is postulated. Thus, an act can be meaningful and fully understood by a person regardless of whether it is believed to be a result of Martian or Earthly origins. In this view, experience is itself a theory.

20. The best discussion of the generation of plausible accounts can be found in Cicourel (1968), Garfinkel (1967), and Lyman and Scott (1970). Most recently, an interesting distinction between disclaimers (which are seen to be future-oriented justifications) and accounts (which are perhaps best thought of as past-oriented justifications) has been suggested by Hewitt and Stokes (1975).

21. On the anticipation side of an actor's temporal frame, Lewin's (1938) ahistorical motivation theory is very similar to the view taken here. In a slightly modified form, the theory is now referred to as expectancy or instrumentality theory (see Vroom, 1964; Porter and Lawler, 1968; and Mitchell and Biglan, 1971). Although the theory has been shown to have some predicative validity, it is incomplete since (among other reasons) it does little more with an actor's past than to assert its existence. But expectancy theory does make explicit Rollo May's notion that 'what a man seeks to become determines what he has been'.

22. The search for verification of one's constructed theme resembles what Mannheim (1952) calls the 'documentary method'. This method, under most conditions, allows the individual to integrate temporally discrete events and therefore order his experiences. See also McHugh (1968) for a discussion of documentation as used here.

23. In many work situations, the entry level job taken by a recruit represents a sort of terminal career node. Coal miners, garbage collectors, secretaries, and social workers, enter jobs at a level from which hierarchical advancement is not the norm. To a degree then these jobs represent a very determinant career. However, there almost always exists the possibility of achieving, from the individual's standpoint, a better assignment, freedom from close supervision, higher pay, tenure, and perhaps increasing recognition for a job well done. Thus, what on the surface may seem to be a preset and deadend organizational career, is in fact a career with varied indeterminant possibilities.

24. Indeed, in some cases, being able to see ahead may be more of a curse than a blessing. The so-called 'mid-life crisis' represents perhaps the epitome of thematic revision wherein an individual must come to grips with the fact that he has already lived longer than one can expect to live in the future—the implicit theme from childhood of immortality, becoming one of mortality.

25. See Roth (1963) for a full account of the notion of timetables as used in this paper.

26. This point is well made by McHugh (1968) who notes that 'it must be possible for the (actor) to participate actively in the sense that he is *doing definition*, that he is engaged even when the outcome is determined by history ... it is a mistake, as Wittgenstein (1965) once pointed out to think that if only nothing keeps me from walking, I shall walk'. (McHugh, 1968, p. 40)

27. Despite Marx or Jesus, neither anomie nor alienation is an objective condition representing class membership or a fall from grace. As the terms are used here, they must be distinguished theoretically from their postulated empirical correlates. Moreover, some recent research indicates that alienation and anomie in the work place occurs to a surprising degree among members of the priviledged and specialized managerial class (see Bailyn, this volume).

28. I use the term 'background expectancies' to refer to the merging of space and time perspectives simply because individuals rarely are able to articulate specifically all their thematic assumptions and normality assessments. They stand, as it were, in the background, ordering and making intelligible the unknowable. A simple example will suffice perhaps. We typically never question the impression someone gives be-

cause we suspend doubts about the person's sincerity—providing of course that the person's appearance in the particular setting is more or less normal and somewhat predictable. While it is indeed impossible to know whether or not the other person is actually sincere (i.e. 'to get inside the other's head'), we must assume that we do know if we are to proceed with our everyday life. Thus we warrant such knowledge on the basis of our background expectancies (Silverman, 1972; Garfinkel, 1967).

29. Although this paper is not the most appropriate place to discuss in detail the kinds of themes available to an actor, let me suggest three generic possibilities that are consistent with the approach taken here. First, a theme can be of the engaging or fulfilling variety in that the individual derives a great deal of satisfaction from his vocational life and, in fact, bases a large part of his self-identification upon his work role. The prestigious occupations such as law or medicine are obvious examples of pursuits where this sort of theme would be expected. Second, a theme can be seen to be alienating in that the individual derives virtually no satisfaction from his occupational efforts and, in fact, makes a conscious effort to provide some distance between his work identity and self-identity (Goffman, 1961). Themes associated with what Hughes (1958) called 'dirty work occupations' (e.g. dishwashers, garbagemen, gravediggers, assembly-line operators, etc.) are perhaps good examples in this regard. Third, and somewhere between these two poles, lies a sort of gray conglomeration of work themes—themes which are neither engaging or alienating. No doubt most pursuits fall into this category. And it is here where one would expect the intermittent pattern of alienation discussed in the text to appear.

PART II

Understanding Organizational Careers and Individual Differences

As researchers have time and again demonstrated, any one occupation turns out to be many occupations involving different kinds of individual skills and talents and taking people along different paths over the course of a career. Indeed, we cannot tag a career simply by denoting an agreed upon occupational label. Such a tactic ignores the well-grounded knowledge held by practitioners in any occupational category that there are many pathways to follow across time. Some pathways may lead to greater specialization in a particular field, others to less specialization, some may lead upward in a hierarchy, others downward, some may lead to greater involvement in the work world, others to less involvement, and so on. The point here being that careers can be expected to vary considerably within as well as between occupations. Thus, we need to develop finely-grained taxonomies to describe career paths—taxonomies that do more than simply label one particular line of work a career.

One way in which we can accomplish this task is to make the most reasonable assumption that within any given occupation or organization, careers differ because people differ. Therefore, an important objective of career studies is to discover relevant internal dimensions upon which people can be expected to vary, and, more importantly, to demonstrate just how these dimensions are associated with a given career path.

In Part I, it was suggested that individuals must locate themselves within their experienced organizational environment before they can take action. However, the issue concerning whether or not individuals were particularly satisfied or productive within their respective situations was glossed over. Here we devote substantial attention to this issue. The question to be addressed in Part II is essentially: 'What kinds of careers are associated with what kinds of people?' Although the question itself is rather classical in its formulation, the answers provided by the various authors are not.

Without going into detail, in recent years, there has been a resurgence of interest in the way a person learns, thinks, solves problems, emphasizes certain outcomes over others, and, in general, pays attention to different clues originating in the environment. The research presented in the following three chapters represents an important step in understanding the effects that different personal styles or cognitive styles have upon an individual's choice of, progress in, and attitude toward a particular career. Whereas in Part I we related experience to cognition, in Part II, we relate cognition to behavior. Indeed, here we assume that people have developed a more or less consistent pattern of addressing the world of their concern—an orientation stylized by their past experiences and biological heritage. Thus, what the authors of the next three chapters are interested in knowing is how these different patterns of interest and abilities help shape individual careers.

Chapter 2

Career Anchors and Career Paths: A Panel Study of Management School Graduates[1]

Edgar H. Schein

INTRODUCTION

A panel study of 44 Sloan School of Management alumni was launched in 1961 in order to study the interaction of personal values and career events in the lives of managers in organizations. The original purpose of the study was to determine the mechanisms and effects of organizational socialization— in what manner and through what means would the values of these students be influenced by their organizational experiences? Would certain sets of individuals with certain sets of values be more or less socialized? Could one determine what kinds of value syndromes would lead to careers in which the individual would innovate, i.e. would change organizations rather than be changed by them?

In order to answer these questions we selected an all male panel to be studied prior to graduation and at various points during their subsequent careers. A major reinterview and resurvey of the panel was completed in 1973–1974. All 44 panelists were located, interviewed, and given the same attitude surveys as in the early 1960's. The present report deals with one aspect of the results. It was found that each of the panelists could be understood best in terms of a concept of 'career anchor'—a syndrome of motives, values, and self-perceived talents which guides and constrains the person's career. This report spells out this concept, classifies the panelists into groups based on different anchors, and reports some correlates of these groupings.

THE PANEL STUDY PROCEDURE

Selection of the panel

Once a panel study had been decided upon in early 1960, it was important to avoid as much as possible whatever biases might be inherent in people volunteering for such a study. Therefore, we took an entire class list for each year, 1961, 1962, 1963, and selected 15 names at random from that list. Prior to that selection we eliminated certain categories of students: (*a*) foreign students; (*b*) students who were to enter the military shortly after graduation;

and (c) students who were going directly into a Ph.D. program following graduation. Once we had located 15 names, we sent an invitation to each of these students to participate in the study. If he refused, we selected another name at random until we had 15 acceptances. This process could have introduced bias if there had been a large number of refusals, but in each class we had to replace only one or two people. It is quite likely, therefore, that the panelists are reasonably representative of the graduating classes from which they were drawn. We ended up with 15 members of the class of 1961, 15 members of the class of 1962, and 14 members of the class of 1963, because of one person dropping the study at a point where it was too late to replace him.

The entire process described above was completed in the fall term of the student's second year of their two-year masters program. The spring term was devoted to the actual interviews and survey procedures.

INITIAL DATA GATHERING

Each panelist was interviewed for two or three hours. The interview covered his educational and occupational history, the origins of his interests in business/management, his plans for the future, his ambitions, his work values, his self-concept, and other information pertinent to unravelling the value syndromes which were operating in the person. In addition, each panelist took two to three hours worth of specially designed attitude and value questionnaires in order to permit us to get a complete picture of his attitudes and values in relation to his career. Such data were obtained prior to any concrete decisions about where or in what kind of job the person would be working.

Reinterviews and Resurveys

The first major post-graduation data gathering occurred one year following graduation. The purpose was to obtain information about the problems of entry into careers. Results have been partially reported in a number of prior publications (Schein, 1962, 1963, 1964). We did not observe major changes or critical career events which seemed to be tied specifically to panelists' attitudes and values, hence did not undertake a major data analysis at that time. Instead, we decided to keep close track of the panel so that we could restudy them at a later time.

After approximately three to five years into their career (depending upon which class we were referring to), we sent a brief questionnaire dealing with career history and a set of the attitude and value surveys to all the panel members. In the spring of 1973, plans were made for a personal follow-up which would include a complete interview at MIT, followed by a retaking of the attitude and value questionnaires. Such interviews were conducted throughout the summer and fall. All 44 men were successfully located and all of them agreed to visit MIT for at least a half day. Interviews again took from two to three hours and covered in considerable detail the career history since graduation, perceptions of the present and future, changes a person saw in himself, relations between work concerns, family concerns, and self-concerns, and reactions to some feedback based on the original interviews.[2] At the end of the interview we also gave each panelist a copy of his original interview transcript in order to give him further feedback.

Data Analysis

The present paper is based on data obtained in the reinterviews. Each interview was tape-recorded, but in addition careful notes were kept around the career history, the reasons for movement, attitudes, and values, and so on. At the end of each interview I dictated a summary based on the notes. These summaries serve as the prime data for the present analysis. The ratings of career anchors which will be reported below are based upon a careful analysis of the interview notes and interview summary.

A Note on Validity

It should be pointed out that one of the reasons for undertaking a panel study of a small sample, in the first place, was to insure a close enough relationship between myself and the panelists to be able to elicit full cooperation from them. I invested considerable energy at the outset of the study in getting to know the panelists and establishing an easy open relationship with them. Their involvement in the study grew as they invested in it and became curious about their own and their peers' careers. I felt in the 1960's that I was getting a pretty accurate picture of where each panelist stood, insofar as he was able to articulate his position, and I felt that the contact over the years had been a worthwhile investment because of the ease of picking up the relationship in the reinterviews. Each of the panelists seemed relaxed, glad to have come to MIT, anxious to tell about himself and his career, and quite frank about his problems and concerns. Several of the panelists had experienced marital difficulties or personal difficulties for which they had sought psychiatric aid. There seemed to be no hesitation on their part in sharing those data with me. On the whole, therefore, I have reasonable confidence that the picture I obtained from each person was about as accurate as he himself could make it. In every case the individual said that it had been an exciting and valuable experience to talk about himself, his career, and life in such great detail. The implications of this point for career counseling or the lack thereof within organizations should be noted.

DEVELOPING A TAXONOMY OF CAREERS—THE CONCEPT OF CAREER ANCHORS

In order to understand clearly how values either determine or are determined by career experiences, it was essential to develop a typology or taxonomy of career paths which reflected important dimensions of the career. The career can be thought of as a set of stages or a path through time which reflects two things: (a) the individual's needs, motives, and aspirations in relation to work, and (b) society's expectations of what kinds of activities will result in monetary and status rewards for the career occupant. In other words, work careers reflect both individual and societal definitions of what is a worthwhile set of activities to pursue throughout a lifetime.

In delineating career types within a given broad occupational category like 'business' or 'management', it is necessary to remember this dual basis for defining the career. Most of the labels one encounters to describe careers reflect only societal or organizational definitions in the form of occupational or positional labels such as supervisor, manager of marketing, executive vicepresident, and so forth. We will use a somewhat broader set of categories, a set which also reflects the individual's subjective view of what his job is and how he relates to it.

In a sense one can speak of two sets of 'anchors' of a career. On the one hand, it is anchored in a set of job descriptions and organizational norms about the rights and duties of a given title in an organization. The 'head of production' is expected to perform certain duties, he carries certain sets of responsibilities, he is held accountable for certain areas of organizational performance. On the other hand, the career is anchored in a set of needs and motives which the career occupant is attempting to fulfill through the work he does and the rewards he obtains for that work—money, prestige, organizational member-ship, challenging work, freedom, etc. The rewards he seeks can be thought of as his job values—what he is looking for in a job. These values reflect an underlying pattern of needs which the individual is trying to fulfill. Thus, as 'head of production', he may be trying to exercise his basic need for in-fluencing and controlling a wide number of people and resources, or he may be trying to meet the challenge of successfully building something or getting something accomplished which is a proof of his competence. Motivational typologies such as those of Maslow or McClelland are useful in categorizing the kinds of underlying needs which serve as one basis for career anchors. For some people, it is achievement or accomplishment *per se*, a drive toward com-petence; for others it is the exercise of a certain talent such as quantitative analysis; and for still others it is a need to find security—to link oneself with a stable and predictable future via an occupation or an organization. The drive for money, as many previous analyses have shown, is difficult to unravel because of the many meanings which money has for people. For some it is a means of achieving security, for some it is an evidence of a social or an occupa-tional status achieved, for some it is a means of exercising power, and for some it is simply a measure of how well they are doing. A drive for money often masks an underlying need, and our categories must attempt to take the underlying need into account.

The career anchor, as defined in this paper, result from an *interaction* between the person with his needs and talents, and the work environment with its opportunities and constraints. During the first few years of his career, the person learns more concretely what he is good at, what he values, and what he needs. He also learns what kinds of jobs or work environments frustrate him because he does not have the talent, motivation, or values needed to function in that environment. As his experience accumulates, the person learns what kinds of jobs or work environments to seek and which to avoid. The underlying syndrome of motives, values, and talents now serves as a guide and constraint on career decisions. The career anchor is more than a motive because it now includes aspects of the self-image based on work experiences.

The interviews revealed a number of themes as to what people are looking for in their career. In fact, the 44 panelists could be classified into five types. The names given to the five career anchors reflect the major motive or need underlying the anchor but it must be remembered that the anchor is not merely a motive. Ultimately it can be thought of as a 'master motive' or the thing the person will not under any circumstances give up.

Anchor 1. Managerial Competence

A number of the respondents make it very clear that their career is organized around the competences and values which make up the fundamental idea of management'. The most important components of this concept are: (*a*) *interpersonal competence*—the ability to influence, supervise, lead, manipulate, and control people toward the most effective achievement of organizational goals; (*b*) *analytical competence*—the ability to identify, analyze, and solve complex conceptual problems under conditions of uncertainty and incomplete information; and (*c*) *emotional stability*—the capacity to be stimulated by emotional and interpersonal crises rather than becoming exhausted or debilitated by them, and the capacity to bear high levels of responsibility and power. The person who wants to rise in the organization, who is seeking higher and higher levels of responsibility must, in other words, be good at handling people, an excellent analyst, and emotionally able to withstand the pressures and tensions of the 'executive suite'. This kind of person 'needs' to be a manager in the sense of needing opportunities to express the *combination* of interpersonal, analytical, and emotional talents delineated above. In terms of organizational categories he is usually thought of as a 'line' manager or a 'general' manager depending upon his rank. Occasionally, a senior functional manager fits this concept if he is getting his prime satisfaction from managing rather than from the technical part of his job.

Anchor 2. Technical–Functional Competence

A number of respondents make it very clear that their career is organized around the challenge of the actual work they are doing—whether that work be financial analysis, marketing, systems analysis, corporate planning, or some other area related to business or management. What distinguishes this group from the previous one is that the anchor is the technical field or functional area, not the managerial process *per se*. If the person has supervisory responsibility, he is usually supervising others in the same technical area as himself, and he makes it clear that it is the area, not the supervising which 'turns him on'. This kind of person is not interested in being promoted out of the technical area he is in; his roots are in the actual analytical work he is doing. In terms of organizational titles such people are spread over a wide range of functional managers, technical managers, senior staff, junior staff, and some external consultants, etc. People with this anchor will leave a company rather than be promoted out of their technical/functional area.

Anchor 3. Security

A number of respondents have tied their career to particular organizations. Though one must infer it, it is reasonable to assume that the underlying need is security and that the person is seeking to stabilize his career by linking it to a given organization. The implications are that he will accept to a greater degree than the other types, an *organizational* definition of his career. Whatever private aspirations or competence areas the individual may have had, he must increasingly rely upon the organization to recognize such needs and competencies and to do the best by him that is possible. But he has lost some degrees of freedom because of his unwillingness to leave a given organization if his needs or talents should go unrecognized. Instead, he must begin to rationalize that the organization's definition of his career is indeed the only valid definition.

If such an individual has technical/functional talent he may rise to a senior functional manager level; but if part of his psychological make-up is a degree of insecurity, that very insecurity is likely to make him 'incompetent' with respect to higher levels of management where emotional security and stability become prime requisites for effective performance. It should be noted that length of time with a given organization is not a sufficient criterion for defining this career anchor. One must know something of the reasons why an individual has remained with a given organization before one can judge whether it is insecurity or a pattern of constant success which is operating.

We do find some individuals who are security oriented yet who are moving from one company to another. However, there are strong similarities between the types of companies and the types of career slots which the individual exchanges. For example, in one person, the pattern of seeking security and stability expressed itself partly in seeking to remain in a given community where he and his family were very happy. Over a period of years this person switched companies three times, but in each case picked a similar company and was willing to start in that new company at an equal or lower level in terms of rank. He is clearly willing to sacrifice some of his autonomy in the career in order to stabilize his total life situation.

Anchor 4. Creativity

A number of respondents have expressed a strong need to create something of their own. This is the fundamental need operating in the entrepreneur and it expresses itself in the desire to invent a new business vehicle, find a new product, develop a new service, or in some other way create something new which can be clearly identified with the individual. In our sample, we can clearly see that the need has varied outlets—one person has become a successful purchaser, restorer, and renter of town houses in a large city; one person has developed a string of financial service organizations which use the computer in new and more effective ways in a region of the country where such services were not available; this person is also purchasing and developing large tracts of land and is currently coowner of a large cattle ranch; one person is operating within a corporate framework taking a new protein product and organizing the marketing, production, and sales of that product in several countries in the Far East and South America; one person is looking for products which he feels he could successfully manufacture, operating as free-lance consultant while he is searching; finally, one person acquired a good deal of capital through some fortunate stock transactions, used his money to buy and set up a small manufacturing firm which he subsequently sold, and is currently looking for other products to develop while operating as a salesman and distributor of sail boats. One of the people, the real-estate dealer, is also a general manager but his drive to build his own ventures supersedes his managerial needs.

One gets the impression that the creativity/entrepreneurial pattern is also closely related to the next one to be discussed—the need for autonomy and independence. All of the entrepreneurs strongly express the desire to be on their own and free of organizational constraints; but the decisive fact about them is that they have not left the world of business to achieve their autonomy. Instead they have chosen to try to express their business and managerial skills through building their own enterprises. The commitment to business shows up in the manner in which this group expresses its ambitions—they want a great deal of money. But the money is not sought for its own sake or for what it will buy—only one of the people mentioned above lives in an opulent fashion. Instead, one gets the distinct impression that total financial assets is a measure that the person uses to define his degree of success as an entrepreneur. The strong urge to be on one's own is probably related to the need to be able to attribute one's success to one's own efforts. There is a degree of self-centeredness or narcissism in the entrepreneurs combined with a strong sense of security, self-confidence, and analytical skill. They vary greatly in the degree to which they possess interpersonal competence, but all of them have some capacity to influence others.

Anchor 5. Autonomy and Independence

A number of respondents are primarily concerned about their own sense of freedom and autonomy. They have found organizational life to be restrictive, irrational, and/or intrusive into their own private life and are seeking careers that have more autonomy associated with them. One of the respondents has become a university professor in areas related to business; one person is a free-lance writer who not only has rejected business as an arena but has rejected the success ethic which he associates with it. For him it has become more important to develop himself—he lives very frugally working as a ghost writer when the mood strikes him. Among the consultants in our sample we find several people who are clearly there because of needs for autonomy, but not all consultants have that need. We have previously noted that some consultants are motivationally entrepreneurs; some are technical/functional specialists who have found that they can pursue their line of work best as a consultant; and some are in transition toward a managerial position. The last-named group have been managerially oriented all along but find that a period of time in management consulting provides much needed experience and contacts. For them consulting is a transitional role rather than a career alternative.

Summary

We have tried to define five basic career anchors from the point of view of the individuals in our panel study: (a) managerial competence; (b) technical/functional competence; (c) organizational security; (d) creativity; and (e) autonomy. For most of our respondents it is possible to identify one major anchor which seems to be the guiding force in their career, even though they are concerned in varying degrees about other motives as well. Viewed as motives, the five categories could be used as a basis for drawing a profile of each person. Viewed as career anchors, however, only one ultimately fits a given person. It is that which he will ultimately not give up.

THE RELATION OF CAREER ANCHORS TO OCCUPATIONAL/ ORGANIZATIONAL TITLES

What the person wants to be competent in or what he is seeking out of his career will not necessarily be reflected in the occupational or organizational titles which he holds. Indeed, one of the important results of this study is to recognize that formal titles or career paths which are overtly similar may reflect important differences in what the career occupants are anchored to. Each panelist was classified into one of the career anchor groups on the basis of his present interview. I took into account any statements of what he was looking for in his work, his explanations of why he moved from job to job or company to company, his view of his present level of success and aspirations for the future, and any other indicator.

Table 2.1 shows the present job titles of the panelists in the different anchor groups. As can be seen from the table, the bulk of the panelists are anchored in technical/functional competence. That is, their major concern in developing

Table 2.1 Job titles and organizational membership of panelists in different career anchor groups

---

Anchor 1. Managerial Competence

1.1 (1961)   *Manager of Factoring Systems*; Corporate Hq's, large financial corporation
1.2 (1961)   *Sales Manager and Part Owner*; Family furniture business
1.3 (1961)   *Sales Manager*; Industrial Foods Division, large conglomerate
1.4 (1961)   *Director of Corporate Plan Administration*; large airline
1.5 (1963)   *President and Part Owner*, Small manufacturing firm
1.6 (1963)   *Manager of Marketing and Assistant to General Manager*, large division of large corporation
1.7 (1963)   *Director of Administration*; Insurance Services Division of large financial corporation
1.8 (1963)   *Vice President for Finance and Administration*; Medium size service organization

---

Anchor 2. Technical/Functional Competence

2.1 (1961)   *Manager of Data Processing and Part Founder*; large consulting R and D firm
2.2 (1961)   *Research Associate to Vice-president for Academic Affairs*, medium size university
2.3 (1961)   *Director of Required Earnings Studies*; large national utility
2.4 (1961)   *Manager of Engineering*; Large product line of medium size manufacturing company
2.5 (1961)   *Member of Technical Staff*; R and D division of large national utility
2.6 (1961)   *Principal Programmer*; Technical unit of large systems design and manufacturing company
2.7 (1961)   *Market Development Engineer*; New venture group, Chemical corporation
2.8 (1962)   *Project Manager*; Aero-space division of large electronics corporation
2.9 (1962)   *Treasurer*; Small growth company
2.10 (1962)   *Commerce Officer*; Large government department, Canadian government
2.11 (1962)   *Assistant Professor of Operations Research*; Management department, US Naval Academy
2.12 (1962)   *Senior Consultant*; small management consulting firm
2.13 (1963)   *Assistant Director*; White House Office of Telecommunications
2.14 (1963)   *Plant Manufacturing Engineer*; Large consumer products division of large corporation
2.15 (1963)   *Manager, Market Support Systems, Europe*; Information Services Division of large corporation
2.16 (1963)   *Teacher and Department Head*; Regional rural Canadian high School
2.17 (1963)   *Project Supervisor*; Technical division of large chemical company
2.18 (1963)   *Director, Cost Analysis Group*; Large technical systems consulting firm
2.19 (1963)   *Principal*; Large management consulting firm

Anchor 3. Organizational Security

3.1 (1961)   *Manager, Forward Product Planning Research*; Large automobile company
3.2 (1962)   *Marketing Sales Representative*; Large data services company
3.3 (1962)   *Advisory Marketing Representative*; Large computer manufacturing corporation
3.4 (1963)   *Chief Engineer*; Small family steel fabricating company

Anchor 4. Creativity

4.1	(1961)	*Founder* of several financial, service, and real estate businesses
4.2	(1961)	*Founder* of one firm and developer of second firm in chemical industry
4.3	(1962)	*Marketing Development Staff*; Overseas development of new ventures for industrial protein products of large consumer company
4.4	(1962)	*Marketing Consultant*; self-employed, searching for new enterprises to buy or develop (one previous unsuccessful venture)
4.5	(1963)	*President and Co-Founder*; planning and consulting firm
4.6	(1962)	*Senior Vice President*; Media Services, large advertising firm; real-estate developer

Anchor 5. Autonomy and Independence   .

5.1	(1961)	*Senior Consultant*; small management consulting firm
5.2	(1962)	*Communication Consultant*; self-employed, looking for entrepreneurial opportunity in communications field
5.3	(1962)	*Proprietor and Owner of retail hardware and wholesale pumping equipment business*
5.4	(1962)	*Assistant Professor of Business and Economics*; Regional campus of a large state university system
5.5	(1962)	*Self-employed Consultant*; Operations Research field emphasizing applications to health care
5.6	(1963)	*Senior Consultant*; Specializing in taxation work, large accounting firm
5.7	(1963)	*Self-employed free-lance writer*

their career is that they be able to continue the kind of work which they enjoy and are good at.

We should not assume from this kind of grouping of people that others are less concerned about developing their expertise or care less about the kind of work they do. What we are saying is that in each person one can find a *predominant* concern which will function as an anchor in the sense of pulling the person back if he strays too far from fulfilling that concern. Thus, a person in the autonomy group (e.g. a professor) is certainly concerned about his area of specialization and certainly wants to be good at it. But his career is not necessarily anchored in that concern. If he were given a chance to pursue that line of work in a large organization at a much higher salary and with much better equipment or resources, he would not take the opportunity if he viewed that organizational setting as one in which he would have to sacrifice his autonomy. It is the autonomy need which is the true anchor in that case.

Eight out of the 44 panelists are anchored in *managerial competence*. Not all of them have made it to higher levels of management, but their interviews clearly indicate that it is those higher levels which they are seeking, and that they get their primary satisfactions out of managerial activity *per se*. Within the group we can note two career patterns: (a) working one's way up within large organizations (persons 1·1, 1·3, 1·4, 1·6, and 1·7); and (b) seeking larger jobs within smaller organizations (person 1·2, 1·5, and 1·8). In both groups there are individuals who have moved from company to company and who have sometimes interrupted the pattern with stints in management consulting. But in the former group, the individual always ended up in another large organization, while in the latter group there was a clear decision to move toward smaller organizations, in one case a family business. Only one man has made it to the level of general manager (1·5) but the others are clearly striving in that direction.

In the *technical/functional competence* group we have a great variety of organizational titles and career paths. The commonest of these is middle level functional or technical management (11 people); next most common is senior or middle level staff roles (five people); two people are in straight consulting roles; and two people are in teaching, one at university, one at high-school level. It must be remembered that if the concept of career anchor is valid, these 19 people are *not* in transition toward managerial roles *per se*. They may rise within functional/technical management ladders, but the theoretical assumption is that they would refuse to be promoted into a role which would entail giving up the kind of work they are presently doing.

Many of the panelists in this group sense that they are violating the 'success ethic' of the business world and feel somewhat conflicted and guilty over their lack of ambition and success. They talk of their work and their family as being really important, and they say that they enjoy their present life, but they wonder whether they are missing something, whether they are doing as well as their peers, etc. As one man puts it, 'Is it better to jump into a fast-moving river to see whether or not you can swim in it, or is it better to wade around in a slow-moving stream—safer but less exciting?' Our prediction would be that none of these men will move out of their present orientation but that they will have to find ways of dealing with their conflicts about what they feel they may be giving up.

Only four people could be classified as *security* oriented *per se*. Three of these people have spent the bulk of their career within a single organization; one of them has moved frequently but it had always been within the same geographical area, and the moves have always been into similar types of jobs (with one exception—an abortive venture into trying to start up a company with a group of others). These men talk of their work, their family, their overall satisfaction with a geographical area in which they have settled, and their sense of having achieved enough to satisfy them. The one man who is in the family business had been in a large corporation before moving back into the family business, and is not entirely happy with his present situation, he may move back into the large corporation in a fairly junior level. Such a move would not concern him so long as he remained in his present home town where he has made a well-ordered life for himself.

The group concerned with *creativity* contains the entrepreneurs. Four of these men are successful in that they have been able to launch enterprises which have succeeded and have brought to their founders either fame or fortune or both. The kinds of activities represented vary greatly—but they all have in common that they are clear extensions of the person and his identity is heavily involved in the vehicle which is created.

Finally, in the *autonomy* group, we have four consultants, one owner/proprietor of a small business, one professor, and one free-lance writer. In many respects this group resembles the technical/functional competence group except that there are no functional managers or staff roles represented in it. What clearly distinguishes the autonomy group is that there is little conflict about missed opportunities or failure to aspire higher. All of these people are very happy with what they are doing and are truly enjoying their freedom. All of them feel that they need to be on their own, to have a sense of their own professionalism, and to be able to link the results of their work to their own efforts (a feeling which they share with the 'creativity' group). It is not easy to differentiate the autonomy from the creativity group on the surface because the entrepreneurs also enjoy a great deal of autonomy and freedom. However, when one listens to the entrepreneurs it is the building of something which clearly preoccupies them most, whereas in the autonomy group it is the *need to be on their own* and *free of constraints* which preoccupies them most. The autonomy group is not concerned with making money or building empires— only with feeling competent and free in whatever they are doing.

SOME BACKGROUND CHARACTERISTICS OF DIFFERENT 'ANCHOR' GROUPS

Grade Point Average and Business Aptitude Test Scores

One obvious factor to be related to the different groups identified above is intellectual aptitude and performance. We can compare groups that have in common a given career anchor on undergraduate grade point average, the verbal and quantitative scores on the Admissions Test for Graduate Study in Business (ATGSB) and grade point average while at MIT (see Table 2.2).

Because the numbers are extremely small for statistical comparison, we will be more concerned with the consistency of the results than the absolute differ-

Table 2.2 Undergraduate Grade Point Average,[a] Business Aptitude Test Scores, and Graduate Grade Point Average of career anchor groups

Career anchor	UG GPA	ATGSB Total	Verbal	Quant.	Grad. GPA
Managerial comp. ($N = 8$)	4·0	574	29	39	4·4
Tech./funct. comp. ($N = 19$)	3·9	590	34	38	4·2
Security ($N = 4$)	3·7	573	31	38	4·2
Creativity ($N = 6$)	3·2	555	31	36	4·0
Autonomy ($N = 7$)	3·5	628	37	41	4·2
Total	3·9	587	33	38	4·2

[a] GPA based on 5-point scale.

Table 2.3 Ranking of A.T.G.S.B. scores of
creativity and autonomy groups

Rank	Autonomy	Creativity
1	680	
2	670	
3	657	
4	615	
5		611
6		610
7	607	
8	594	
9	576	
10		551
11		535
12		526
13		494

ences in GPA and test scores. In terms of undergraduate GPA it is the managerial and technical/functional groups which have the highest grades, while the creativity group clearly has the lowest grades. In terms of aptitude, as measured by the ATGSB, it is the autonomy group that shows up with the highest scores, both in the verbal and quantitative areas, while the creativity group again shows the lowest scores. In terms of GPA at MIT, the groups resemble each other closely except for the lower average of the creativity group. The two salient features in the results are the consistent low performance of the creativity group and the very high aptitude test score of the autonomy group. To highlight this difference we show in Table 2·3 the ATGSB scores of the two extreme groups—note that they are virtually nonoverlapping distributions, and that all but one of the autonomy groups falls above the total group mean of 587, while all but two of the creativity groups fall below the group mean.

One can conjecture that the entrepreneurs probably learned early in life (high school and before) that they would not do outstanding academic work (note their lower college GPA), and consequently developed much broader interest patterns which are now reflected in the variety of creative activities they are engaged in. Their skills have become those of leadership, salesmanship, influencing others, and seeing opportunities that are feasible, as contrasted with the more intellectually oriented autonomous individual who is seeking elegance of solution and knowledge in depth. The entrepreneurs want to be generalists; the autonomous men want to be specialists. The managerial, technical/functional, and security groups do not differ in important ways from each other in terms of intellectual aptitude or performance.

Parent's Level of Education and Occupation

The managerial competence group is average in father's education, low in mother's education, high in business and managerial fathers, and high in percentage of housewife mothers. In contrast, the technical/functional competence group is high in parental education but is more diversified in parental occupations. The security group is low in father's education and high in mothers' education, high in percentage of business and managerial fathers, and average in number of housewife mothers. One can conjecture that the security orientation reflects a feeling on the part of the alumnus that once he has completed graduate school and made it into some level of management, he already has achieved success by climbing higher on the socioeconomic ladder than his father.

The creativity group shows high levels of education for both fathers and mothers and a high percentage of business/managerial fathers. Perhaps the broad interests of this group derive from the breadth that is associated with the higher level of education of both parents.

The autonomy group, average for parental education and level of mothers' occupation, stands out in having the lowest percentage of business/managerial fathers and the highest percentage of professional fathers. The autonomy pattern may already have been set in these families in that among the fathers' occupations were farmer, associate professor, chief engineer of a company, electrical contractor, insurance agency owner, and executive vice president of a family business. Only the latter two jobs are business and managerial, and they both involve ownership; none of the fathers was a manager in the traditional sense.

CAREER SUCCESS OF CAREER ANCHOR GROUPS

Success is a complex and difficult variable to define and measure because of the fact that it can be objectively defined by societal standards or subjectively defined by personal standards and goals.

In this paper, I will report one indicator of *objective* success—the income of the panelists, broken down by career anchor groups. Table 2.4 shows the average income, median income, and income range of the panelists based on their report during the interview. In many cases the numbers are a baseline and exclude annual bonuses, the value of stock options, and other perquisites.

Table 2.4 Income of career anchor groups

Career anchor	Mean ($)	Median ($)	Range ($)
Managerial Comp. ($N = 8$)	35,000	31,000	27,000–50,000
Tech./Funct. Comp. ($N = 19$)	25,800	26,000	16,000–42,000
Security ($N = 4$)	23,000	24,500	18,000–25,000
Creativity[a] ($N = 6$)	29,000	26,000	17,000–40,000
Autonomy ($N = 7$)	19,000	17,000	10,000–25,000
Total	26,000	25,000	

[a]The two successful entrepreneurs report assets in excess of a half million dollars.

In the case of the entrepreneurs we also have to supplement the annual income with figures on the total value of the assets which they say they have accumulated.

As might be expected, the most successful group in pure income terms is the managerial competence group, because the climbing of the managerial ladder is congruent with society's definition of success. The successful entrepreneurs are similarly high if one includes their assets, but even the most successful of them only reports an annual *income* of $40,000. Perhaps for this group it is more important to build their total assets than to consume what they have amassed. The technical/functional competence group and security group make up the average of the income range in our sample, while the autonomy group is clearly at the low end. As many other studies have shown (Bailyn and Schein, 1972; Le Jeune, 1973) the individuals who leave large organizations to become teachers, writers, and consultants may, in this process sacrifice opportunities for high incomes. However, those consultants and professionals who develop special areas of knowledge and skill may be expected, at a later time, to rise sharply in income as their talents become better known. In a recent survey of Sloan School alumni conducted in 1973, the graduates of 1958 to 1962 were pulled out as a group (Le Jeune, 1973). Their mean income was $26,500 which is virtually identical to the mean income of our group. This similarity supports our earlier claim that we are dealing with a reasonably representative sample of our total alumni pool.

CONCLUSIONS

In this paper I have tried to introduce and elaborate the concept of *career anchors*, viewed as a syndrome of motives, values, and self-perceived competences which function to guide and constrain an individual's entire career. Panelists were classified into career anchor group on the basis of the reasons they gave for career choices, moves from one company to another, what they were looking for in life, how they saw their future, and so on. Actual job history and earlier interview data were *not* used in order to minimize bias. The relationships which we have reported between career anchor, intellectual aptitude, school performance, parental background, current job, and current income are therefore real relationships, i.e. the classification into career anchor group was made before any of the correlative data were examined.

What has been shown in this analysis is that the concept of career anchor is viable in that it permits a sensible categorization of the panelists. Furthermore, the categories are to some degree psychologically and socio-economically homogeneous. If career anchors function as stable syndromes in the personality, it becomes crucial for employing organizations to identify those syndromes early and to create career opportunities which are congruent with them. It does little good to offer a promotion into management to someone who basically does not want to be a manager. Organizations will have to learn to think more broadly about the different kinds of contributions which people can make, and to develop multiple reward systems as well as multiple career paths to permit the full development of diverse kinds of individuals who work in organizations.

NOTES

1. This research was supported by the Organizational Effectiveness Research Program of the Office of Naval Research under Contract No. N0014-67-A-0204-0073. A brief earlier statement on the concept of career anchors can be found in Schein (1975).
2. We had made rather careful analyses of the major value themes which were reflected in the original interview but had never given any of those data to the panel members. At this 10 to 12 years out point, I decided that such feedback could not bias the data too much, and hence told each person what we had seen in his interview back in graduate school. This feedback was given at the very end of the interview and the person was asked how he felt about it, whether it sounded true, whether it suggested new thoughts about how he had changed or not changed, etc. In most cases this discussion led to some important new insights which had previously not come out.

Chapter 3

The Experiential Learning Theory of Career Development

David A. Kolb and Mark S. Plovnick

INTRODUCTION

While much is known in increasing detail about the processes and stages of development in children and adolescents, there has been comparatively little research on the developmental regularities in the lives of adult men and women. This scarcity of empirically based scientific models of development is paralleled by the primitive nature of popular common sense images of adult life, (e.g. 'they were married and lived happily ever after') and the notion of a 'success ladder' to be climbed rung after rung.

One major reason for the failure to formulate more articulate models of adult development has to do with the difficulty of conceptualizing adult development. While the worlds of children and even adolescents are structurely similar, the worlds of adults becomes highly differentiated along a great number of dimensions. This problem of complexity has led to either generalized self-environment process models of career development (e.g. Super and coworkers, 1963) or deterministic models of personality development that trace different career paths to formative experiences in those well-known early years of development (e.g. Roe, 1956; McClelland, 1962) or to linear, one-track models of adult development that describe a normative path for human growth that is precipitated through periodic crises of environmental adaptation (e.g. Erickson, 1959) or to the familiar trait-factor approach to career development that focuses on some one or more personal variables as the determinants of career choice which is seen as only one decision, such as the first job choice (e.g. Holland, 1973). While it is not our task here to examine and criticize these different approaches in detail, suffice it to say the approach of the chapter is to integrate what we feel to be the strengths of each of the above-mentioned theoretical strategies. More specifically we are attempting in the formulation of the ex-periential learning theory of adult development to create an approach that: (*a*) gives a central role to self-environment interaction, (*b*) describes differentiated paths of adult development, (*c*) maintains an emphasis on a normative model of human fulfillment, and (*d*) focuses on certain specific personal variables that can be used to understand and influence the career development process.

STABILITY AND CHANGE IN CAREER DEVELOPMENT

Any comprehensive theory of career development must explain not only the emergence of stable enduring career paths, but it must also explain the dynamics and directions of career change. In the experiential learning theory of adult development stability and change in career paths is seen as resulting from the interaction between internal personality dynamics and external social forces in a manner much like that described by Super and coworkers (1963). The most powerful development dynamic that emerges from this interaction is the tendency for there to be a closer and closer match between self characteristics and environmental demands. This match comes about in two ways—(a) environments tend to change personal characteristics to fit them (i.e. socialization), and (b) individuals tend to select themselves into environments that are consistent with their personal characteristics. Thus career development in general tends to follow a path toward accentuation of personal characteristics and skills (Feldman and Newcombe, 1969; Kolb, 1973b) in that development is a product of the interaction between choices and socialization experiences that match these dispositions and the resulting experiences further reinforce the same choice disposition for later experience. Many adult life paths follow a cycle of job, educational, and life-style choices that build upon the experiences resulting from previous similar choices. Indeed the common stereotype of the successful career is a graded ladder of similar experiences on which one climbs to success and fulfillment.

Yet accentuation represents only the warp of the fabric of adult career development. The woof is formed by the career changes that mark transitions from one career path to another.

Given this primary developmental force toward stable, linear career paths, we suggest that change or deviation from this career path can occur in only three ways as discussed in the following sections.

The Individual May Err in his Choice of a Matching Socialization Experience

For example, the woman with scientific interest may not choose a scientific career on the 'good advice' that there are few jobs for women in science. Or an individual may decide to become an engineer because he has been told how glamorous it is, even though he at present does not like mathematics or science very much.

The Socialization Experience May Cease to Reward the Choice Dispositions and Skills that Brought the Individual to it

This is the career *cul de sac* where the individual is rewarded for accentuation of his personal skills and dispositions up to a given point where further advancement or development is precluded unless he or she is prepared to develop new knowledge, skills, or attitudes. For example, engineers in most organizations reach a point where further advancement or promotion is possible only by moving into management. Studies of engineers and managers (e.g. Sofer, 1970; Jaffe, 1971) indicate that lack of success and advancement are major factors in mid-career crises. The woman in the housewife or mother role experiences this change in another way. A husband's increasing success and development can cause her role as a wife to change dramatically, leaving homemaking satisfactions abandoned. Similarly, as children grow up and leave home, the nutrient mother role becomes irrelevant. Gail Sheehy (1974b) describes well how complex these dynamics can be:

'Now invigorated by his new-found confidence, no longer in constant need of having his loneliness "taken care of" and having become bored by a substitute mother, he changes the instructions to his wife; now you must be something more too. Be a companion instead of a child or mother be capable of excellence like me. "Why don't you take some courses" is the way it usually comes out, because he doesn't want her to stray too far from the caretaking of him (and children if they have or plan them). But what he sees as "encouraging" her, she perceives as threatening her, getting rid of her, freeing himself from her, because this relationship has become mutually restricting.

'She is at war with her own age 30 inner demons, but ill equipped to be "something more." As part of their earlier collusion, she was told she didn't have to get out in world in any full sense. She could become her mother in her own married household. So long as she does not individuate, she can partake in all those illusions which she brought along from her own mother that make her feel safe. Anyone who pushes the other way is goading her toward danger.' (Sheehy, 1974b, pp. 34–45)

The Individual as a Result of his Own Maturation and Personality Development may find that his Personal Style and Choice Dispositions Change, Placing these new desires in conflict with the Accentuating Socialization Process he has chosen.

For example, there is a general tendency for undergraduate students to move away from interests in science to the social sciences, arts, and humanities (Davis, 1965). Our own research (Plovick, 1971, 1972; Kolb, 1973b) and counseling with students at MIT has illustrated how difficult and traumatic this conflict can be. A sophomore engineering student who has suddenly discovered the excitement of psychology and human behavior must now face the difficult decision of transfering to another school or making do with the resources at hand. The corresponding conflict can occur for the practicing engineer whose years of impersonal isolation in the world of things becomes boring and he finds new interest in personal relationships with family and friends, and coworkers.

EXPERIENTIAL LEARNING THEORY AND ADULT DEVELOPMENT

From a psychological perspective the developmental cycle of choices and experiences is seen as a process of learning. Experiential learning theory provides a means of conceptualizing the learning process that allows for the identification of different learning styles and corresponding environments

68

that are congruent with these learning styles. Thus the theory offers a framework for mapping career paths that follow the accentuation pattern (i.e. toward a greater match between learning style and its corresponding environment) and those paths that deviate from this pattern. The learning model is a dialectic one, founded on the Jungian concept of styles or types that states that fulfillment in adult development is accomplished by higher level integration and expression of nondominant modes of dealing with the world (Jung, 1923). This concept of fulfillment forms the basis for predictions about the directions of career transition.

The theory is called 'experiential learning' for two reasons. The first is historical, tying it to its intellectual origins in the social psychology of Kurt Lewin in the 40's and the sensitivity training and laboratory education work of the 50's and 60's. The second reason is to emphasize the important role that experience plays in the learning process, an emphasis that differentiates this approach from other cognitive theories of the learning process. The core of the model is a simple description of the learning cycle, of how experience is translated into concepts which in turn are used as guides in the choice of new experiences.

Learning is conceived as a four-stage cycle. Immediate concrete experience is the basis for observation and reflection. These observations are assimilated into a 'theory' from which new implications for action can be deduced. These implications or hypotheses then serve as guides in acting to create new experiences. The learner, if he is to be effective, needs four different kinds of abilities— *Concrete Experience* abilities (CE), *Reflective Observation* abilities (RO), *Abstract Conceptualization* abilities (AC), and *Active Experimentation* (AE) abilities. That is, he must be able to involve himself fully, openly, and without bias in new experiences (CE), he must be able to reflect on and observe these experiences from many perspectives (RO); he must be able to create concepts that integrate his observations into logically sound theories (AC) and he must be able to use these theories to make decisions and solve problems (AE). Yet this ideal is difficult to achieve. Can anyone become highly skilled in all of these abilities or are they necessarily in conflict? How can one be concrete and immediate and still be theoretical?

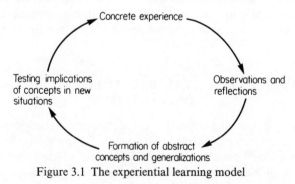

Figure 3.1 The experiential learning model

A closer examination of the four-stage learning model would suggest that learning requires abilities that are polar opposites and that the learner, as a result, must continually choose which set of learning abilities he will bring to bear in any specific learning situation. More specifically, there are two primary dimensions to the learning process. The first dimension represents the concrete experiencing of events at one end and abstract conceptualization at the other. The other dimension has active experimentation at one extreme and reflective observation at the other. Thus, in the process of learning one moves in varying degrees from actor to observer, from specific involvement to general analytic detachment.

Many cognitive psychologists (e.g. Flavell, 1963; Bruner, 1960, 1966; Harvey, Hunt, and Schroder, 1961) have identified the concrete/abstract dimension as a primary dimension on which cognitive growth and learning occurs. Goldstein and Scheerer (1941) suggest that greater abstractness results in the development of the following abilities:

(1) To detach our ego from the outer world or from inner experience
(2) To assume a mental set
(3) To account for acts to oneself; to verbalize the account
(4) To shift reflectively from one aspect of the situation to another
(5) To hold in mind simultaneously various aspects
(6) To grasp the essential of a given whole: to break up a given whole into parts to isolate and to synthesize them.
(7) To abstract common properties reflectively; to form hierarchic concepts
(8) To plan ahead ideationally, to assume an attitude toward the more possible and to think or perform symbolically (Goldstein and Scheerer, 1941, p. 4).

Concreteness, on the other hand, represents according to these theorists, the absence of these abilities, the immersion in and domination by one's immediate experiences. Yet the circular, dialectic model of the learning process would imply, abstractness is not exclusively good and concreteness exclusively bad. To be creative requires that one be able to experience anew, freed somewhat from the constraints of previous abstract concepts. In psychoanalytic theory this need for a concrete childlike perspective in the creative process is referred to as regression in service of the ego (Kris, 1975). Bruner (1966) in his essay on the conditions for creativity further emphasizes the dialectic tension between abstract and concrete involvement. For him the creative act is a product of detachment and commitment, of passion and decorum, and of a freedom to be dominated by the object of one's inquiry.

The active/reflective dimension is the other major dimension of cognitive growth and learning. As growth occurs, thought becomes more reflective and internalized, based more on the manipulation of symbols and images than overt actions. The modes of active experimentation and reflection, like abstractness/ concreteness, stand in opposition to one another. Reflection tends to inhibit action and vice-versa. For example, Singer (1968) has found that children who have active internal fantasy lives are more capable of inhibiting action for long periods of time than are children with little internal fantasy life. Kagan and coworkers (1964) have found, on the other hand, that very active orientations toward learning situations inhibit reflection and thereby preclude the development of analytic concepts. Herein lies the second major dialectic in the learning process—the tension between actively testing the implications of one's hypotheses and reflectively interpreting data already collected.

INDIVIDUAL LEARNING STYLES AND THE LEARNING STYLE INVENTORY

Over time, accentuation forces operate on individuals in such a way that the dialectic tensions between these dimensions are consistently resolved in a characteristic fashion. As a result of our hereditary equipment, our particular past life experience, and the demands of our present environment most people develop learning styles that emphasize some learning abilities over others. Through socialization experiences in family, school, and work we come to resolve the conflicts between being active and reflective and between being immediate and analytical in characteristic ways. Some people develop minds that excel at assimilating disparate facts into coherent theories, yet these same people are incapable of, or uninterested in deducing hypotheses from the theory. Other are logical geniuses but find it impossible to involve and surrender themselves to an experience. And so on. A mathematician may come to place great emphasis on abstract concepts while a poet may value concrete experience more highly. A manager may be primarily concerned with the active application of ideas while a naturalist may develop his observational skills highly. Each of us, in a unique way, develops a learning style that has some weak and strong points. We have developed a simple self-description inventory, the Learning Style Inventory (LSI), that is designed to measure an individual's strengths and weaknesses as a learner. The LSI measures an individual's relative emphasis on the four learning abilities—Concrete Experience (CE), Reflective Observation (RO), Abstract Conceptualization (AC), and Active Experimentation (AE) by asking him, several different times, to rank in order four words that describe these different abilities. For example, one set of four words is 'Feeling' (CE), 'Watching' (RO), 'Thinking' (AC), 'Doing' (AE). The inventory yields six scores, CE, RO, AC, and AE plus two combination scores that indicate the extent to which an individual emphasizes abstractness over concreteness (AC–CE) and the extent to which an individual emphasizes active experimentation over reflective observation (AE–RO).

The LSI was administered to 800 practicing managers and graduate students in management to obtain norms for the management population. In general these managers tended to emphasize Active Experimentation over Reflective Observation. In addition, managers with graduate degrees tended to rate their abstract (AC) learning skills higher.[1] While the individuals we tested showed many different patterns of scores on the LSI, we have identified four statistically prevalent types of learning styles. We have called these four styles—the Converger, the Diverger, the Assimilator, and the Accommodator.[2] The following is a summary of the characteristics of these types based both on our research and clinical observation of these patterns of LSI scores.

The *Converger*'s dominant learning abilities are Abstract Conceptualization (AC) and Active Experimentation (AE). His greatest strength lies in the practical application of ideas. We have called this learning style the 'Converger' because a person with this style seems to do best in those situations like conventional intelligence tests where there is a single correct answer or solution to a question or problem (Torrealba, 1972). His knowledge is organized in such a way that, through hypothetical–deductive reasoning, he can focus it on specific problem. Liam Hudson's (1966) research in this style of learning (using different measures from the LSI) shows that convergers are relatively unemotional, preferring to deal with things rather than people. They tend to have narrow interests, and choose to specialize in the physical sciences. Our research shows that this learning style is characteristic of many engineers (Kolb, 1973a).

The *Diverger* has the opposite learning strengths of the convergers. He is best at Concrete Experience (CE) and Reflective Observation (RO). His greatest strength lies in his imaginative ability. He excells in the ability to view concrete situations from many perspectives and to organize many relationships into a meaningful 'gestalt'. We have labelled this style 'Diverger' because a person of this type performs better in situations that call for generation of ideas such as a 'brainstroming' idea session. Divergers are interested in people and tend to be imaginative and emotional. They have broad cultural interests and tend to specialize in the arts. Our research show that this style is characteristic of persons with humanities and liberal arts backgrounds.

The *Assimilator*'s dominant learning abilities are Abstract Conceptualization (AC) and Reflective Observation (RO). His greatest strength lies in his ability to create theoretical models. He excells in inductive reasoning; in assimilating disparate observations into an integrated explanation (Growchow, 1973). He, like the converger, is less interested in people but he is also less concerned with the practical use of theories. For him, it is more important that the theory be logically sound and precise. As a result, this learning style is more characteristic of the basic sciences and mathematics rather than the applied sciences. In organizations, this style is found most often in the research and planning departments (Kolb, 1973a; Strasmore, 1973).

The *Accommodator* has the opposite strengths of the Assimilator. He is best at Concrete Experience (CE) and Active Experimentation (AE). His greatest strength lies in doing things; in carrying out plans and experiments and involving himself in new experiences. He tends to be more of a risk-taker than people with the other three learning styles. We have labeled this style 'Accommodator' because he tends to excel in those situations where he must adapt himself to specific immediate circumstances. He tends to solve problems in an intuitive trial and error manner (Growchow, 1973), relying heavily on other people for information rather than his own analytic ability (Stabell, 1973).

GROWTH AND DEVELOPMENT IN THE EXPERIENTIAL LEARNING MODEL

In addition to providing a framework for conceptualizing individual differences in styles of adaptation to the world, the experiential learning model suggests more normative directions for human growth and development. As we have seen in the previous section individual learning styles effect how people learn not only in the limited educational sense but also in the broader aspects of adaptation to life such as decision-making, problem-solving, and life style in general. Experiential learning is not a molecular educational concept but rather is a molar concept describing the central process of human adaptation to the social and physical environment. It is an holistic concept much akin to the Jungian theory of psychological types (Jung, 1923) in that it seeks to describe the emergence of basic life orientations as a function of dialectic tensions between basic modes of relating to the world. As such it encompasses other more limited adaptative concepts such as creativity, problem-solving, decision-making, and attitude change that focus heavily on one or another of the basic aspects of adaptation. Thus creativity research has tended to focus on the divergent (concrete and reflective) factors in adaptation such as tolerance for ambiguity, metaphorical thinking, and flexibility, while research on decision-making has emphasized more convergent (abstract and active) adaptive factors such as the rational evaluation of solution alternatives.

From this broader perspective, learning becomes a central life task and how one learns becomes a major determinant of the course of his personal development. The experiential learning model provides a means of mapping these different developmental paths and a normative adaptative ideal—a learning process wherein the individual has highly developed abilities to experience, observe, conceptualize, and experiment.

The human growth process is divided into three broad developmental stages. The first stage, *Acquisition*, extends from birth to adolescense and marks the acquisition of basic learning abilities and cognitive structures. The second stage, *Specialization*, extends through formal education and/or career training and the early experiences of adulthood in work and personal life. In this stage development primarily follows paths that accentuate a particular learning style. Individuals shaped by social, educational and organizational socialization forces develop increased competence in a specialized mode of adaptation that enables them to master the particular life tasks they encounter in their chosen career (in the broadest sense of that word) path. This stage, in our thinking, terminates at mid-career although the specific chronology of the transition to stage three will vary widely from person to person and from one career path to another. The third stage, *Integration*, is marked by the reassertion and expression of the non-dominant adapative modes or learning styles. Means of adapting to the world that have been suppressed and lay fallow in favor of the development of the more highly rewarded dominant learning style now find expression in the form of new career interests, changes in life styles, and/or innovation and creativity in one's chosen career.

Through these three stages, development is marked by increasing complexity and relativism in dealing with the world and one's experiences and by higher level integrations of the dialectic conflicts between the four primary adaptive modes—Concrete Experience, Reflective Observation, Abstract Conceptualization, and Active Experimentation. A major dimension of personal growth is associated with each of these four modes. Development in the Concrete Experience adaptive mode is characterized by increases in *Affective Complexity*. Development in the Reflective Observation mode is characterized by increases in *Perceptual Complexity*. Development in the Abstract Conceptualization and Active Experimentation modes are characterized respectively by increases in *Symbolic Complexity* and *Behavioral Complexity*.

In the early stages of development, progress along one of these four

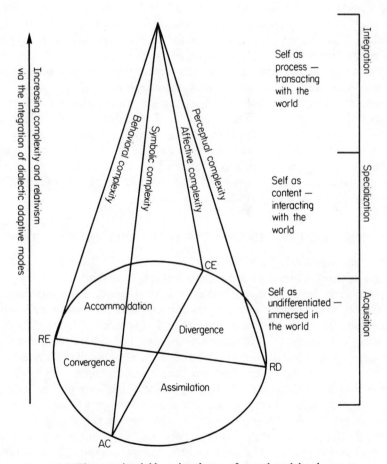

Figure 3.2 The experiential learning theory of growth and development

dimensions can occur with relative independence from the others. The child and young adult, for example, can develop highly sophisticated symbolic proficiencies and remain naive emotionally. At the highest stages of development, however, the adaptive commitment to learning and creativity produces a strong need for integration of the four adaptive modes. Development in one mode precipitates development in the others. Increases in symbolic complexity, for example, refine and sharpen both perceptual and behavioral possibilities. Thus complexity and the integration of dialectic conflicts among the adaptive modes are the hallmarks of true creativity and growth.

Figure 3.2 graphically illustrates the experiential learning model of growth and development as it has been outlined thus far. The four dimensions of growth are depicted in the shape of a cone the base of which represents the lower stages of development and the apex of which represents the peak of development—representing the fact that the four dimensions become more highly integrated at higher stages of development. Any individual learning style would be represented on this cone by four data points on the four vertical dimensions of development. Thus a converger in developmental stage two (specialization) would be characterized by high complexity in the symbolic and behavioral modes and lower complexity in the affective and perceptual modes. As he moved into stage three of development his complexity scores in the affective and perceptual modes would increase.

While we have depicted the stages of the growth process in the form of a simple three layer cone, the actual process of growth in any single individual life history probably proceeds through successive oscillations from one stage to another. Thus a person may move from stage two to three in several separate subphases of integrative advances followed by consolidation or regression into specialization. [For a more detailed description of this developmental model see Kolb and Fry (1975)].

RESEARCH ON LEARNING STYLES AND CAREER PATHS

One focus on the Experiential Learning Theory of Career Development is the relationship between an individuals learning style and the type of career he chooses. If we examine the undergraduate majors of the individuals in our sample of 800 practicing managers and graduate students in management a correspondence can be seen between their LSI scores and their initial career interests. This is done by plotting the average LSI scores for managers in our sample who reported their undergraduate college major (See Figure 3.3; only those majors with more than ten people responding are included). The distribution of undergraduate majors on the learning style grid is quite consistent with theory.[3] Undergraduate business majors tend to have accommodative learning styles while engineers on the average fall in the convergent quadrant. History, english, political science, and psychology majors all have divergent learning styles. Mathematics and chemistry majors have assimilative learning styles along with economics and sociology. Physics majors are very

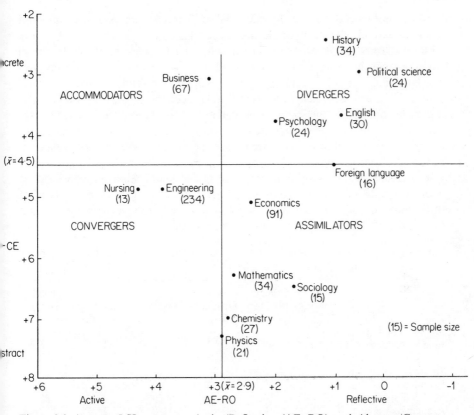

Figure 3.3 Average LSI scores on Active/Reflective (AE–RO) and Abstract/Concrete (AC–CE) by undergraduate college major

abstract falling between the convergent and assimilative quadrant. What these data show is that one's undergraduate education is a major factor in the development of his learning style. Whether this is because individual's are shaped by the fields they enter or because of selection processes that put people into and out of disciplines is an open question at this point. Most probably both factors are operating—people choose fields which are consistent with their learning styles and are further shaped to fit the learning norms of their field once they are in it. When there is a mismatch between the fields learning norm's and the individual's learning style people will either change or leave the field.

In order to further explore the relationship between learning style and academic and/or career choices the LSI was administered to the freshman and senior classes of a large eastern medical school (Plovnick, 1974, 1975). Our assumption was that the differences between the various medical specialities and types of medical careers available to these students would be reflected in their relative attractiveness to students with varying learning styles.

We hypothesized that academic medical careers stressing research and teaching would attract assimilators more than other learning style types while those practicing oriented careers requiring frequent patient interaction would attract the more active types. In addition we expected that subspecialty practices (e.g. cardiology) having a more 'scientific' orientation would attract convergers more, whereas practices in family medicine or primary care involving more concern for the socio-emotional aspects of patient care would attract accommodators more. We expected psychiatry to attract divergers because of its 'humanistic' orientation and because of the more reserved, reflective nature of the practitioner role in psychiatry.

The results of this study indicated that of the senior students whose career choices matched those predicted, 97 per cent indicated they were 'certain' of their choices, while 40 per cent of the seniors choosing careers other than those predicted indicated they were 'uncertain' of their choices.

Table 3.1 Percentage distribution of career choices of different learning style types among medical school seniors who indicated that they were certain of their choices

	Accommodators ($N = 14$)	Divergers ($N = 10$)	Convergers ($N = 11$)	Assimilators ($N = 12$)	Total Sample ($N = 47$)
Family medicine and primary care	43[a]	30	9	17	26
Surgery	36	30	27	8	25
Psychiatry	7	10[a]	0	8	6
Medicine specialty	14	20	55[a]	25	28
Academic medicine	0	0	0	25[a]	7
Pathology	0	0	0	17[a]	4
Radiology	0	10	9	0	4
Total	100	100	100	100	100

[a] It was predicted, prior to analyzing the questionnaire results, that these would be high-frequency choices for the learning style type in question compared with other learning style types.

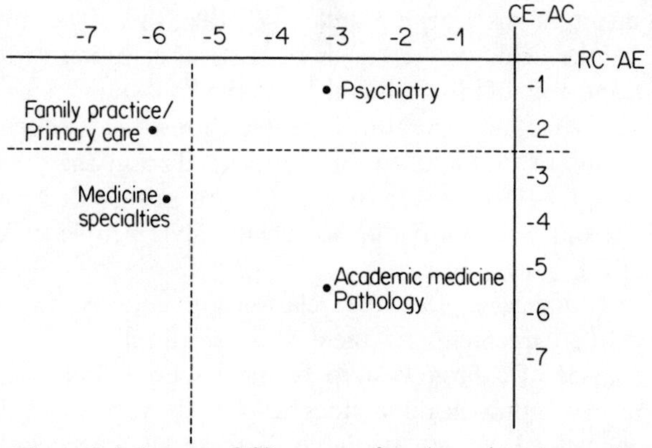

Figure 3.4 Average LSI scores of seniors choosing various medical careers

The actual distribution of senior career choices generally supported the predicted pattern (see Table 3.1 and Figure 3.4).

The frequency of accommodators and divergers choosing careers in surgery proved to be the only unexpected result. In retrospect, however, it appears that surgery appeals to these types because it is seen literally as a 'hands-on', more here-and-now field (and thus more concrete) than medicine, pediatrics, and the other fields represented by the students.

Finally, to test the assumption that there is a process of selection and/or socialization occurring in medical school with respect to learning styles and career choices we compared the career choices of the freshmen with those of the seniors. The results indicated that seniors chose the predicted careers nearly twice as frequently as freshmen.

As in the case of the management population, the results from this sample of medical students leads us to the conclusion that through the process of career choice and through the learning process within a career field, an individual's learning style tends toward a 'match' with the requirements of his work.

To examine if there was a correspondence between learning styles and the kind of jobs individuals held in mid-career we studied about 20 managers from each of five functional groups in a mid-western division of a large American industrial corporation. The five functional groups are described below followed by our hypothesis about the learning style that should characterize each group given the nature of their work.

(1) Marketing ($n = 20$). This group is made up primarily of former salesmen. They have a nonquantitative 'intuitive' approach to their work. Because of their practical sales orientation in meeting customer demand they should have accommodative learning styles (i.e. concrete and active).

(2) Research ($n = 22$). The work of this group is split about 50/50 between pioneer research and applied research projects. The emphasis is on basic research. Researchers should be the most assimilative group, (i.e. abstract and reflective) a style fitted to the world of knowledge and ideas.

(3) Personnel/Labor Relations ($n = 20$). In this company men from this department serve two primary functions, interpreting personnel policy and promoting interaction among groups to reduce conflict and disagreement. Because of their 'people orientation' these men should be predominantly divergers, concrete and reflective.

(4) Engineering ($n = 18$). This group is made up primarily of design engineers who are quite production oriented. They should be the most convergent subgroup, (i.e. abstract and active) although they should be less abstract than the research group. They represent a bridge between thought and action.

(5) Finance ($n = 20$). This group has a strong computer, information system bias. Finance men, given their orientation toward the mathematical task of information system design, should be highly abstract. Their crucial role in organizational survival should produce an active orientation. Thus finance group members should have convergent learning styles.

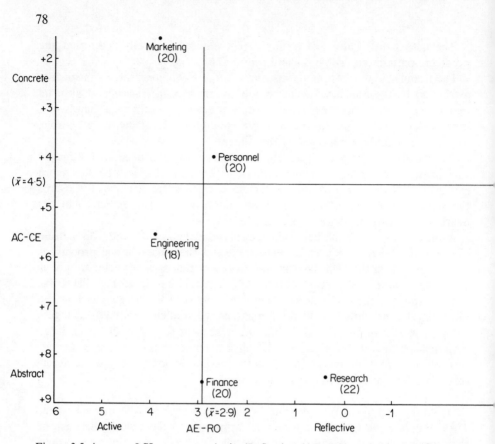

Figure 3.5 Average LSI scores on Active/Reflective (AE–RO) and Abstract/Concrete (AC–CE) by Organizational Function

Figure 3.5 shows the average scores on the active/reflective (AE–RO) and abstract/concrete (AC–CE) learning dimensions for the five functional groups. These results are consistent with the above predictions with the exception of the finance group whose scores are less active than predicted and thus they fall between the assimilative and the convergent quadrant.[4] The LSI clearly differentiates the learning styles that characterize managers following different career paths within a single company.

EVIDENCE FOR ACCENTUATION IN EARLY CAREER

While the above data are suggestive of some general correspondence between learning styles and careers, they do not offer conclusive evidence for the accentuation process. In a first attempt to examine the details of this process, Plovnick (1971) studied a major university department using the concepts of convergence and divergence defined by Hudson (1966). He concluded that the major emphasis in physics education was on convergent learning. He predicted that physics students who had convergent learning styles would be more uncertain of physics as a career and would take more courses outside of the physics department than their convergent colleagues. His predictions were confirmed. Those students who were not fitted for the convergent learning style required in physics tended to turn away from physics as a profession, while those physics students having a convergent style tended to continue to specialize in physics, both in their course choices and their career choices.

In an unpublished study, we examined the accentuation process as it operated at the molecular level of course choice. This research examined the choice of sensitivity training by MIT graduate students in management. When we tested the learning styles of students who chose an elective sensitivity training laboratory, we found that they tended to be more concrete (CE) and reflective (RO) than those who chose not to attend the lab. When these individuals with divergent learning styles completed the training sessions their scores became even more concrete and reflective, accentuating their disposition toward divergent learning experiences.

In a large survey of MIT seniors (Kolb, 1973b), we examined the correspondence between the learning styles of these students and their departmental majors and then compared these scores with the scores of those students who were continuing graduate study in their chosen major. The results of these analysis are shown graphically in Figure 3.6 for departments with ten or more students. Analysis of variance for the six learning style dimensions by departmental majors shows that Reflective Observation, Active Experimentation, and the combination score active–reflective all vary significantly by departmental major. Differences on the abstract–concrete dimensions show no significance. This lack of significant differentiation may well be because of more uniform selective and normative pressures toward abstraction that operate across all the MIT departments.

The correspondence between learning style and undergraduate major in this study are similar to the previous findings. Humanities falls in the diverger quadrant while mathematics is assimilative. Management is clearly accommodative. Although the engineering departments all fall on the lower edge of the accommodator quadrant rather than the converger quadrant as we would predict, this is most likely a function of the general abstract bias of MIT just noted. Physics and chemistry are not as abstract and reflective as predicted, although if the LSI scores of only those students planning to attend graduate school are used (as indicated by the arrowheads in Figure 3.6) the pattern is more consistent with prediction. Economics is somewhat more abstract and active than in our previous sample though this is somewhat a function of the unique nature of the MIT department. The architecture department's position in the divergent quadrant is also to some extent a function of the unique nature of the department with its emphasis on creative design and photography as well as the more convergent technical skills of architecture. We did not make predictions about the biology and earth-science departments.

Figure 3.6 also contains data about career paths of the students in each of

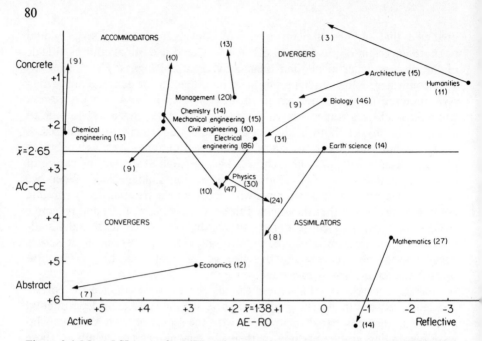

Figure 3.6 Mean LSI scores for MIT seniors on Abstract/Concrete and Active/Reflective by departmental major. Arrowheads indicate mean scores for those seniors in that department who are planning to attend graduate school. Sample size is indicated in parentheses

the departments. The arrowheads indicate for each department the average LSI scores for those students who are planning to attend graduate school. Our prediction was that those who chose to pursue a given discipline further through graduate training should show accentuation of the learning style characteristic of that discipline. That is, the arrows for those departments falling in the accommodative quadrant should point toward the concrete and active extremes of the LSI grid, the arrows for divergent departments toward the concrete and reflective, the arrows for the assimilative departments toward the abstract and reflective, and the arrows for the convergent departments toward abstract and active extremes of the LSI grid. The actual results are not so clear-cut. Chemical engineering, mechanical engineering, management, humanities, mathematics, and economics all show in varying degrees the predicted accentuation pattern. Potential graduate students in chemistry, civil engineering, and electrical engineering score in the convergent quadrant rather than becoming more accommodative. Architecture, biology, and earth science potential graduate students move toward the convergent rather than becoming more divergent. Physics moves into the assimilative quadrant.

The above results should be viewed as only suggestive since several measurement problems prevented a more accurate test of the accentuation hypothesis.[5] To deal with these problems in the measurement of the accentuation process we selected four departments for more intensive case study. Several criteria were used to choose four departments whose learning style demands matched the four dominant learning styles. The four departments chosen and their learning style demand were Mechanical engineering = Accommodator, Humanities = Diverger, Mathematics = Assimilator, and Economics = Converger.

To study the career choices of the students in the four departments each student's LSI scores were used to position him on the LSI grid with a notation of the career field he had chosen to pursue after graduation. If the student was planning to attend graduate school his career field was circled. If the accentuation process were operating in the career choices of the students we should find that those students who fall in the same quadrant as the norm of their academic major should be more likely to pursue careers and graduate training related to that major while students with learning styles that differ from their discipline norms should be more inclined to pursue other careers and not attend graduate school in their discipline. We can illustrate this pattern by examining students in the mathematics department (Figure 3.7). Ten of the 13 mathematics students (80 per cent) whose learning styles are congruent with departmental norms choose careers and graduate training in mathematics. Only two of the 13 students (15 per cent) whose learning styles are not congruent plan both careers and graduate training in mathematics (these differences are significant using the Fisher Exact Test $p < 01$). Similar patterns occurred in the other three departments.

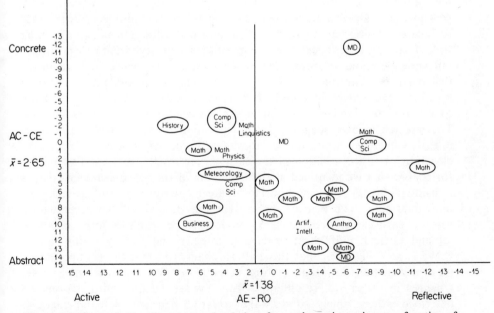

Figure 3.7 Career field and graduate school plans for mathematics majors as a function of their learning style. (Circles indicate that the student is planning to attend graduate school)

To further test the accentuation process in the four departments, we examined whether the student's choice/experience career development cycle indeed operated as an accentuating positive feedback loop. If this were so then those students whose learning style dispositions matched and were reinforced by their discipline demands should show a greater commitment to their choice of future career field than those whose learning styles were not reinforced by their experiences in their discipline. As part of a questionnaire, students were asked to rate how important it was for them to pursue their chosen career field. In all four departments the average importance rating was higher for the students with a match between learning style and discipline norms (the differences being statistically significant in the mechanical engineering and economic departments). Thus it seems that learning experiences that reinforce learning style dispositions tend to produce greater commitment in career choices than those learning experiences that do not reinforce learning style dispositions.

SUMMARY AND CONCLUSIONS—THEORETICAL CONSIDERATIONS

From the above research we draw two main conclusions. First the experiental learning typology seems to provide a useful grid for mapping individual differences in learning style and for mapping corresponding differences in the environmental demands of different career paths. As such it is a potentially powerful tool for describing the differentiated paths of adult development. Secondly, the above data present enticing, if not definitive, evidence that early career choices tend to follow a path toward accentuation on one's learning style. Learning experiences congruent with learning styles tend to positively influence the choice of future learning and work experiences that reinforce that particular learning style. On the other hand, those students who find a learning environment incongruent with their learning style tend to move away from that kind of environment in future learning and work choices. The research to date suggests that accentuation is the most powerful force in early career development. Correspondingly, the major cause of change or deviation from accentuation in the early career results from the first reason for change that we identified at the beginning of the research review, that is individual choice errors in choosing a career environment that matches the individual style. The primary reason for the strength of the accentuation forces in early career seems to stem from identity pressures to simply choose *a* job and *a* career. Fulfillment needs seem to be second priority at this time.

We expect, however, that this pattern changes in mid-career. Specifically we expect that as individuals mature, accentuation forces play a smaller role. Changes in career will result more from the second and third reasons we described earlier, namely withdrawal of reward for accentuation and emerging needs for personal fulfillment. Fulfillment needs will take the form of a desire to express non-dominant learning styles, (e.g. concrete and reflective skills for convergent engineers). The origins of these needs stem both from intrapersonal developmental processes (e.g. maturation) and external pressures for better managing life tasks (e.g. a man has so emphasized his convergent skills at work that he has neglected home and family).

For many individuals, however, withdrawal of reward for accentuation may be a precondition for the emergence of fulfillment concerns. Our notion here is that rewards for accentuation are often so powerful and overwhelming that the individual develops what we call a role-encapsulated ego. That is, rewards for specialized role performance tend to prevent the emergence of nondominant fulfillment needs. Thus, in many cases, withdrawal of these rewards may have to precede the awareness of fulfillment needs.

The direction of career transition can be predicted from the experiental learning theory of adult development. Since this theory suggests that the process of career change is a learning process that requires not only the acquisition of new skills but also the development of a modified learning style, career transitions to adjacent learning styles (e.g. from converger to accommodator or assimilator) should be easier than transitions to opposite learning styles (e.g. from diverger to converger). In addition our clinical observations, although few in number, suggest that it is easier to move from abstract to concrete and from reflective to active than the reverse.

PRACTICAL CONSIDERATIONS

As the rates of social and technological change continue to increase in American society the relationships between education and work will of necessity be dramatically altered. At present, however, social responses to these changes have lagged far behind. The public and private educational system remains structured to respond to traditional stable notions of career development that are no longer appropriate. Although today the career paths of many men and women may pass through two, three, or four distinct phases, each of which requires major new learning of knowledge skills and attitudes, educational programs remain primarily oriented to the early stages of life. In most educational institutions, adult and continuing education are low status, low priority activities done half-heartedly in the name of community service. The provision of mid-career educational programs has been left primarily to private industry. While this is, in some cases, as it should be and some of these programs are of quite high quality, all too often the implicit price for admission is a further commitment to one's previous career path. Changing careers is somewhat harder. For example, selection criteria for mid-career programs often include previous experience in that career, and tax laws allow deductions for training that is job related, but not for changing jobs.

The failure to provide avenues for career change produces great losses both in social productivity and in human satisfaction. Organizations do not benefit by locking their employees into careers that long ago ceased to be rewarding and challenging. Society loses the creativity and productivity of those who are barred from entry into new careers in mid-life. This is particularly true for the female half of the population. Traditional adult developmental patterns for women have included a phase where marriage and family keep them from the job market in their early career. Though social norms are changing, entry into careers in mid-life when family demands are less pressing still remains most difficult for women.

While structural and legal changes are essential to insure access to education and learning throughout our life span, it is equally important that men and women in our society gain a greater awareness and insight into the problems and possibilities of adult development. Underlying our selection of a *learning* theory as the primary theoretical framework for our work is the assumption that managing and adapting to change is a central task of adult development in contemporary society. In an earlier time personal identity and continuity were sustained in relatively stable environments of expectation and demand. Career and life style were ascribed not chosen. Once on a life path, personal choice was primarily a process of affirming expectations. In today's 'future shock' world, environmental complexity and change have denied us this easy route to personal identity. Now, more than ever, identity and continuity are forged through personal choices. These choices go beyond the computational selection of one alternative over another according to some predetermined values. They require the selection of the basic values themselves. In addition to asking, 'What is the right thing to do?' we now ask 'What do I believe is right?'. In addition to 'Who am I?' we ask 'Who do I want to be?'

Not surprisingly, the most common response to the dizzying freedom implied by these choices is the search for some *a priori* heuristic for reducing this freedom.[6] A primary function of the self-image we create and the opportunities we perceive is to define what we are *not* and to exclude by definition all that is *not* possible. Counseling and educational programs are needed to provide learning environments that allow the individual to raise to the conscious level his choices of these heuristic, freedom-reducing images. Said another way, we need career development programs with learning as a focus that would not only examine the 'content' of the self (i.e. abilities, interests, aspirations, and needs) but would also focus on the self as 'process'—an examination of the psychological principles and structures that determine *how* people choose career and life directions.

For some time now, the authors have been evaluating many of the existing career development programs in industry and universities from this learning theory perspective. We have identified several important limitations in many of these programs:

(1) They are too work oriented. By placing work/income in a central focus (this fits for many but not all people), other life interests are placed in an *a priori* peripheral and compensatory role. Such a bias precludes a fundamental reassessment of one's life and life style and places in a secondary position

the primary problem experienced by many individuals—that of integrating the many diverse elements of their lives.

(2) They are too specialization oriented. Many programs based their future planning on an analysis of past accomplishments and an assessment of already established abilities. Thus the limiting image that is perpetuated is that of climbing the ladder to the top of that specialized field that you have been best in. The opportunities for the expression of nondominant interests and abilities and more basic change in one's life path are not explored.

(3) They are too planning oriented. Planning and goal-setting are but one mode for achieving personal continuity and direction. Many achievement-oriented individuals prefer this mode. But for others this mode is antithetical to their life style (e.g. some find their sense of meaning in the Gestalt of the here and now, for them goals are merely abstractions).

(4) They are too outcome oriented. This is perhaps the major limitation, as we see it, of existing programs—they emphasize outcomes at the expense of process. Where you are going and what you want to accomplish are more important than how you are getting there. As a result, the individual may still be ill-prepared to cope with a future set of career and life choices.

Although we have certainly been too critical in our analysis of current career development programs, the creation of this 'straw man' has helped us to identify more clearly the themes for a career development program based on experiential learning theory. Briefly stated these are:

(1) *A focus on life rather than occupation*: Career development and life planning should start from a holistic analysis of the person's life space and examine the relationship among work, family, leisure, spiritual/development needs, etc. The term career therefore is used in its broadest sense—the self-mediated progress through time of transactions between person and environment.

(2) *Career as a here-and-now issue*: An individual's goals and his interpretations of his own personal history represent his attempts to make sense and meaning of his present existential life situation. Major tasks in coping with change are the reinterpretation of personal history and the readjustment of goal images in the context of new emerging life circumstances. In this sense, previous accomplishments and developed abilities and life goals are as much determined by life experiences as they are causes of these experiences.

(3) *Emphasis on choices versus planning*: Implicit in the above is an emphasis on immediate personal choice as opposed to longer range planning. An aim of the program should be to bring the individual into closer contact with his choice-making process. This is accomplished by increasing awareness of choice-making and control over the choice-making process by shortening the time lag between choices and consequences (e.g. seeing a first job choice in terms of its immediate consequences as well as a long-term determining decision).

(4) *Emphasis on the learning process as opposed to outcomes*: The problem of managing and adapting to change as a central task of adult development in contemporary society is, at its most fundamental level, an issue of the process by which people learn. A career program with learning as a central focus helps participants examine not only the 'content of the self'—abilities, interests, aspirations, and needs—but also helps them to focus on the 'self as process'—the process by which one makes choices among various alternatives. The participant is thereby helped to increase his range of choices not only in terms of outcomes but also in terms of the processes whereby he can achieve these outcomes.

In conclusion, the theoretical and practical considerations discussed point to the importance of further study of career development, particularly the mid-career transition process, from the perspective of an adult developmental model. Experiential learning theory is one such model that has yielded some interesting results and prospects.

NOTES

1. The details of the inventory construction along with preliminary reliability and validity studies are described in Kolb (1971). The inventory itself along with management norms appears in Kolb, Rubin, and McIntyre (1971).
2. The reason that there are four dominant styles is that AC and CE are highly negatively correlated as are RO and AE. Thus individuals score high on both AC and CE or on both AE and RO with less frequency than do the other four combinations of LSI scores.
3. Many of these differences in LSI scores among disciplines are statistically significant at a very high level, especially when they are grouped into physical sciences, social sciences, and the arts (see Kolb (1971) for details).

   Some cautions are in order in interpreting these data. First, it should be remembered that all of the individuals in the sample are managers or managers-to-be. In addition most of these people have completed or are in graduate school. These two facts should produce learning styles that are somewhat more active and abstract than the population at large. (As indicated by total sample mean scores on AC–CE and AE–RO of $+4.5$ and $+2.9$, respectively.) The interaction between career, high level of education and undergraduate major may produce distinctive learning styles. For example, physicists who are not in industry may be somewhat more reflective than those in this sample. Secondly, undergraduate majors are described only in the most gross terms. There are many forms of engineering or psychology. A business major at one school can be quite different from that at another.
4. 't' tests for significance of difference between groups on the abstract/concrete dimension yields the following one-tail probabilities that are less than 0.10. Marketing is more concrete that personnel ($p < 0.10$), engineering ($p < 0.05$), research ($p < 0.005$), and finance ($p < 0.005$). Finance and research are more abstract than personnel (on both comparisons $p < 0.005$). On the active/reflective dimension research is more reflective than marketing ($p < 0.05$), engineering ($p < 0.05$), and to a lesser extent finance ($p < 0.10$).
5. The first problem was that it was difficult to determine whether a student was in all cases planning graduate training in the subject he majored in. It was difficult, for example, to determine whether a mathematics student planning graduate work in artificial intelligence would continue studying mathematics or not. While most students

clearly planned graduate training in the field of their major, the few borderline cases do contaminate the results. A second measurement problem lies in the fact, already demonstrated, that graduate study in general for MIT students is associated with an abstract and active orientation. Since all six of the departments that did not follow the accentuation prediction showed a tendency toward abstractness and four of the six showed a tendency toward the active orientation, this general tendency for graduate study may well have overshadowed the accentuation process in those departments. The final measurement problem has to do with the prediction of learning demands for those departments like electrical engineering who score close to the middle of the LSI grid.

6. As an example of this phenomenon, Plovnick (1974, 1975) discovered that students with different learning styles tended to utilize different limited sources of information and influence in making important career choices. He found that accommodators and divergers relied on concrete work experiences and identification with a single charismatic role model while convergers tend to scan across a variety of role models. Assimilators relied most heavily on such things as course work and reading for their career influences.

Chapter 4

Cognitive Style and Career Specialization

Peter G. W. Keen

INTRODUCTION: THE MANAGEMENT OF EXPERTISE

Management careers in the field of business are usually discussed in terms of the line manager, whose training and career path emphasize a broad exposure to a range of functional areas and techniques. However, in recent years the role of the specialist in business has grown immensely and while it may still be true that senior executives remain generalists in their orientation, they increasingly draw on a range of professional, technical, and staff personnel who have substantial impact on the organization's decision making and who are also now reaching senior positions within the management hierarchy. For example, specialists in operations research, corporate planning, and research and development, are to be found at the senior vice president level in many major companies. These are individuals whose careers run counter to the traditional line manager pattern; they have concentrated on their complex, professionalized specialty and often have had virtually no exposure to any of the main business functions of marketing, production, accounting, or finance. Because this role of the specialist in business is relatively recent, it is difficult to pick out common career patterns or to summarize the main differences between the managerial and the professional orientation.

This chapter discusses career specialization in terms of a narrow, but in-sightful perspective. It examines the cognitive 'styles' associated with particular disciplines and skills. The specialist is 'different' from the manager not just because he has an advanced degree in a mathematical area; the difference goes far deeper and seems to reflect an entirely different way of thinking—of conceptualizing, analyzing, problem-solving, and explaining. Examining the management science specialization from this viewpoint has been a very illuminating one (McKenney and Keen, 1973). The aim here is to extend that analysis to the wider issue of career specialization in general. The framework in no way amounts to a 'theory' of specialization, but it does serve to highlight what it is that is distinctive about the specialist, what his or her role should be and the opportunities and constraints involved in specialized careers. There are many factors influencing career paths. Cognitive style is only one of these, but by focusing on how specialists' minds work, we can get a much clearer idea of the main forces influencing their activity, effectiveness, and career growth. The Management of expertise requires, at the very least, this understanding.

COGNITIVE STYLE: AN OVERVIEW

The term 'cognitive style' refers to the distinct and consistent strategies people show in their approach to information and problem-solving. These styles are integral personality traits, analogous to 'introversion' or 'self-control'. There are a number of different (though overlapping) models of styles, but regardless of the particular labels and categories, it seems clear that cognitive style in general is important in both people's choice of, and ability in, particular jobs, especially those that require specialized intellectual skills. Many people do not show an extreme style, just as many people are so mildly introverted or extroverted that it is not meaningful to classify them in those terms. An extreme cognitive style reflects an imbalance in intellectual responses that makes it particularly well-suited to jobs that similarly involve specialized information, analysis, and communication.

The effectiveness of a cognitive style obviously depends on how well-matched it is to its context. The idiosyncratic skills of a proofreader are ill-suited to a job requiring speed-reading or selective scanning of large amounts of written information but are, on the other hand, ideally fitted to the specialized task of galley-proofing. The proofreader's skills are rare; people with a more balanced set of cognitive abilities may perhaps be more effective over a broad range of jobs, but in this one they cannot equal the seemingly instinctive responses of someone who may be no more attentive, intelligent, or verbal than themselves. It must be stressed that virtually all cognitive style studies find no correlation between style and intelligence or general level of academic performance, though, of course, they report strong correlations between particular styles and particular academic fields (especially mathematics).

It is very hard indeed to estimate the fraction of the population that has a distinct cognitive style. The author's own research, focused on MBA graduates, middle managers, and computer professionals in the 20–30 age range, suggests that at least 30 per cent of people have a style that is marked enough to show significant variations in performance and approach over a wide range of problem-solving tasks. In addition, they show several marked personality characteristics.

It may be felt that a distinct cognitive style is a weakness, in that it indicates an incapacity in dealing with some problems, and that the more extreme the style, the narrower the area of strengths. It is certainly true that the cognitive specialist is limited in his skills, and that his relatively unusual mode of thinking can make it difficult for others to work with him. On the other hand, the specialist can cover that small but sometimes very important set of problems that those with more general skills fail at. For example, computer programmers are notorious for their 'quirks' in thinking; the job of structuring, coding, and debugging a program involves complex demands on memory and method and it seems that the skills required cannot be easily taught. While the standard Programmer Aptitude Test (PAT) is almost universally castigated as a poor device for selecting potential programmers, there is still general agreement that programming does involve 'aptitude', a natural compatibility of cognitive skills and habits that is not directly related to intelligence. It is the very imbalance of cognitive abilities that makes the programmer so useful—and so irritating to deal with at times. Very few people could be comfortable with the programmer's job. Even if they could learn his tricks of technique, they would be under some definite mental strain—the job is not 'natural' for them.

The author's research on cognitive style has used a particular model that will be discussed later. However, the main concern here is to establish a general perspective on the nature and value of cognitive specialization and it is hoped that the arguments hold regardless of the particular model of style one may adopt.

Thinking is a compromise. People adapt to tasks and informational environments, developing strategies that ease cognitive strain. One cannot do everything; accuracy and precision can be increased at the expense of speed and vice versa. A few alternatives can be examined in depth or many alternatives at a more global but less focused level. A cognitive style may well emerge from continuous exposure to particular types of information and problems over a long period of time; the strategies that develop and that are effective harden and the set of skills implicit in those strategies are extended and refined while other abilities atrophy. For example, a fourteen-year-old who is top of his class in mathematics and mediocre in English and languages will generally choose courses that build on his mathematical skills, and just try to get by in the other subjects. It seems plausible that a cognitive style emerges through early exposure in this way to specialized informational environments. Certainly, the meritocratic education systems of Britain and France seem to encourage very apparent patterns of style: the verbal 'divergent' conceptualizing of the Oxbridge tradition and the 'convergent' logical precision and formalism of L'Ecole Polytechnique. American education generally delays the point at which a student can limit his studies to a single subject or type of discipline. Even so, Altemeyer's study of undergraduates at Carnegie–Mellon shows the rapidity with which students adjust their cognitive responses to the demands of their environment. He found virtually no differences in cognitive characteristics between the engineering and liberal arts students at the freshman level, but by the junior year the two groups showed substantial and very consistent distinctions (Altemeyer, 1966).

Of course, one implication of this mutually reinforcing pattern of specialized studies and specialized cognitive style in an individual is that he or she is likely to develop a very 'marketable' set of skills. Cognitive specialization seems to be associated in particular with a number of professions; the author's research has concentrated on the computer field where cognitive style and its implications are fairly easy to observe. Other studies have similarly focused on medical professionals, lawyers, engineers, and so on. The evidence is fragmented but consistent; specialized jobs seem to be associated with particular styles (e.g. Cullen and coworkers 1969 and Levy, 1969). The discussion here will mainly focus on just one career example, that of the management scientist, both because it is important in itself and because it highlights many of the central issues of cognitive and career specialization.

MANAGERS AND MANAGEMENT SCIENTISTS: THE PROBLEM OF MUTUAL UNDERSTANDING

Management scientists are a strange breed and tend to be an unpopular one. They bring to their job a powerful ability to formalize their thinking. They are methodological, approaching problems by structuring them in terms of a program for a solution. Because of this, they are able to take fuzzy, messy problems and clarify or simplify them. They tend to make others feel defensive because of the sense of structure and certainty they show in their way of thinking—and of behaving—and are generally associated with a technique-based approach to problems, what has been called the 'have technique, will travel' syndrome. Management science has had some stunning successes. There are problem areas, such as inventory management, resource allocation, and production scheduling, that 20 years ago were little understood and for which 'artists' were hired (at substantial salaries). The powerful methodology implicit in the management scientist's way of thinking, his ability to build explicit conceptual, as well as physical models has made these problems relatively trivial, even automatable.

At the same time, management science has had little impact on problems that do not seem so structurable: policy making, strategic planning, marketing, and public sector decision making. There is a substantial body of literature attacking, often in angry tones, the failures of management science in these areas (Keen, 1975). It was mentioned earlier that the effectiveness of a cognitive style depends on how well-matched it is to its context. A major theme in the attacks of management scientists is that their modes of thinking and assumptions about problem-solving are often unfitted to the reality of the *manager*'s world. Even within the management science profession itself, it is often argued that the skills and approach of quantitatively trained specialists are not useful to the managers and decision makers they are hired to support. The blame is generally placed on the education system that produces them; a point to raise here and leave hanging for later discussion is whether a shift in training could resolve the issue if in fact the real problem is the cognitive style—the 'mentality'—of the management science specialist, with its clear value and suitability to the world of optimizable problems and its limitations in the wider area of decision making under uncertainty, ambiguity, time-pressure, and vagueness.

Grayson's paper in the *Harvard Business Review* (Grayson, 1973) is perhaps the most-quoted summary of the attack on management science as a specialization:

'Managers and management scientists are operating as two separate cultures, each with its own goals, languages and methods. Effective cooperation—and even communication—between the two is just about minimal.' (Grayson, 1973, p. 41)

His conclusion is that both managers and management scientists should be educated towards a common middle ground. The argument implicit in the discussion so far is the opposite of this; we need the limited, powerful abilities of the cognitive specialist. The issue then is how to manage these specialists, to recognize their characteristics, and to match them to a context where they can be effective. The starting point for this is obviously descriptive, to develop an understanding of the link between style and career. If one identifies the communication problems managers find in dealing with staff professionals as being due to their specialized knowledge, then training in and exposure to each other's activities should eliminate the difficulty. The key point in the argument here, led up to so leisurely, is that this approach will not work and is, in fact, undesirable. The auditor, the proofreader, the computer programmer, lawyer, librarian, and engineer are valuable *because* of, not in spite of, their cognitive styles. While, of course, it is desirable for them to get some understanding of their clients' very different mode of thinking and while a cognitive style can perhaps shift given time and exposure to other environments, organizations need the 'green eye-shade' crew of auditors whose pedantry, deliberateness and single-minded focus on 'just what the data says' allow them to spot a double-debit among a million ledger entries or the operations researcher whose response to the plea 'help me save my marriage' is 'define your objective function!'

TWO MODELS OF STYLE

The argument so far has avoided presenting a specific model of cognitive style. In a way it would be preferable to continue to do so. There are several competing paradigms and the research on measuring styles is exploratory and tentative in its conclusions. The particular labels one may choose to categorize style are less important than the more general implications of the notion of style and specialization; in fact, style seems easier to recognize than to measure. There is, however, a common pattern in the various theories, a distinction between an extreme mode of problem-solving that is 'convergent' and one that is 'divergent':

'In convergent thinking the aim is to discover the one right answer to the problem set. It is highly directed, essentially logical thinking of the kind required in science and mathematics. It is also the kind required for the solution of most intelligence tests. In "divergent" thinking, on the other hand, the aim is to produce a large number of possible answers, none of which is necessarily more correct than the others, though some may be more original. Such thinking is marked by its variety and fertility rather than by its logical precision.' (Zangwill, 1970, p. 145)

Liam Hudson (1966), among others, has explored in detail the distinct differences between convergent and divergent high-school age students, in terms of personality, academic preferences, and ability. The differences are marked and explain much of these students' day-to-day behavior. They are too young for the impact their style will have on their career choices to be apparent, except that already they have made several critical decisions: the convergers to select engineering and hard sciences and the divergers to choose the humanities. Thomas Kuhn (1963) has, however, extended Hudson's diverger–converger classifications in discussing varying types of scientific researcher. More recently, Ian Mitroff (1975) in his study of the Apollo Moon Scientists suggests that such differences in style are important determinants of both scientists' research approach, career path, and even their opinion of their colleagues.

Herman Witkin's (1962) paradigm of cognitive style is somewhat different from Hudson's. His field-dependence/field-independence distinction is by far the best known of all the style models. Witkin and his colleagues have amassed an impressive range of data on the relation between style and career choice. His model is perhaps less rich than Hudson's in that it does not apply so well to complex problem-solving but focuses on perceptual behavior: an individual's ability to analytically isolate an item from its context, its field. One of Witkin's experiments amusingly demonstrates the extent to which a person's cognitive style is a major aspect of his whole personality and not just a measure of intellectual functioning. His Rod-and-Frame test involves a subject being placed in a totally darkened room in which he can see only a square frame and a rod, both covered with luminous paint. He is required to adjust the rod to an upright position. 'Field-dependent' subjects tend to align the rod with the frame, which may be tilted from the upright. The results are often striking; in a variant of the test, the room itself is tilted and subjects are asked to align their own body to the upright: 'Astonishing as it may seem, some people actually can be tilted as much as 30 per cent and in that position report that they are perfectly straight, stating that 'this is the way I sit in class' (Witkin, 1973). Witkin reports that field-dependent people are likely to be particularly responsive to social frames of reference and thus to favor careers which are 'people-oriented', such as teaching, sales, and counseling and to study in fields like sociology, clinical psychology, and the humanities. They are more likely than field-independent individuals to change their majors during college. The latter, by contrast, usually have a definite career in mind when they enter college and tend to choose jobs which require a fairly impersonal analytic approach, especially in science and engineering. Within specific occupations Witkin found distinct differences in specialization; for example, surgical nurses tend to be field-independent and psychiatric nurses field-dependent.

While most of Witkin's research has been in the area of education, his disciples have accumulated a wealth of data on career-related issues. A particularly interesting implication of his model is that field-dependent individuals seem to need personal guidance and orientation; they thus seem especially open to the socialization experiences discussed by Van Maanen (1976). By contrast, field-independent individuals are likely to resist or ignore these cues and pressures. The field-independent, analytic, relatively impersonal management scientist is thus difficult to integrate into the organizational milieu, while the field-dependent personal director builds his reference points through socialization. The implications of this are important; the field-independent analytic specialist, with whom managers find it hard to communicate, needs to maintain his own distance from the organization and simply cannot relate to it or learn about its operations through conventional patterns such as orientation or training programs, group pressures, apprenticeship model, and the like. By contrast, the field-dependent 'people' specialist, in personnel or sales activity, actively seeks to adapt to the organization's climate.

THE McKENNEY–KEEN MODEL OF COGNITIVE STYLE

Both Hudson's and Witkin's models suggest that cognitive style is an important influence on career choice. The model that was used in the author's research has several overlaps with both of their theories (and with Kolb's (1971) Learning Style model). An important distinction, however, is that it is two-dimensional. One of the major weaknesses of cognitive style research has been its effort to summarize wide ranges of cognitive skills along a bipolar spectrum. These skills include perception, conceptualization, problem-solving, and memory; a dichotomized single dimension such as 'concrete-abstract', 'levelling-sharpening', or 'field-dependent-independent' seems unlikely to capture the overall complexity these individual skills comprise. For this reason, the McKenney–Keen model (Figure 4.1), like Kolb's, summarizes cognitive functioning in terms of two dimensions. The first of these defines individuals' information-gathering in terms of a bipolar scale of Receptive and Preceptive modes of behavior. The second dimension, information evaluation, distinguishes between Systematic and Intuitive problem-solving.

An individual's style is categorized in terms of the quadrant in which he falls, e.g. Systematic–Receptive, Intuitive–Preceptive. [For a fuller description of the theory and measurement, see Keen (1973).]

The information-gathering dimension relates essentially to the perceptual processes by which the mind organizes the diffuse and verbal stimuli it encounters. The resultant 'information' is a very *personalized* summary of data. It is easy to underestimate the complex coding involved in this process and the strategies we use—often unconsciously—to ease 'cognitive strain'. Of necessity,

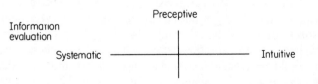

Figure 4.1 The McKenney–Keen model of cognitive style

(a)   (b)   (c)

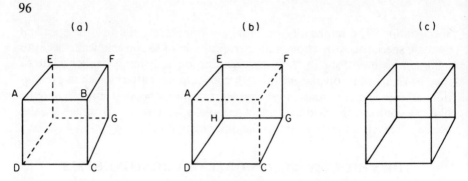

Figure 4.2 Perceptual example: shape classification

information gathering involves rejecting some of the data encountered, summarizing and organizing the rest. The strategies used are critical; for example, we all exploit the redundancy of the English language in reading— we read much, much faster than our eyes can physically take in the letters on the page. Of course, this makes us vulnerable to error. Few people will spot a duplication in a word, such as 'this is the month of Appril'. We are generally aware of our perceptual processes only when for some reason they fail to work. We have perceptual programs for classifying shapes. Figure 4.2 (a) is easily recognized as a cube with the plane ABCD facing forward and Figure 4.2 (b) as a similar cube with EFGH to the front. Figure 4.2 (c) is a transparent composite of (a) and (b) and our mental program generally has trouble reaching a conclusion.

THE PRECEPTIVE–RECEPTIVE STYLES

The McKenney–Keen model captures, at a molar level, strategies of information gathering, defined in terms of Receptive and Preceptive modes of style.

Preceptive individuals tend to have very powerful concepts and strategies that they use to filter data; they focus on patterns of information and look for deviations from (or conformities with) their expectations. The precepts act as both cues for information-gathering and heuristics for cataloguing and classifying. By contrast, Receptive thinkers are much more sensitive to the data-stimulus itself; they focus on detail rather than pattern and try to derive the implications of the data from direct examination instead of its fitting their precepts. An almost prototypical example of the Receptive mode of thinking is the auditor. His job requires focusing on information very deliberately without presuppositions, without organizing precepts. Thus, given a set of *pro forma* financial statements, for instance, he must ask 'what *exactly* does this say?' and build up from the data itself a complete and clear definition of its meaning. The preceptor, given the same data, is far more likely to scan it quickly, building up a set of mental frames such as 'high margin, high overhead', 'small volume consumer goods company', etc. He can then use these precepts as a frame of reference against which to examine the data more closely. He needs some sense of context and pattern. The Receptor in this particular situation is certainly better suited to the demands of the task. His inductive approach is less likely to jump to incorrect conclusions or to overlook relevant detail. In general, the Receptor is attentive, specific and his style well-suited to situations where a small volume of information must be painstakingly combed.

The strength of the Preceptor lies in his ability to deal with large volumes of heterogeneous data. He is concerned with pattern at the expense of detail. His powerful organizing focus is especially effective in fitting together a jigsaw puzzle of information. For example, many marketing managers are strong Preceptors; they are often able to build a sense of their market and to spot trends or shifts because their precepts act as cues to alert them to subtle details among all the heterogeneous data of their day-to-day activities—salesmen's reports, trade journals, market analyses, customer requests, and so on. The Receptor is ill-suited to such situations; his mode of information-gathering treats all data as potentially relevant, while the Preceptor screens and filters data very quickly. The Receptor also works best with well-defined small volumes of information; he is unlikely to be able to develop a sense of the pattern and overall dynamics of the market.

Each mode of style has its advantages in specific situations and equally includes risks of overlooking the potential meaning of data. It is worth stressing that a person's cognitive style is his way of coping, of feeling comfortable and effective in his information-processing. It is an integral part of his 'reality-testing'—making sense of what is happening and acting on her basis of his interpretation of the situation. Competent individuals generally have an accurate sense of their relative capabilities and gravitate to jobs in which they feel comfortable. It is easy to think of situations where a Preceptor, say, cannot operate in his preferred mode—the auditor's or proofreader's jobs and obvious examples. It seems clear that the Preceptor thrives in situations in which he must develop and continually test out a concept of his environment, and in which the data he has to deal with has a high noise-to-signal ratio and must therefore be filtered and screened. Conversely, the Receptor is most effective in jobs where his information environment is mainly signal and where he needs a careful attention to the precise implications of data, where a small detail may be highly important, and where approximations or generalizations

Table 4.1 Careers well-suited to receptors and preceptors

Receptor	Preceptor
Architect	Advertising
Engineer	Liberal arts teacher
Computer programmer	Computer systems analyst
Auditor	Psychologist
Proofreader	Librarian
Production manager	Marketing manager

can be risky. The list given in Table 4.1 is obviously not comprehensive but hopefully does suggest the nature and relevance of differences in modes of information-gathering (Keen, 1973).

THE SYSTEMATIC-INTUITIVE STYLES

The second dimension of the McKenney–Keen model is perhaps easier to identify and measure. It distinguishes between a Systematic and an Intuitive mode of problem-solving. The differences between the two relate mainly to planning. Some individuals are very methodological (which is in no way the same as methodical); their response to a problem is to explicitly define *how* they will approach it. Their main effort goes to laying out the constraints of the problem, selecting and then implementing a strategy. Their analysis is basically sequential, zeroing in on a solution through steps of increasing refinement. This systematic mode of response is thus marked by several distinctive features:

(1) a conscious awareness of where any substep fits within the overall plan;
(2) an ordered sequence of search and analysis;
(3) the justification of a solution largely in terms of method.

In many ways, the Systematic thinker's plan amounts to a program, in the computer meaning of the word. Before the program is run, all the rules for action have been specified so that the rest of the problem-solving process is mainly computational or analytic; in a sense, the methodology guarantees the solution.

Part of the difficulty in discussing the Intuitive style is that, unlike Systematic thinking, it lacks conscious definition and visible structure. Its most obvious feature is a reliance on unverbalized responses. The main principle governing the Intuitive's sequence of thought is a continuous global sense of the whole problem. Once the Systematic thinker has defined the problem and his methodology for dealing with it, he can largely leave the original problem-statement behind. He can also break the process up into a series of discrete substeps — his plan provides the framework for fitting them together. The Intuitive, by contrast, continually relates a step in his analysis to the overall problem, implicitly asking 'does it fit together? does it make sense?' as he proceeds. This allows him to work with much more ambiguity in the problem. For instance, a manager who is asked to forecast consumer preferences over the next two years for men's shirt styles has an ill-defined problem that is hard to fit into any Systematic plan. The Intuitive's response may well be initially to scan over a range of ideas and information, developing a sense of the issues and testing out some concepts well before he even defines the problem as such. He might, for example, review his own buying habits and his wife's influence on them, scan Sears–Roebuck catalogues for the last two years and read through an industry report on men's fashions. The search is not random, but it is hardly planned. He may draw tentative conclusions from each area of this initial analysis and the process of fitting them together or resolving some contradictions among them may *then* lead him to define the real 'problem', which he now may feel is to identify the lagged relationships between shifts in style in women's fashions and men's. He may, at that point, be able to articulate a systematic plan, perhaps in the form of instructions to a staff analyst. It is important to note that when he began his analysis he had no direct reference point for determining the relevance of each step. The Systematic can assess the value (and purpose) of reading the Sears catalogues by reviewing his methodology; the Intuitive's rationale is much more one of 'let's see what I can get out of this'. His reference point has to be his sensitization to the overall implications of the problem and an alertness to the meaning of what he has just done at each stage in the process. It is in this sense that he mainly relies on 'feel' and cues where the Systematic uses method and plan.

In this example, the manager evaluates a wide range of information, whose relevance cannot be anticipated. He cannot afford to review it exhaustively and must be ready to discard lines of exploration that are unpromising very quickly. Largely for this reason, the Intuitive does not verbalize his problem-solving to anywhere near the same extent that the Systematic thinker does. He operates almost at the fringe of consciousness, ranging quickly and lightly over a wide range of ideas, but able to pause and bring information into more conscious awareness when he hits on some worthwhile line of exploration. It is in this way that his strategy, with its potentially high fraction of false starts, redundancy, and dead-ends can be successful. The Systematic's conscious understanding of what he is trying to do and of the direction of his analysis means that he will process only the data that is likely to be relevant—his plan in

Table 4.2 Characteristics of each mode of cognitive style

Systematic thinkers tend to:

Look for method and make a plan for solving a problem;
Be very conscious of their approach;
Defend the quality of a solution largely in terms of the method;
Define the specific constraints of the problem early in the process;
Move through a process of increasing refinement of analysis;
Conduct an ordered search for additional information;
Complete any discrete step in analysis that they set out on.

Intuitive thinkers tend to:

Keep the overall problem continuously in mind;
Redefine the problem frequently as they proceed;
Rely on unverbalized cues, even hunches;
Defend a solution in terms of 'fit';
Consider a number of alternatives and options simultaneously;
Explore and abandon alternatives quickly.

itself screens out noise and wasted effort. The Intuitive must operate with immensely more speed because he has no such mechanism for screening; the speed can only come from avoiding the substantial time lapses implicit in verbalization. A common phenomenon in his thinking is the 'hunch', an unarticulated sense that some information or line of thought contains a vital cue. Quite often, that hunch comes a few seconds after the cue itself; he then tries to recapture it by backtracking and reconstructing his line of thought. For a tabulation of the characteristics of Systematic and Intuitive Thinkers see Table 4.2.

THE CAREER IMPLICATIONS OF EACH STYLE

The author's research, mainly using MBA students and middle managers as subjects, has found distinctive and consistent differences between Systematic and Intuitive thinkers that have immense implications for both career choice and for effective working together. Each type prefers different careers, performs very differently on complex problems (differently in terms of process, approach, and even of language, rather than in terms of answers) and shows marked personality traits. There is space here only to summarize these differences. (See Keen (1973) for a fuller discussion.)

Systematic thinkers are convergers. They learn by developing *methods* and are very effective in structuring problems. They are attracted to careers in engineering, production, management science, and administration. Intuitives much prefer open-ended jobs in which their ability to create solutions out of nonstructured, ill-defined or ambiguous situations can be best used; they seem particularly attracted to such professional positions as librarian, psychologist, lawyer, journalism, and advertising. The occupations preferred by Systematics are marked by their being largely administrative, technical, or business positions involving planning, control, and supervision. The Intuitive's preferred occupations are more heterogeneous and less structured. They involve much less feedback and lack the characteristic of clear criteria for action with clear feedback of results found in the Systematic thinker's choices (Table 4.3).

One of the author's experiments, using a small sample of MBA students, each of whom had a distinctive style amounting to a cognitive specialization,

Table 4.3 Occupation preferred by systematics and intuitives

Systematics	Intuitives
Engineering	Psychology
Production	Librarianship
Management science	Law
Computer programming	Journalism
Finance	Advertising
Military	Arts

Table 4.4 Undergraduate major and work experience of MBA sample (Keen, 1974)

Systematics		Intuitives	
Major	Work experience	Major	Work experience
Engineering	Construction engineering	Economics	Military intelligence
Glass science	Engineering	Engineering	Teaching math and economics
Mechanical engineering	Computer hardware design	Chemical engineering	Technical sales
Civil engineering	Construction engineering	Mechanical engineering	Technical writer
Nautical engineering	Construction project manager	Production management	Teaching in U.S. Navy
Electrical engineering	Computer programming	French literature	Law
Engineering	U.S. Coast Guard	Law	Sales and marketing
		Philosophy	market research
		Economics	Sales representative

revealed an interesting difference between the Systematic and Intuitive thinkers (Keen, 1974). Both groups consisted mainly of engineering majors. However, while the Systematic engineers invariably had chosen work in technical or engineering-related fields for their first jobs, virtually none of the Intuitives had done so. The sample in small (20 students), but the pattern is distinctive Table 4.4 shows the undergraduate majors and work experience of those students who had worked full-time after college.

This sample of students was also given a set of very varied problems to solve; the aim was to examine the types of problems preferred by Systematics as against Intuitives and the *approach* to problems made by each group (instead of just comparing quality of answers). The students were encouraged to talk aloud if they wished. The differences between the Systematics and Intuitives were striking. The Systematics tended to choose problems that had a clear structure, solved them in a manner that was deliberate, sequential in thought and consciously organized. The Intuitives, by contrast, preferred open-ended problems that had no one 'right' answer. They tended to think aloud, to look for an organizing idea or approach, to shift from one topic to another, and to base answers on their own feelings rather than on external validity such as logic.

The differences between the two groups in terms of language were revealing. The Systematic subjects almost invariably began their answers by defining *how* they were going to solve the problem while the Intuitives frequently stated some analogy or metaphor. The convergent Systematic bounds the problem before starting in on it:

'What I'm going to do is count the letter frequencies.'
'The problem seems to be . . .'
'To come up with some explanation, you'll have to weight the inputs . . .'

Having structured the problem in this fashion, the Systematic has a set of guidelines, a methodology for analysis. The divergent Intuitive, however, needs to cue himself—he often seems to jump in overhastily, trying something quickly that generates some self-correcting feedback to clarify what is involved:

'When I read this the first time, it reminded me of the Olympics; you know— the Arabs and Israelis.'
'This situation is similar to . . .'
'I have a feeling that the way the problem's set up, you should probably make the decision to be anti. . . . But I would decide pro.'
'I've got to do all this? What am I supposed to do?'
'I'm not sure why I chose this. I don't even understand it.'

The approaches used by the two groups on the same problems differed in almost every way. On some problems, one mode of style was clearly more effective; in decoding a cipher, for instance, the Intuitives did overwhelmingly better than the Systematics. The convergent Systematic has a precise method, letter-by-letter substitutions, that takes far too long. The divergent Intuitive is much more sensitive to pattern, tries out a range of ideas in parallel, and is more alert to clues (for example, one part of the cipher read 'XE AEMS XE'— there are few such combinations in English; 'as . . . as', 'to . . . to', and 'of . . . of' are the most obvious ones).

The subjects in this sample were all very intelligent. Their ability to find good answers (especially in exams and academic achievement tests) obscures their differences in problem-solving. They all in fact describe themselves in similar terms as 'attentive to detail', 'logical', etc. They also tend to take for granted that what is self-evident to themselves should be so to other. However, it is clear, both from the experiment discussed above and from some follow-up personality tests given to several larger samples, that they often cannot even understand the other's reasoning. The Systematics tend to be Thinking and Judging in personality (these are Jung's categories of psychological type, measured by the Myers–Briggs Type Indicator—Myers (1962)]. They reach decisions through a logical process that relies on impersonal finding and that stresses 'realism, analysis, logic, critical faculty'. The criteria the Systematic uses to determine a 'good' solution (and to determine 'self-evident') is thus logical consistency and a demonstrable chain of reasoning. This is entirely different from the Intuitives, who are Feeling and Perceiving in psychological type. Because so much of their reasoning is divergent, unverbalized, and lacking any conscious plan, they need to be very sensitive to their own 'sense' of things. In the experiment described earlier, a number of the Intuitives justified solutions essentially by saying 'it feels right'. The Intuitive's frequent use of hunches reflects this reliance on internalized emotive responses rather than on external validation. It should be stressed that in all the research using the McKenney–Keen Model of Style, there is no evidence that either Systematics or Intuitives are in any way 'better' (or more intelligent) than the other, though each can be more effective in particular contexts. In certain extreme situations, one mode of style may totally outperform the other.

The author's original research aimed at identifying and measuring cognitive style in a homogeneous population, the fabled college students without whom psychological research would hardly exist. Follow-up studies in the 'Real World' have extended and confirmed most of the original findings. In particular, these have looked at extreme situations—jobs where one style seems much, much more suitable than the other. Management science is the most obvious of these, but all the situations that were studied revealed a phenomenon that seems very common indeed when skilled specialists have to work on a joint problem. They have 'difficulties in communication' which can often become quite acrimonious. In describing the other, each of these obviously competent, obviously intelligent professionals will dismiss him or her, not as ill-tempered, uncooperative, or obnoxious, but as 'stupid'. The Systematic gets irritated at the Intuitive's apparently ill-thought-out ramblings with its high rate of false starts; his thinking seems sloppy, even irresponsible. Equally, the Intuitive objects to the narrow-minded, snail-paced pedantry of the Systematic, who will not jump ahead but painstakingly plods through each step in an obvious sequence. Our own reasoning is logical—the other's misses the point. The author has recorded a variety of encounters in which this mutual dismissal occurs, even though it is obvious that the participants are simply *different*, not stupid. The situation seems worse with specialized professionals—a CPA and a marketing manager, or a lawyer and an engineer. A specialized problem-solver such as a CPA is valuable *because* of his specialized cognitive style which allows him to deal with problems his client finds difficult, but this makes him hard to work with and hard to understand.

MANAGEMENT SCIENCE AND SYSTEMATIC THINKING

The management science profession as a whole represents perhaps the prototypical Systematic approach to problems. The management scientist is an expert in methods and a model builder—these are not just computer models but conceptual abstractions that can make explicit someone else's vague notions and that permit complex problems to be formalized and analyzed. This Systematic approach is immensely powerful and it seems fair to say that management scientists as a whole are among the most intelligent group to be found in any field. However, management science has not had anywhere near the impact it could have on organizations' planning and decision making.

Far more models are built than are used; the reasons for this lack of adoption are rarely technical. There is in fact a crisis of implementation. Horror stories abound and expenditures of over several millions of dollars for elegant, never-to-be used models are not uncommon. In the past five years, a number of researchers have argued that one of the main reasons for this problem has been the differences in cognitive style of model-builders and the intended users of the models. Management scientists have often viewed their role as normative and educative; they feel that managers are fuzzy-minded and lack clear concepts and an analytic approach to problems. They thus build a 'good' model, based on their own view of the problem. The Intuitive manager views such a model as a misrepresentation of a complex situation, overstructured and not useful to himself as he tries to think through the problem. He has learned to make effective decisions even where he consciously does not understand the environment in which he has to operate. He cannot present the precise conceptualization the management scientist views as essential and dismisses him as lacking in any understanding of the management reality.

Much of the research on cognitive style has been aimed at suggesting to the management scientist that managers think differently from the way he himself does and that the difference is in no way an inadequacy in the manager. In addition, it has been recommended that the manager recognize he is drawing on a scarce, skilled style of problem-solving and that he adjust to it or at least realize where and if it can help him. The point ought to be obvious. That it is not, indicates the extent to which skilled problem-solvers project their own logic onto other individuals' activities and assume that there is some one 'right' way of thinking (that happens to be their own).

The difficulties managers and management scientists have had in working together are paralleled in many fields. It is both frustrating and amusing to listen to lawyers and engineers talk past each other in trying to reach a decision on where to site an offshore 'multiuse' platform—frustrating in that each belabors the 'obvious', amusing in that each talks more and more to the other as one would to a child—patiently, elaborately, and ineffectually.

THE ROLE OF THE SPECIALIST

The role of the specialist in our fragmented, differentiated society seems to be increasing rather than stabilizing. There are some problems—forecasting energy requirements, analyzing investment opportunities, or determining an effective welfare policy—that simply cannot be solved by reasonable people doing their best; they need the idiosyncratic—even warped—viewpoint of the specialist, the individual who brings an unusual mode of thinking to the situation. The professional is almost invariably a cognitive specialist. He has a special talent for a narrow range of problems that lie outside the scope of the generalist. A major problem is how to make use of these talented individuals; outside their own specialization they can be dangerous—they may assume that *all* problems fit into their distinctive frame of reference. One of the main values

of research on cognitive style, regardless of the particular labels it may use—
'field dependence', 'Systematic–Intuitive', etc.—is that it focuses attention on
the nature and importance of the specialist's competence. In many ways, the
thesis that researchers on cognitive style present is simple to the point of
triviality—when the concept of cognitive style becomes part of the jargon of
management studies it will then have established its argument, that differences
in modes of thinking are of dominant impact on individuals' effectiveness in
particular situations and on their ability to help and communicate with others.

Obviously, we do not yet have enough empirical data to lay out in more
detail the links between cognitive style and career. The argument here raises
rather than resolves an issue. It is apparent though, even on a very general
level that cognitive style has direct implications in career counseling and career
planning (e.g. Clas, 1971). The specialist needs, too, to recognize very consciously what his or her skill is and what it implies in day-to-day dealings with
others—the range of jobs and problems it is really suited to, the difficulties it
generates in communication and mutual understanding and its strengths and
vulnerabilities. Cognitive style is only one of many dynamic factors in personality and career. It has, however, been easily overlooked. For groups or careers
that involve a general range of cognitive skills, this poses no problems. However, the cognitive specialist operates idiosyncratically; to make most effective
use of such specialists, we must understand how they operate. It also seems
essential that organizations be very careful in promoting specialists. There
is a tendency to look at jobs in terms of their broad function, such as 'EDP'
or 'Marketing'. However, the cognitive skills of the EDP programmer are not
those most needed by the EDP systems analyst. Similarly, the intuitive abilities
of the field sales manager may be less well-suited to the task of marketing forecasting. The specialist's career path should be centered around the cognitive
demands of his job. The imbalance in skills that makes him distinctive can
also result in his being less adaptive than the generalist; he may be as dramatically ineffectual in his new job as he was outstanding in his previous one. An
understanding of his cognitive style can clarify such problems—and opportunities—in his career development and help him exploit his peculiar talent.

This chapter has focused on a narrow aspect of a broad and complex field.
Cognitive style is, of course, not the 'answer' to the question of the dynamics
of career development. Nonetheless, it is clearly a major factor in the career
growth of people who have an increasingly important role to play in most
organizations. It is a factor that is at the same time obvious and too often
overlooked, and for that reason alone needs to be brought to our attention.

While it will obviously be some time before the present demonstrations of
links between particular styles and particular jobs can be generalized to a wider
theory of career specialization, the empirical data accumulated so far clearly
suggests both the conceptual and practical relevance of cognitive style for
understanding the dynamics of professional and technical careers.

PART III

The Individual's Orientation Toward Work
Across the Career

Much of our deductive and empirical work directed toward understanding behavior in organizations has used the nature of the work performed and/or the characteristics of the organization in which a person is employed as the major explanatory concepts that somehow account for human actions in work settings. Thus, for example, people have been viewed uniformly as responding in a positive fashion to roles that are challenging, autonomous, varied, responsible, and/or rich with intrinsic and extrinsic reward. Yet, observation and personal experience dictate that roles merely entitle one to act in a particular manner, they most certainly do not coerce or compel one into a given behavioral style. This is an important point and one we should not take casually. Social actors—unlike pigeons or rats—pursue many ends, only some of which are related to the work world.

When examining careers, we see this point most clearly. People do shift in their orientation toward work. Many times this shift occurs without any change at all in the person's task or organization. Take, for instance, the research scientist who, unmarried, at age 25, spends most of his waking hours in the laboratory. This same scientist, at age 30, now married perhaps with one or two children, will be quite unlikely to spend the same amount of time in the laboratory even though the work role has remained the same—indeed, the role may have grown more exciting. Certainly we would not argue that the job in this case 'causes' the scientist to change his work orientation. Yet many of our current theories of individual behavior in work organizations have precisely this context-free character.

What is required of course is a profound and studied appreciation of the many roles a person is asked to play within a lifetime. Whereas, in the past, we have looked upon the individual's relationship to work as if it were a closed system, separable in theory and practice from other streams of life, we must now begin to consider not only the changes in one's orientation toward work as a function of career stage, but also to consider one's orientation toward work as a function of the other roles to which the person is committed.

The selections presented here are premised upon just these considerations. Each of the following three chapters addresses some of the obvious, but unavoidable strains associated with work careers over time. While there are few, if any, universal patterns to be found, each chapter suggests that the shaping of one's psychological response to the workplace is an interdependent, holistic phenomena intimately tied to a person's total life situation. Clearly, people do not respond to personal, family, and occupational concerns as if they were mutually exclusive, rather they respond to a life in its full and mysterious complexity.

Chapter **5**

Involvement and Accommodation in Technical Careers: An Inquiry into the Relation to Work at Mid-Career

Lotte Bailyn

INTRODUCTION

We live in an era of peculiar complexity. Traditional modes of behavior are being widely questioned, and a great variety of styles affecting fundamental aspects of living has become realistically available. Perhaps nothing reflects the range and intensity of these developments more sensitively than the current debate about the role of work in people's lives. At one extreme are those who are fearful of the demise of the 'work ethic'—a loss of interest in and concern about work. Part of this fear, of course, is not new: social analysts have studied alienation from menial work for well over a century. But recently the same fear has been expressed about the attitudes of people at the highest levels of the occupational hierarchy. Alienation from jobs usually considered to 'provide scope for wider and deeper aspirations than do jobs at the bottom' (Fox, 1971) must reflect a far-reaching withdrawal from work, it is argued. At the other extreme the trouble is seen to stem from *too much* emphasis on work. The term 'Workaholic' has entered our vocabulary to signify the victim of a newly-recognized social disease presumably responsible for the disintegration of the family, for severe distortion of full personal development, and for the excesses of industrial growth.

The existence of such divergent concerns reflects the wide range of choice in attitudes toward work available to the individual today, and it creates for the researcher a complexity that earlier investigators of the role of work were spared. This paper tries to deal with some of the complexity by studying a group of men for whom these issues would seem to be particularly salient—a group of highly educated, technically trained people in their late thirties and early forties. These people work in fields that were accepted as essential for the nation's welfare and for social betterment at the time of their education, but whose value is now being questioned. They are also in a problematic phase of their lives, a phase that has been called the 'mid-life crisis' (e.g. Jaques, 1965; Levinson and coworkers, 1974; Vaillant and McArthur, 1972). Their relation to their work, therefore, has a double interest: it reflects both the general problem of work in current society and the specific problems of mid-career tensions. The group exemplifies, as we shall see, the many directions a technical career can take, and the individual dilemmas that are involved in each.

*   *   *

The data used in this paper stem from a survey of three classes of alumni of the Massachusetts Institute of Technology: graduates of the years 1951, 1955, and 1959.[1] The more than 1,300 respondents in this study are men who, relatively early in their lives, decided to pursue some of the most demanding occupations in our society. They pursued a rigorous course of technical study and undoubtedly began their careers with the expectation that work would satisfy their inner needs for self-fulfillment as well as their instrumental needs. In 1970, when these data were collected, ten to twenty years had passed since their graduation and presumably they were approaching the height of their careers and the maximum return on their educational and personal investment in their work.

Our study looks at the relation these men have to their work in two ways: from the point of view of involvement and from that of accommodation.[2] The first is a relatively straightforward reflection of the strength of each respondent's work orientation. The measure was derived empirically from an analysis of the intercorrelations of many items in a questionnaire. The second is more theoretically based. It was designed to probe each man's orientation to his family relative to his concern with professional achievement and success at work. The attempt will be to establish the extent to which these technically trained people are involved with their work and the extent to which they accommodate to the needs of their families, and, more importantly, to investigate the correlates of these attitudes and their interrelation with each other.

THE MEASUREMENT OF INVOLVEMENT

The individual's level of involvement with his work was ascertained by his responses to the series of questions presented in Table 5.1. These items were combined in such a way that a resulting score was obtained for every person ranging between 1·0 and 5·0 (advancing by intervals of 0·5), with 5·0 indicating a highly involved relation to work, and 1·0 indicating one of very low involvement.

For a person to receive a score of 5·0, he would *strongly agree* with the statements 'I like to think about my work, even when off the job' and 'my main satisfactions in life come from the work I do' and *strongly disagree* with the statements 'my only interest in my job is to get enough money to do the other things that I want to do' and 'I wish I were in a completely different occupation', and would rank his *career or occupation* as giving him the *most* satisfaction in his life. Thirty-two people (some 2 per cent of the sample) did indeed answer in this way, indicating very high involvement with their work, to the exclusion of almost every other aspect of their lives, and 257 respondents (almost 20 per cent of the sample) had a score of 4·5.

Table 5.1 Involvement with work

___

I. Work orientation

___

Please indicate the extent to which you agree with the following statements by circling the appropriate number.

	Strongly disagree			Strongly agree
I like to think about my work, even when off the job 1	2	3	4	5
My only interest in my job is to get enough money to do the other things that I want to do....................1	2	3	4	5
I wish I were in a completely different occupation 1	2	3	4	5
My main satisfactions in life come from the work I do......1	2	3	4	5

___

II. Career satisfaction

___

Which *three* aspects of your life give you the most satisfaction? In the following list, place a *1* next to the item that gives you the most satisfaction in life; a *2* next to the one that gives you the *next* most satisfaction, and a *3* next to the *third* most satisfying aspect of your life.

CAREER or OCCUPATION

(Creative or other activities not related to career or occupation)

(Leisure time recreational activities)

(Family relationships)

(Activities directed at community, national, or international betterment)

___

At the other extreme, in contrast, only one person had a score of 1·0: *strongly disagreeing* with the statements about thinking continuously about his work and gaining his main satisfactions from it, *strongly agreeing* with those indicating purely instrumental interest in work and showing a desire to be in a different occupation, and *not* ranking career or occupation as among the top three aspects of his life that give him the most satisfaction. And only 22 people (not quite 2 per cent of the sample) had an average score of 1·5. All in all, at the low end of the involvement scale, just over 12 per cent of the respondents had average scores *below* the mid-point of 3, and another 13 per cent had an average score of 3·0.

Thus the distribution of scores in this sample seems to be skewed toward the involved end—the mean score is 3·6—as might be expected, given the character of the population surveyed. It is best, however, not to try to interpret such scores in any precise fashion. Instead, for purposes of analysis, the distribution has been trichotomized into one group (a little over one fifth of the sample) whose scores were 4·5 or more—on the very involved end of the scale; another (just over a quarter of the sample) whose scores were ≤3·0, indicating lack of involvement with their work; and the remaining half who fall into a middle range (Table 5.2).

Table 5.2 Involvement with work of MIT alumni

	N	Percentage
Involved (≥ 4·5)	289	22%
Medium (3·5–4·0)	687	52%
Uninvolved (≤ 3·0)	335	26%
Total	1311	100%

The meaning of this measure can be further clarified by looking at some of the ways in which the uninvolved group differs from the involved one (Table 5.3): they are much less satisfied with their present jobs (Item 1); they see themselves as much less successful in their work (Item 2); they indicate hardly any frustration at the hypothetical prospect of having to change the kind of work they do (Item 3). Further, they show a certain lack of response to the cues stemming from their work situation (Item 4). About one sixth of the sample, when asked how long they expect to stay in their present jobs, responded with an emphatic 'forever' or 'till I die'—an indication, presumably,

Table 5.3 Comparison of involved and uninvolved groups on other aspects of their relation to work

	Involved $(N = 289)^a$	Uninvolved $(N = 335)^a$
1. Job satisfaction		
Percentage very satisfied with their jobs	39%	10%
Percentage not satisfied	12%	50%
2. Perceived success		
Percentage very successful now or at height of career	46%	23%
Percentage not successful now or at height of career	7%	17%
3. Reaction to change in work		
Percentage very frustrated	20%	1%
Percentage not at all frustrated	16%	40%
4. Job permanence		
Percentage definitely expecting to stay with their present jobs	18%	16%
of those very satisfied:	30%	19%
of those not satisfied:	9%	15%

^{a}Reduced by those not answering a given item.

of a positive reaction to their working conditions. This response, not unexpectedly, occurs considerably more frequently among those respondents who are very satisfied with their present jobs than it does among those whose jobs do not particularly please them. Not unexpectedly, that is, except for those who are *not* involved in their work, among whom there is no relation between expressed intention to stay permanently in their jobs and the satisfaction derived from them. It seems almost as if these people have withdrawn from active consideration of the implications of what happens to them on the job.

In general, the responses of this uninvolved group are quite different on these items from those of the involved segment of the sample. The index of work involvement seems, therefore, to capture an orientation that encompasses various aspects of a person's reaction to the working part of his life.

CORRELATES OF INVOLVEMENT

Involvement with work is therefore *not* a uniform characteristic of the people in this sample, despite the fact that all are part of a highly trained, obviously capable population in which the probability of finding challenging and satisfying work would seem to be maximal. Nor are the backgrounds of the men in the sample, though homogeneous in this general sense, uniform in all details. Notwithstanding the standard core curriculum which all participated in, the respondents did major in different fields. Further, they differed in the education they received after their undergraduate years: some stopping, some going on for masters degrees or doctorates. And though they were destined for a relatively circumscribed set of technically based careers when looked at from the point of view of the total spectrum of jobs available in our society, the range of possibilities was certainly wide enough to encompass quite a number of different career paths.

All of these subdivisions in the background and career experiences of the group affect the respondents' relation to their work. In particular, graduates of the Schools of Engineering and Management end up less involved with their work than do alumni who majored in the sciences or in architecture (Table 5.4).[3] Also, the more graduate education an alumnus received, the

Table 5.4 Involvement with work by undergraduate major

	Per Cent Involved	Per Cent Uninvolved
Management ($N = 168$)	14%	31%
Engineering ($N = 852$)	20%	27%
Humanities and social science ($N = 31$)	29%	23%
Science ($N = 211$)	35%	17%
Architecture ($N = 49$)	31%	14%

Table 5.5 Involvement with work by highest degree

	Per Cent Involved	Per Cent Uninvolved
Bachelors degree ($N = 539$)	17%	32%
Masters degree ($N = 441$)	19%	25%
[MBA ($N = 132$)]	[19%]	[19%]
Doctorate ($N = 331$)	33%	16%

Table 5.6 Involvement with work by first job[a]

	Per Cent Involved	Per Cent Uninvolved
Engineering ($N = 622$)	20%	29%
Engineering management ($N = 109$)	16%	26%
Nontechnical management ($N = 104$)	23%	25%
Science ($N = 125$)	40%	13%

[a]Information on first jobs is missing for 148 people. The remaining 203 had first jobs in business staff positions or taught, consulted, or did research in unspecified fields or in architecture, medicine, law, or social science.

more likely he is to be involved with his work (Table 5.5). Further, those whose first jobs were in science, as opposed to engineering or management, are much more involved with their work over a decade later (Table 5.6). Since 61 per cent of the graduates from science departments received doctorates as opposed to only 21 per cent of those whose undergraduate degrees were in engineering, it is obvious that these distinctions are not independent of each other. They indicate that alumni initially headed for technical careers of the more scientific–professional kind are now more work involved than those whose emphasis was initially more on the applied-engineering end of the spectrum.

Table 5.7 Involvement with work by current profession[a]

	Per Cent Involved	Per Cent Uninvolved
Staff engineer ($N = 299$)	10%	39%
Business staff ($N = 69$)	7%	36%
Engineering manager ($N = 230$)	20%	27%
General manager ($N = 312$)	20%	21%
Scientist ($N = 78$)	30%	18%
Professor ($N = 135$)	44%	10%

[a]The remaining 188 people are in architecture and planning, in consulting firms, or in other professions such as medicine or law.

All of these distinctions are highlighted when one looks at the present occupational roles of the sample. Here the differences in relation to work are fairly striking. Staff engineers, followed closely by business staff, are the least involved group; scientists, and particularly academics are the most involved (Table 5.7).[4]

INVOLVEMENT IN ENGINEERING-BASED CAREERS

In order to separate the influence of occupational role from factors of training and initial work experiences, it was necessary to select from the total sample a group quite uniform in their early career history. Engineering-based careers were the most useful since they represented the largest homogeneous group in the sample. Further, the problems of engineers at mid-career have been of particular concern lately (cf. 1975 IEEE Manpower Report), and hence this group was also a particularly interesting one to study. The specific selection criteria actually used were developed by a former engineer, now in a managerial role, himself interested in the effect of different occupational roles on engineers (Madrazo, 1974). These criteria used undergraduate major, higher degree, and initial job to define the category of engineering-based careers (see Table 5.8). The category was limited, first, to those who graduated from the School of Engineering (some two thirds of the MIT graduates in the 'fifties—a figure, interestingly, reduced in the early 'seventies to only one third, though at mid-decade up again to close to half). Second, it included only those who neither went on to get a doctorate (though they might have a masters or an engineering degree) nor a degree in management or business

Table 5.8 Engineering-based careers

	N	
Graduates of School of Engineering	878	(65% of total sample)
Who did *not* get Doctorate or MBA	619	(70% of engineering graduates)
Whose first jobs were in engineering in private industry	374[a]	(67% of non-Ph.D. non-MBA engineering graduates with information on first jobs)
These men are currently in:	General management	84	(22%)
	Technical management	87	(23%)
	Staff positions	158	(43%)
	Other professions	45	(12%)

[a]58 did not give information about first jobs.

administration. And, finally, it concentrated on those whose first jobs were in engineering staff positions in private industry and eliminated those initially employed in government or nonprofit labs, as well as those who started in non-technical positions. Almost half of this group are still—some ten to twenty years after graduation—in engineering staff positions; the other half are more or less evenly divided between those in engineering management and those who have left the technical area altogether and are managers in a nontechnical, functional area or are in positions of general management.[5]

Obviously, any such selection reduces the sample size considerably. But it enables one to ascertain the effects on a person of his occupational position, while holding constant certain background characteristics, such as college attended, undergraduate major, degree attained, and first job, that are usually associated with a particular occupational role. If one then looks at the relation of work involvement to occupational position in this group, one finds that the differences in involvement seen previously persist: engineers who hold staff positions well over a decade into their careers are less involved in their work than are those whose jobs also include managerial duties (Table 5.9).

But Table 5.9 also shows that not all engineers follow this pattern; some, indeed, are very much involved in their work. It makes sense, therefore, to try to isolate the conditions under which such involvement does or does not occur. Previous research on engineers (e.g. Ritti, 1971; Perucci and Gerstl, 1969; Gerstl and Hutton, 1966) has sought to locate the reasons for the 'alienation' of the engineer in certain very general structural conditions of employment: obsolescence, under-utilization of technical knowledge, lack of decision-making powers have all been blamed. This study by reversing the usual research design and dealing with engineers in different job environments but with the same educational and early career backgrounds, allows one to ascertain some of the specific individual factors that are related to an engineer's lack of involvement in his work.

Table 5.9 Involvement with work of respondents in engineering-based careers

Percentage who are:	Present position		
	General management	Technical management	Engineering staff
Involved	23%	23%	13%
Medium	51%	49%	45%
Uninvolved	26%	28%	42%
Total	100%	100%	100%
	$(N = 78)^a$	$(N = 87)$	$(N = 156)^a$

[a]Respondents who did not answer all the questions included in the work involvement index are excluded from the table.

First, however, it is necessary to raise the question of whether differences in income account for the differences in relation to work in these three occupational roles. On the whole, alumni whose professional incomes are lower tend to be less involved in their work: 30 per cent of those whose total professional income is under $15,000 (1970 figures) are in the uninvolved group, as opposed to 14 per cent of those with incomes over $50,000. Further, people in staff positions are paid less than those whose duties include managerial responsibilities. Only 5 per cent of the managerial groups have professional incomes of $15,000 or less as compared to 22 per cent of the staff engineers; and *none* of the staff engineers in this selected group makes more than $30,000 a year; almost one third of the general managers (31 per cent) and close to one eighth of the technical managers (12 per cent) exceed this amount.

The question arises, therefore, whether these income differences account for the differences that exist in the relation to work of these alumni. Apparently not, it seems. Even among the highest paid engineers, over 30 per cent are *not* involved in their work, and at virtually all income levels—particularly among the majority in the middle range—the proportion of the engineers in the uninvolved group is higher than that of the managerial groups at the same level of income. For all groups, in other words, low incomes are associated with less involvement, but income does not explain the differences between the occupational roles, since these persist even within groups in which income has been controlled.[6]

There are, however, some conditions that do reduce the percentage of staff engineers who are in the uninvolved group below the 30 per cent point, down to the level of the managerial groups (Table 5.10). Some of these factors (Items 4, 5, 6) are those previously shown to be aspects of a person's relation to his work. In other words, there is a group of engineers who are well satisfied with their work, who would feel frustrated if they had to change it, and who see themselves as very successful in it. And this group is no more 'alienated' than the equivalent managerial groups. But though these differences elucidate

Table 5.10 Conditions of reduced 'alienation' in staff engineers

		Percent Uninvolved
1. Undergraduate grade average B or higher	($N = 60$)	28%
2. More interested in working with things than people	($N = 63$)	25%
3. Cosmopolitan orientation	($N = 24$)	29%
4. Frustrated if had to change work	($N = 29$)	21%
5. Already very successful	($N = 17$)	24%
6. Very satisfied with current job	($N = 22$)	18%
Total group	($N = 156$)	42%

the meaning of involvement with work, they do little more than reiterate the fact that there are some staff engineers who can overcome the potential for alienation in their jobs.

Some items, on the other hand—less closely related to the definition of the relation to work—tell us more about what kinds of engineers can most successfully do this. First, it develops that engineers with higher undergraduate grade-point averages (averages of A or B) are less likely to be uninvolved in their jobs (Item 1, Table 5.10). Since we have excluded engineers with doctorates, the higher grade-point average does not indicate a higher level of education. It may, however, indicate a greater capability for engineering work—a better absorption of the necessary technical and scientific knowledge on which engineering is based—though it is possible that high undergraduate grades merely establish the engineer's *confidence* in his technical competence.

The decisive factor seems to be the professionalization of the engineer. Engineers with a cosmopolitan orientation (Item 3, Table 10)—by which is meant those who see their professional colleagues, rather than their employers, as their reference group—show reduced 'alienation'. Hence the professionally oriented and technically most competent engineers are the ones most able to retain their involvement with work. In other words, though it has sometimes been stated that only a move to management can satisfy the engineer, these results indicate that for some engineers, those whose orientation is more scientifically professional, technical work can continue to be involving. These are the people, presumably, who are more interested in working with things than with people (Item 2, Table 5.10). Their orientation was and remains technical, and, given the right conditions, they remain involved with their technical duties even many years into their careers.

In contrast, those engineers in staff positions who are less technically oriented and more interested in working with people, have a more problematic relation to their work. Whether they have always had these inclinations and hence would have been better off in a different field from the beginning, or whether these tendencies represent new developmental stages which point to the desirability of a mid-career change after an involving initial decade or so of technical work, we do not know. At this point in their careers, however, this group, as opposed to the more professionally oriented one referred to before, would benefit less from opportunities for technical up-dating than from training that would help them make a mid-career transition—training in management, for example.

Thus the 'plight' of the engineer at mid-career is a complex phenomenon, and there is no one 'solution' for it. It requires diagnosis on the level of the individual and flexibility in response to his (or her) needs: there must be not one kind of arrangement between engineers and their employing organizations regarding their future careers but several, and a discriminating approach to selecting these paths.

But what about other facets of a person's life? It is misleading to view work as an isolated part of one's life. Indeed, we assume that attitudes to work can

Table 5.11 Work and family in engineering-based careers

	Percent satisfied with their family situations	
Present position	Involved	Uninvolved
General managers	67% ($N = 18$)	95% ($N = 20$)
Technical managers	70% ($N = 20$)	83% ($N = 24$)
Staff engineers	67% ($N = 21$)	78% ($N = 64$)

only be realistically understood if they are examined in the full context of the individual's total life situation. It is important, therefore, to know whether lack of involvement in work is compensated for in other areas of a person's life, or, at the other extreme—with obviously much more serious consequences for the individual—whether it is part of a generally 'problematic' life. In particular, we are interested in knowing whether a person's family plays an effective compensating role.

On the whole, some such compensating mechanism seems to be operating. There is a general tendency, in the sample as a whole, for the uninvolved group to be more satisfied with their family situations than are those more involved in their work. But when one looks separately at the three groups in the engineering-based career pattern, one finds this trend to hold true to a somewhat different degree in each occupational role (Table 5.11). Virtually all of the uninvolved general managers are fully satisfied with their current family situation.[7] Whatever the reason may be for a general manager not to be involved in his work, he at least has a family situation that he likes and in which a number of his needs are presumably met. This is much less true of those in the more technical occupational roles, particularly the staff engineers. More than 20 per cent of the uninvolved engineers indicate a real discrepancy between their present family arrangements and their ideal.[8]

There is an indication, therefore, that a person's family situation is related to the level of his work involvement in a complex way. It thus becomes crucial to examine this relationship in a more thorough fashion, which we shall do, in the remainder of this paper, by means of the concept of accommodation.

ACCOMMODATION AS A CAREER STRATEGY

The concept of accommodation evolved from an effort to investigate the way men deal with the major socialization tasks that face them as educated adults: those that involve work and those that concern family. Much study has been devoted to each of these areas separately, but it is only quite recently that the *interrelation* of work and family in a man's life has come to be seen as worthy of study. Furthermore, most of the work that has been done on men's strategies for reconciling career and family demands (e.g. Rapoport and Rapoport, 1969; Bailyn, 1970) has concentrated on the effect of men's family–career orientations on their marriages and the quality of their family life. Scarcely anything has been done on the implications of such strategies for the professional part of men's lives and the dilemmas that contradictory implications for these two areas could pose for them.

To deal with this problem, we limited ourselves to the currently married respondents in the sample (over 90 per cent of the total), and tried to classify them according to the extent to which they accommodated their careers to the needs of their families. We wanted to differentiate men for whom career success is of major importance and for whom family considerations are clearly secondary, from those, at the other extreme, for whom family considerations are primary and whose occupational decisions are guided by a hierarchy of values that places family needs ahead of those of career. The first extreme is the position of nonaccommodation, the attitude of extreme achievement orientation traditionally associated with men's roles in industrial societies. The opposite extreme, in contrast, is fully accommodative; it is associated with a career pattern in which the demands of work are subordinated to those of the family.

The accommodative career represents a strategy for easing conflict between these two areas. Such a strategy is particularly important to study because it parallels new social developments. For example, accommodation has been deemed a necessary precondition for true equality of occupational opportunity between the sexes (cf. the report of the Swedish Government to the United Nations on The Status of Women in Sweden, 1971); and in its shift away from success and achievement as the major motivating forces in life it reflects both the new values of the 'youth culture' (Yankelovich, 1972) and of the years surrounding the 'mid-career crisis' (Tarnowieski, 1973).

IMPLICATIONS OF ACCOMMODATION FOR MEN'S FAMILIES

Before turning to the analysis of the extent to which accommodation exists in various technical careers and the attitudes toward work that accompany it, it is important to get a feel for the effect of such a strategy on a man's family. Without this, the data on the implications of accommodation for work cannot be evaluated in their full context.

In general, and not surprisingly, accommodation has highly beneficial results for a man's family. In a study of family and career patterns of a sample of English university graduates of 1960,[9] for instance, it was shown that wives of accommodative men are more satisfied with their lives and with the options available to them. That study showed that wives of career-oriented men are more likely to be working outside the home, while more of the wives of family-oriented men are at home, playing traditional feminine roles.[10] But this result hides the important distinction that the wives of family-oriented men react more positively to their role, whatever it may be. When they are *not* working, most of them are satisfied with their traditional roles, whereas more than half of the non-working wives of career-oriented men express some dissatisfaction with their non-working status. Also, there is a difference in the attitudes of the *working* wives of these two types of men. A majority of the working wives of career-oriented men say that they are *not* in favor of married women having careers at all, even if these are clearly secondary to their husbands'. To work in the face of such an attitude can only be considered a dissatisfaction—or at best a lack of full satisfaction—with the role of the working wife. In contrast, the bulk of the working wives of family-oriented men exhibit an attitude that might be termed secondary commitment: they favor careers for married women, though they feel they must be secondary to their husbands'.

To repeat: the wife of the family-oriented man is more satisfied with whatever role she chooses, as housewife or as careerist. The presence of such a facilitative effect is further supported by the finding that marriages between family-oriented men and women who try to combine careers with family life are much happier than marriages of such women to men more oriented to their careers (Bailyn, 1970). In various ways, then, accommodation in men has very positive consequences for the families involved. This is an important fact to keep in mind as we investigate the work correlates of this strategy in technically-based careers.

THE MEASURE OF ACCOMMODATION

The measure of accommodation in the MIT sample is based on four items (see Table 5.12) chosen on theoretical grounds. First, the married men were classified according to whether career or family relationships contributed more to their satisfaction in life (Item 1). But we wanted also to probe the extent to which the respondents were oriented to success, since, as indicated above, the extreme accommodative position was envisioned as being accompanied by a partial rejection of the traditional pressure on men toward achievement and career success. Therefore two items were included to cover this aspect of accommodation: one concerning the importance of success (Item 4) and the other dealing with career aspirations (Item 3). Finally, an attempt was made to go beyond attitudes in order to discover the extent to which family considerations are taken into account in making career decisions. The best item for this purpose was the question concerning the value of a 'job which leaves sufficient time for family and personal life'—one in a list of job characteristics whose importance 'with regard to your present and future jobs' each respondent was asked to rate on a five-point scale (Item 2).

All in all, 1,155 married men in the sample answered these four questions. Their responses to each were grouped into four categories, from least to most accommodative, and combined into a simple additive index ranging from 0 (extreme nonaccommodation) to 12 (extreme accommodation). The mean of the index for all married respondent is 4·5. For most of the analysis the distribution has been trichotomized into the *accommodators*, the top 20 per cent of the distribution; the *nonaccommodators*, the bottom 20 per cent; and the 60 per

Table 5.12 The strategy of accommodation

---

1. Which *three* aspects of your life give you the most satisfaction? In the following list, place a 1 next to the item that gives you the *most* satisfaction in life; a 2 next to the one that gives you the *next* most satisfaction; and a 3 next to the *third* most satisfying aspect of your life.

   CAREER or OCCUPATION
   (Creative or other activities not related to career or occupation)
   (Leisure time recreational activities)

   FAMILY RELATIONSHIPS
   (Activities directed at community, national, or international betterment)

2. The list below shows a number of characteristics of a job. Please circle the appropriate number to show how important you feel each characteristic is to you with regard to your present and future jobs.

   Job which leaves sufficient time for family and personal life

   Not at all important   Very important
       1   2   3   4   5

3. Below is a list of abilities and traits that people possess to varying degrees. Please indicate the degree to which you NOW possess each of the listed factors. Rate yourself by circling the number from 0 to 4 that best describes the extent to which you now possess each ability or trait.

   High aspirations for your career

   Do not possess at all   Possess to a great extent
       0   1   2   3   4

4. How important is it to you to be successful in your work?

   Unimportant   Very important
       1   2   3   4   5

---

cent in the *middle range*. The lowest (nonaccommodative) fifth of the distribution has scores of 0,1, or 2, while the scores of the highest fifth range from 7 to 12.

The differences between the accommodative and nonaccommodative groups are considerable. In terms of their responses to the four defining items they may be characterized in the following way. The *accommodators* rated family relationships as among the most important sources of their main satisfactions in life; they rated importance of time for family and personal life as at least 4 on a five-point scale; they did *not* rate themselves as possessing career aspirations to a 'great extent'; and they did *not* feel that success at work was 'very important' to them. The *nonaccommodators*, in contrast, rated their careers as among the main sources of their life satisfactions; rated time for family three or less on a five-point scale of importance; indicated that they possessed high career aspirations to a 'great extent'; and viewed success at work as 'very important' to them. The middle group, obviously, consists of a variety of patterns: it includes those very active people for whom both family considerations and success aspirations are very important and those more withdrawn respondents who do not indicate great concern with either area, as well as those who are moderate on both.

WORK CORRELATES OF ACCOMMODATION

In a later section we will investigate the relation of accommodation to work involvement for the three different engineering-based careers identified earlier in this chapter. First, however, we deal with all the married respondents and seek the work correlates of accommodation in certain cognitive characteristics of the sample and in aspects of their professional role behavior.[11]

The data show that accommodation has implications for the way in which a person functions cognitively (Table 5.13). When asked to evaluate themselves with respect to certain abilities and traits, the accommodators have a self-image different from that of the nonaccommodators. The nonaccommodators are much more likely than the accommodators to feel secure in their ability to think creatively (Item 1) and to identify and solve problems (Item 2). In contrast, the accommodators perceive themselves as having more tolerance for other people (Item 3) and as more concerned with the problems of society (Item 4). The nonaccommodators are more 'scientifically' oriented, the accommodators more 'humanistically'.

The implications of this difference in orientation depend, of course, on the type of work a person is doing. In the helping professions, for instance, these characteristics of accommodators—which partly account, no doubt, for the good effects of this strategy on a man's family—may be the crucial ones for effective professional functioning. In the technically-based careers in the MIT sample, however, it is the nonaccommodators who seem to function best

Table 5. 13 Accommodation and cognitive orientation

	Accommodation			
Percentage who say they:	High $(N = 242)^a$	Medium $(N = 681)^a$	Low $(N = 232)^a$	D (Low % — High %)
1. Have great ability to think creatively	21%	34%	47%	26
2. Have great ability to identify and solve problems	21%	33%	45%	24
3. Have great tolerance of other people and their points of view	40%	31%	25%	—15
4. Have great concern about social problems	38%	35%	28%	—10

[a] Reduced by those not answering a relevant item.

Table 5.14 Accommodation and professional role behavior

Percentage who say they:	Accommodation			
	High $(N=242)^a$	Medium $(N=681)^a$	Low $(N=232)^a$	D (Low % − High %)
1. Participate in all professional activities	24%	35%	45%	21
2. Have entrepreneurship	8%	14%	22%	14
3. (a) Possess great ability to continue to learn	20%	38%	48%	28
(b) Have a positive attitude to further education	18%	30%	43%	25
4. (a) Have great ability to induce change in others and in organizations	10%	16%	30%	20
(b) Are HIGH on leadership	6%	15%	25%	19

^{a}Reduced by those not answering a relevant item.

professionally. In the occupations represented by this sample the nonaccommodators not only perceive themselves to be better problem solvers but are generally more professionally involved. The accommodators, in contrast, are more passive in their professional role (Table 5.14): they are less likely to be active in professional affairs—to publish or present papers at meetings, or to belong to a professional society (Item 1); they are less likely to be entrepreneurs—to have founded a business or established a professional office or firm (Item 2). They differ also in their perceptions of their leadership ability. The accommodators are less likely than the nonaccommodators to see themselves as good leaders (Item 4). And, from more detailed analysis, we find that even if they think they have leadership ability, they have less desire to use it, in contrast to the nonaccommodators whose leadership desire is great even if their perceived ability is not.

Further, there is evidence that this professional passivity is self-perpetuating. The accommodators are much less likely than the nonaccommodators to feel that they possess the 'ability to continue to learn new things' to any great extent or to have a very 'positive attitude toward further education' (Item 3, Table 5·14). Even where their own jobs are concerned, the passivity is apparent. Each respondent, as indicated above, was asked how long he thought he would remain with the organization he was currently working for. A little more than half the sample gave a noncommittal answer to this question, but almost a fifth of the married respondents indicated that they definitely planned to stay for the rest of their working lives, and a fourth indicated that they were considering leaving their present positions (5 per cent had already made definite plans to leave their present position or organization). Since, obviously, these plans are very dependent on the person's satisfaction with his current job, it is necessary to look at their relation to accommodation separately for those who are very satisfied with their jobs and for those whose satisfaction is not great.

Table 5·15 shows that more of the nonaccommodators who are very satisfied with their present job indicate a definite desire to stay in it than do the accommodators. The accommodators who share this degree of satisfaction are mainly noncommittal about their job permanence. Among those whose job satisfaction is *not* great, just the reverse pattern exists. More than one fifth of the accommodators in this group say they nonetheless plan to stay in the job indefinitely (as opposed to 7 per cent of the nonaccommodators); and only 7 per cent of them have any definite plans to leave the job, despite their lack of satisfaction with it, as compared to the nonaccommodators of whom almost one fourth have such definite plans. Looked at in another way, what this means is that the *definite* plans of the accommodators to stay in their current job or to leave it, show hardly any relation to the extent of their satisfaction with that job. Perhaps these people have responded to the unsatisfactory job situation by accommodation—by withdrawing from the realm of work and emphasizing their orientation toward their families—rather than by attempting to improve the work situation itself.

It is not easy, of course, to interpret these differences. One does not know to what extent this 'passivity' is a problematic response to work leading to impaired performance, or to what extent it represents a positive response to family which is accompanied by a more balanced attitude to work, stripping it of its competitive elements and concentrating on its essentials. The fact that accommodators are less concerned about advancement, high earnings, or other

Table 5.15 Accommodation, job satisfaction, and permanence in present job

	Satisfaction with present job[a]			
	Very great		Not Great	
	ACCOMMODATION			
	High ($N=30$)	Low ($N=106$)	High ($N=111$)	Low ($N=43$)
Percentage who:				
DEFINITELY plan to stay for the rest of their working lives	23%	37%	21%	7%
Are noncommittal	70%	51%	48%	44%
Indicate feelings of transience	7%	12%	31%	49%
[Have definite plans to leave]	[3%]	[0%]	[7%]	[23%]

[a] A middle group which is quite, but not very satisfied with their jobs has been eliminated from this table.

Table 5.16 Accommodation and other aspects of self-imagery

	ACCOMMODATION			
Percentage who indicate:	High $(N=242)^a$	Medium $(N=681)^a$	Low $(N=232)^a$	D (Low % − High %)
1. Great concern about organizational power	24%	39%	59%	35
2. Great overall self-confidence	14%	29%	45%	31
3. Great concern about intrinsic character of work	23%	38%	50%	27

[a] Reduced by those not answering a relevant item.

signs of organizational power may indicate that this latter interpretation is the correct one (Table 5.16, Item 1). But they also have less overall self confidence (Item 2) and show less interest in the intrinsic character of the work they do — whether or not it is challenging or gives them a sense of accomplishment (Item 3). These are aspects of the self-image that might well impair professional performance.

It is the large difference in self-confidence that is of particular concern: only 14 per cent of the accommodators feel that they possess self-confidence 'to a great extent'; almost half of the nonaccommodators give this positive self-assessment. Tangri (personal communication) has suggested that this negative self-image of the accommodators results from behavior not commensurate with the American male sex-role ideal. She feels this

'may be part of the attributional process: "I am not the 'go-getter' this society extolls, therefore, there must be something wrong with me."'

It is of interest, therefore, to investigate the cognitive orientation and professional role behavior of those accommodators who *do* have great self-confidence along with their accommodative stance toward the interrelation of family and career. Obviously, this is a small group: only 34 of the more than 1,000 married alumni in the sample are both accommodative and have great self-confidence. But it is an important group because it is clear that changes in society are lessening sex-role pressures and thus, if Tangri is right, we should see an increase in this group in the future.

A comparison of the first part of Table 5.17 with Table 5.13 shows that this group—accommodators with substantial self-confidence—is every bit as 'scientifically' oriented as the nonaccommodators, and their already greater 'humanistic' orientation is even more pronounced.[12] And, with regard to professional role behavior (Table 5.17, second part), a comparison with Table 5.14 shows that these self-confident accommodators are fully as active as the nonaccommodators in leadership and entrepreneurship, and approach them

Table 5.17 Cognitive orientation and professional role behavior of accommodators with great self-confidence
($N = 34$)

I. Cognitive orientation (cf. Table 5.13)	
Percentage who say they:	
1. Have great ability to think creatively	44%
2. Have great ability to identify and solve problems	53%
3. Have great tolerance of other people and their points of view	56%
4. Have great concern about social problems	50%

II. Professional role behavior (cf. Table 5.14)	
Percentage who say they:	
1. Participate in all professional activities	32%
2. Have entrepreneurship	18%
3. (a) Possess great ability to continue to learn	35%
(b) Have positive attitude to further education	26%
4. (a) Have great ability to induce change in others and in organizations	29%
(b) Are HIGH on leadership	32%

in other manifestations of professional involvement.[13] In this small subgroup of self-confident accommodators, therefore, the 'impairment' in technical functioning seen for the group as a whole is greatly reduced.

ACCOMMODATION IN ENGINEERING-BASED CAREERS

Finally, we come to the question of the extent of accommodation in the engineering-based careers and its relation to work involvement. To deal with this question the analysis is again limited to the married respondents.[14]

It will be recalled that the total engineering-based group consists of graduates of the School of Engineering, without either a degree in management or business administration or a doctorate, whose first jobs were in engineering positions in industry. This group is slightly more accommodative than the total sample: 30 per cent are in the accommodative group (as opposed to the 20 per cent cut-off which defines this category). Representation in the nonaccommodative category, however, is similar to that of the total group. It will be recalled further that this relatively homogeneous group in terms of education and initial career experience is predominantly employed in three positions: general management, technical management, and engineering staff (see Table 5.8). These three occupational roles obviously differ not only in the responsibilities and range of tasks they entail but also in the power and prestige that accompany them. And, as is evident in Table 5.18, these three roles show very different degrees of accommodation. By far the greatest accommodation is found among those in technical staff positions: almost half of these alumni are accommodative and only one in eight is in the nonaccommodating group. In contrast, the general and technical

Table 5.18 Accommodation in engineering-based careers (married respondents only)

		Percentage whose ACCOMMODATION is:		
Organizational role		High	Medium	Low
General managers	$(N = 72)$	19%	49%	32%
Technical managers	$(N = 78)^{a}$	18%	60%	22%
Staff engineers	$(N = 138)^{a}$	44%	44%	12%
All married engineering based	$(N = 328)^{a}$	30%	52%	18%

[a]Excludes those who did not answer all the items included in the accommodation index.

managers have just about the expected proportion in the accommodative group. The general managers, however, are more likely to be nonaccommodative: about a third of them fall into the nonaccommodative category.

What is not known, of course, and what cannot be ascertained from these data, is whether such differences actually result from factors associated with certain organizational roles, or whether they depend on the fact that it is primarily those with a nonaccommodating orientation who get promoted into high organizational positions. It seems most likely that in fact both directions of influence occur—that one is dealing with an interactive process between career events and orientations.[15] Nor is it known whether nonaccommodation has any necessary relation to the way one is able to fulfill positions of general management, or whether this association is merely a by-product of certain shared assumptions of organizations and their employees that reflect no realistic requirements for these roles. All that can be ascertained from the data at hand is that even in this group, which is homogeneous with respect to education and early career events, engineering staff roles are more likely to be associated with accommodation to family, whereas people in managerial roles (particularly those in general management) are more likely to be nonaccommodative with respect to their families.

It has already been shown that these same groups also differ in the extent to which they are involved in their work. It becomes of particular interest, therefore, to look at accommodation separately for each level of work involvement. In order to do this, it is necessary not only to limit the analysis to married alumni in engineering-based careers but also to make an adjustment in the work involvement index in order to assure operational independence between the measures of involvement and of accommodation.[16] As is obvious from Table 5.19, there is a strong negative relation between these two indicators of a person's relation to work: almost none of the respondents with high involvement are accommodative to their families, and this is true no matter what organizational role is involved. Among those who are uninvolved, however, a larger than expected proportion is accommodative in all groups, but this is

Table 5.19 Accommodation and work involvement (reduced) in engineering-based careers (married respondents only)

Percentage with high accommodation of those who are:	Work involvement	
	Involved	Uninvolved
General managers	5 % (N = 19)	40 % (N = 15)
Technical managers	6 % (N = 17)	37 % (N = 19)
Staff engineers	0 % (N = 18)	76 % (N = 45)
All married engineering based	3 % (N = 59)	58 % (N = 93)

most evident among those in engineering staff positions where over three fourths are accommodative.

This last point is of special interest. It has already been demonstrated that engineers have varying work needs at mid-career. And now one sees that the picture is even more complex. Indeed, for some engineers who are not particularly involved in their work and who are accommodative to their families, an increase in work challenge (by whatever means) is likely to be dysfunctional for them as individuals and unproductive for their employing organizations. In such cases it may be more beneficial for organizations to provide a sufficiently flexible schedule and enough free time to ensure the successful pursuit of the employee's non-work concerns. By easing external pressures on accommodative employees, such policies are likely to improve their professional performance. Though such an approach would require an unusual amount of flexibility in the relation between organizations and their technical employees, it may be the approach most likely to maximize the benefits to both.

CONCLUSION

The findings in this paper document a dilemma. In the technical sample analyzed here, a high degree of involvement in work seems to be required for optimal professional functioning, and its absence seems not to be easily compatible with a well-integrated and positive self-image. And yet a person's well-being, particularly in the middle years, cannot be defined solely on the basis of his relation to his work. Other areas, particularly relations with family, can only be ignored at one's peril. And from the point of view of family, we know that accommodation is likely to be a more 'successful' strategy. Thus the dilemma stems from these seemingly contradictory implications for the two areas of greatest importance to a man: his work and his family.

How can this dilemma be resolved? Partly by time. We have seen that in those few cases where accommodation is accompanied by great self-confidence, professional performance is not adversely affected. And the conditions that permit this combination to appear are likely to become more prevalent in the years ahead. But beyond waiting for social values to change, it is crucial, *now*, to test the validity of the organizational and occupational requirements that seem to preclude accommodation. It is interesting to note, for instance, that accommodative employees are more loyal to their employing organizations than those less accommodative (Getchell, 1975), and they thus contribute to the stability that most organizations seek. It is also possible, as indicated above, that encouraging accommodation among some engineers will allow organizations to allocate their technical employees to tasks that differ widely in the extent to which they are routine or challenging in a mutually more satisfactory way. Indeed, it has been found that in entirely different occupations—those of symphony orchestra and professional hockey players (Faulkner, 1974)—accommodation is a functionally efficient response to an inevitable 'plateauing', a phenomenon that develops in some way for most people in all occupations.

Our findings also highlight another crucial point: responses to work differ in different people with different family circumstances and holding different jobs. No one prescription is likely to fit all. We must recognize that 'workaholism' as well as its opposite—the rejection of any involvement with work—are the extremes of a distribution that has a large variance. The challenge is to make it possible for individuals to choose their options in ways that are congruent with their needs and not overly constrained by stereotyped expectations, and for organizations to devise policies that have sufficient flexibility to benefit from the resulting pluralism.

NOTES

1. This research was financed in part by a grant from the Carnegie Commission on Higher Education.
2. These two measures were originally analyzed in separate papers, one prepared for the ILO symposium on which this volume is based, and one for presentation at the meetings of the Eastern Psychological Association in April, 1971. They are, however, based on the same data and stem from a common conceptual concern. They have been revised and put together in this chapter in order to encompass more of a complex problem than was possible for each alone.
3. The low work involvement shown by alumni whose bachelors were in management is probably accounted for by the fact that in the 1950's the management major was a frequent fall-back position for students who did not succeed in other departments. Indeed, almost half (48 per cent) of all management graduates entered MIT with plans to major in something else, whereas 82 per cent of those who graduated with engineering degrees never changed their undergraduate majors—the equivalent figure for the science departments is 68 per cent. Further, those management graduates who, at the time of this survey, were in engineering staff positions (some 10 per cent of the group) are particularly dissatisfied with the course of their careers.
4. About a third of the professors are professors in engineering, half are science professors, and the rest are scattered in various fields in the social sciences and humanities.
5. The 45 people in 'other' professions tend to be either consultants (primarily in engineering) or to hold business staff positions. They are eliminated in most of the subsequent discussion on engineering-based careers.
6. Despite the fact that the data do not meet the necessary specifications, we checked

this assertion by means of a one-way analysis of covariance with total professional income the covariate. This analysis showed that occupational role has a significant effect on work involvement even after adjustment is made for differences in income ($F = 3.78$, $p = 0.02$). The actual and adjusted means of the involvement index are given below:

	Means	Adjusted means
General managers	3·68	3·57
Technical managers	3·68	3·66
Staff engineers	3·35	3·41

7. They are also much more likely than any other group to gain satisfaction from 'creative or other activities not related to career or occupation'.

8. Very few of the single respondents in the total sample are satisfied with their family situations—most would prefer to be married. They are, however, more likely than those who are married to be involved in their work, probably because of a compensating mechanism in the other direction. But the engineering-based alumni who are still staff engineers do not exhibit this compensating behavior. Whereas *none* of the 12 single technical or general managers in this group have low work involvement, nine (60 per cent) of the 15 single staff engineers are uninvolved. The presence of this single group among the uninvolved staff engineers—almost none of whom are satisfied with their family situations—is partly responsible for their 'double jeopardy' situation. In a later section we will be looking only at married respondents and thus will be able to control for this difference.

9. This study is presented in Fogarty, Rapoport, and Rapoport (1970). Material in the present paper on the total sample comes from Chapters 6 and 7. Material based on the couples subsegment of the whole stems from an unpublished research memorandum on career and family orientations of husbands.

10. The married men in the English sample were divided by one question dealing with accommodation, *viz.* the relative importance of career as opposed to family relationships as the source of one's *greatest* satisfaction in life. Those who put career first were considered career-oriented, and those who put family first were considered family-oriented. About three fifths of the married men in the English sample— University graduates from the year 1960—are family-oriented in this sense. The same question was asked in the MIT survey and in the closely equivalent class there (1959), about half of the married men are family-oriented by the same criterion. In both samples, however, the career-oriented men are more likely than their family-oriented counterparts to have working wives. An important modification of this result in the total MIT sample stems from an analysis of working among wives who are trained for full professional work but are constrained by the presence of preschool children (Bailyn, 1973). In this group, where work is likely to be associated with a life-long career, it is not those whose husbands get their main satisfaction from career who are most likely to be working, but those whose husbands get their main satisfaction from their families first, and from their careers second. It should be mentioned, however, that those professionally qualified wives who are *least* likely to be working at this vulnerable time in their lives, are those whose husbands get satisfaction only from family and hardly at all from career.

11. It should be mentioned that accommodation is also related to certain background characteristics of the respondents. In particular, alumni with doctorates are *less* accommodative than those without; those whose undergraduate grades were low are *more* accommodative than those with average or high grades; and, to a lesser extent, those from higher socioeconomic backgrounds tend to be less accommodative than those from lower socioeconomic backgrounds. These differences, however, do not account for the correlates discussed: that is, even when these background characteristics are held constant, the relations discussed in the text persist.

12. These self-confident accommodators are still not as sure of their creative and problem-solving abilities as are the self-confident nonaccommodators. Self-confidence, in other words, increases this part of the self image for everyone. But the difference that accommodation makes is reduced in the self-confident group: the D's of 26 and 24 shown in the top half of Table 5.13 are reduced to 18 and 9, respectively, in this group. In contrast, self-confidence in no way increases the 'humanistic' orientation of nonaccommodators. Thus, among the self-confident, accommodation makes a much bigger difference to tolerance and social concern than it does for the whole sample. The D's in the bottom half of Table 5.13 change from -15 and -10 to -30 and -25 in this self-confident group.

13. In no case, however, are they as professionally involved as the self-confident non-accommodators. In fact, the D's in the self-confident group are only slightly reduced from those given in Table 5.14.

14. This limitation does not change the distribution of work involvement very much, as may be seen when the following figures are compared with Table 5.9:

	Per Cent Involved	Per Cent Uninvolved
General managers ($N = 72$)	24%	28%
Technical managers ($N = 81$)	20%	30%
Staff engineers ($N = 141$)	13%	40%

15. Evans (1974), studying a group of marketing managers (on an organizational level similar to the technical managers), concludes that accommodation to home life is the response of middle managers whose career aspirations have declined, as a result, usually, of some 'failure' on the part of the manager to get a promotion or other formal recognition of success.

16. We eliminate the 'career satisfaction' question of the work involvement index (see Table 5.1, Part II) because this question, in conjunction with the part on family, enters centrally into the accommodation index. When the distribution of this reduced index (trichotomized in a way to bring overall category proportions as close to the original as possible) is compared to that of the full index (see note 14), it is obvious that this reduction does not change the basic relation between organizational role and work involvement:

	Reduced index	
	Per Cent Involved	Per Cent Uninvolved
General managers ($N = 74$)[a]	26%	22%
Technical managers ($N = 81$)	21%	25%
Staff engineers ($N = 141$)	14%	33%

[a]Two people who did not answer the 'career satisfaction' question are included in the reduced index.

Chapter 6

Job Enrichment: Some Career Considerations

Ralph Katz

> '... *to crush, to annihilate a man utterly, to inflict on him the most terrible of punishments, ... one need only give work of an absolutely, completely unless and irrational character.*'   —Dostoevsky

AN OVERVIEW

Over the past decade or so, there has been increasing interest expressed in what has come to be called, 'the quality of work life'. Under this umbrella-like concept, one finds a host of normative models all designed to alter and improve the conditions under which work in this society is performed. Of these various models, job enrichment or work redesign is by and large the most visible, if not the most popular, reform methodology.

Work satisfaction represents one yardstick by which researchers have tried to assess and gauge the effects of job conditions upon individuals. While the interpretation of high satisfaction scores is somewhat ambiguous, low satisfaction scores usually signify some problem, incongruency, or conflict between employees and their employers. Furthermore, evidence accumulated from a variety of settings suggests that low satisfaction has a substantially adverse impact upon individual and collective behavior both inside and outside the workplace. Perhaps the most disturbing data, albeit controversial, have been summarized in the Department of Health, Education and Welfare's task force report *Work in America* (1973) and in Jenkins's *Job Power* (1974).[1]

However, empirical studies documenting distressing levels of worker dissatisfaction, together with warnings of further erosion, are probably not sufficient in and of themselves to have aroused the attention presently commanded by the quality of work life issues. What has been most impressive of late are the dramatic recounts of gains achieved through programs of job enrichment—programs developed explicitly to counteract worker alienation and enhance intrinsic motivation by redesigning the various tasks workers perform in their everyday activities (Glaser, 1975; Walton, 1972; Ford, 1969). Thus, it is the possibility that some concrete actions can be taken to improve work environments and rejuvenate workers that has provoked intense interest and excitement.[2] Yet, despite the apparent fruitful yields from these experimental programs, relatively few of the nation's large corporations have tried to implement comparable job enrichment programs. One survey, Luthans and Rief

(1974), places the figure at around 4 per cent. And, even without these experimenting organizations, only a small minority of their total labor force has been affected. In short, despite all of the theory and professed interest in job enrichment, it has barely managed to dent the 'quality of work life in America'.

One of the biggest roadblocks to the implementation of job enrichment—even after knowledge of its experimental successes has been diffused—is tied to the knotty problem of transposing the results from specific case studies to other locales.[3] In order to achieve this 'know-how', a broader, more inclusive theoretical and methodological framework is needed from which cross-organizational generalizations can be made concerning the reactions of employees to specific task dimensions over time and under varied work conditions. An important step in this direction has been made by J. Richard Hackman and his colleagues at Yale University. They have designed a diagnostic survey instrument to measure the degree to which certain conceptually independent task characteristics are present on particular jobs (Hackman and Oldham, 1975). This instrument quantifies the distinct job attributes of (a) skill variety; (b) task identity; (c) task significance; (d) autonomy, and (e) feedback-from-job. These dimensions presumably coincide with certain psychological states—meaningfulness, responsibility, and knowledge of results—experienced by individuals which, according to the developing theory, are critical for attaining and sustaining high employee motivation, satisfaction and commitment.[4]

Preliminary survey results comfirm that these job characteristics, especially autonomy and skill variety, are correlated strongly with general work satisfaction and are related moderately (but significantly) to absenteeism, overall performance effectiveness, and the quality of performance (Hackman and Lawler, 1971; Van Maanen and Katz, 1974). Such findings are encouraging but we still know little about the pattern of these relationships from a long-range, temporal standpoint. The few longitudinal studies available typically provide only pre- and post-measures (within a very restricted time-frame) as a means of tracking the effectiveness of a particular organizational change program. As such, they are not concerned with how employees react to the various task dimensions over a career span. Thus, the purpose of this chapter is to empirically explore the linkages between work satisfaction and particular job attributes over a broad temporal horizon. That is, how do employees react to certain commonly examined task dimensions throughout their careers—are the relationships stable and invariant, or is there some vacillating pattern that demands further elaboration and explanation.

THEORETICAL BACKGROUND: THE LOCI MODEL ACROSS TIME

Theorists involved in the study of work satisfaction tend to emphasize particular aspects of the employment situation at the expense of others. For instance, proponents of job enrichment or redesign efforts—usually, the domain of the applied behavioral scientist—assume that the set of daily tasks performed by employees are most related to their reported satisfaction level.

At the same time, advocates of the group process or human relations school of thought, primarily the management or personnel specialist, postulate that the interpersonal context of work environments contribute the most to individual satisfaction. Finally, a third approach can be detected and labeled 'structuralist'. Those supporting this third approach, frequently the labor relations expert or union leader, argue persuasively that the organization's (or industry's) policies regarding pay, advancement, scheduling, and so forth are the primary elements associated with employee satisfaction. Without detailing the various studies that support these positions, it seems likely that the applicability of each approach shifts or fluctuates throughout the course of employee careers. Hence, the relative capacity of any of these models for explaining job satisfaction may change over time, either increasing or decreasing in strength.

In a previous study, Katz and Van Maanen (1974) derived empirically a tripart locus of work satisfaction involving job properties, interactional features, and organization policy variables. The study supported the contention that work satisfaction is associated with each of the three generic theories mentioned above. Yet, no one theory in and of itself was sufficient to interpret the data. The three theories were defined operationally and each was considered to be a major locus of work satisfaction. Briefly, the three loci are:

(1) *Job properties:* Characteristics of the everyday task processes involved in a particular line of work.

(2) *Interactional Features:* Characteristics of the day-to-day supervision, agent-client dealings, interpersonal feedback, colleague relationships, and so on.

(3) *Organizational Policies:* Characteristics of the policies enforced in the workplace regarding compensation, promotion, training, and the like.

Each of these loci was shown to be analytically distinct and related to conceptually objective role design features. The task design features of skill variety, identity, significance, autonomy, and feedback from the job were linked only to the satisfaction locus of job properties. Face-to-face dealings, such as feedback from supervisor, were aligned exclusively with the international context locus. And, an additional group of role design features, promotion fairness for example, was associated uniquely with organizational policy satisfaction.

Katz and Van Maanen (1974) argue from these findings that job enrichment is indeed not a panacea for every situation of low satisfaction simply because it is only an appropriate remedy for one of the three possible sources of trouble. In effect, they suggest that in any program aimed at influencing work satisfaction, explicit attention must be paid to all three explanatory loci and corresponding design features. Standing by itself, therefore, job enrichment is limited in scope, pertinence, and effectiveness. Work redesign programs must broaden their focus from concentrating purely on task dimensions to emphasizing all features of work roles, including the interactional and organizational aspects. Consequently, we must shift from programs emphasizing task redesign to programs of role redesign where the concept of role encompasses all three satisfaction loci.

But even this extension is insufficient if it fails to consider the nature of the relationships between role characteristics and work satisfaction over time. In other words, we must investigate and decipher the emerging patterns of influence exhibited by the role design features—those affiliated with the satisfaction loci—throughout one's career, from initial entry to eventual retirement. Of course, these patterns may be constant or dynamic and vary from person to person. However, the point is simply that it is necessary to view the loci from a developmental perspective.[5]

Social scientists interested in socialization processes have long been aware of such temporal considerations. In particular, the work of Parsons (1951) and Brim (1966) draws explicit attention to the changing nature of an individual's relationship to the workplace over the course of their career. More specifically, it has been demonstrated in a variety of work settings that employee needs change in relative importance during their early career years (Van Maanen, 1975; Hall and Nougaim, 1968; Berlew and Hall, 1966). These writers argue that an employee's dominant need upon entering an organization is one of job safety and security. In a similar vein, Schein (1961) suggests that to be accepted by others in the organization as a contributing member ('to prove oneself') represents the major problem faced by a newcomer. It would seem therefore that only after grappling with the problem of establishing a somewhat stable situational identity can the newcomer turn to other matters such as achievement, challenge, and innovation.[6] In other words, people must determine what it is they are to do before they can decide how well to do it.

Some perspective on the nature of individual changes across the career can be gained by relating the loci model to Maslow's (1954) hierarchial need theory. Thus, for example, if an individual were progressing up the need hierarchy, one would expect that the relative influence of each loci upon satisfaction would also be shifting—from a concern for organizational policies, to a concern with the interactional context, to a concern for job properties. Presumably, the longer employees have been at their jobs, the more their needs for pay, security, and fellowship have been fulfilled; hence, they should be advancing up the need hierarchy. One might reason, therefore, that the relationship between overall work satisfaction and each of the task dimensions mentioned by Hackman and Oldham (1975) to increase in strength with prolonged periods of job longevity (i.e. longevity being defined simply by the length of time an individual has been working on the same job). The critical implication is that employees may be amenable to job redesign efforts only during particular phases of their organizational careers—a fact of obvious significance for both theorists and practitioners of job enrichment. Furthermore, there is little reason to believe that the influence of various task features operate with equal strength during particular career stages. Different task dimensions may be more powerful at different career points.

RESEARCH DESIGN

In order to test some of the notions discussed above, data collected from a large attitude survey (administered between October, 1973 and February, 1974) were analyzed for temporal implications. The guiding purpose behind the analysis was simply to investigate the patterns of relationship between overall work satisfaction and each of the role design features (allied with a particular locus) across separate groups of employees distinguished by different lengths of job longevity—job longevity was defined as the length of time an individual had been working on the same job. An emphasis was placed, however, upon the temporal affects of the task characteristics (Job Property locus), for such characteristics represent the primary thrust of job enlargement programs.

The survey was undertaken in four distinct governmental organizations as part of a project designed to examine job satisfaction in the public sector. Each of the governments represents a rather loose confederation of various service departments operating within clearly defined geographical regions (e.g. police and fire departments, public utilities, hospitals, social work agencies, sanitation departments, planning departments, and so on). Within each organization, a stratified random sample was drawn from among the full range of jobs and employees. The stratification was based on the EEOC (Equal Employment Opportunity Commission) occupational categories: administrative, technical, professional, protective service, paraprofessional, clerical, skilled craft, and maintenance. Of the total sample of 3,500 employees, 88 per cent completed the survey instrument. For a more complete discussion of the sampling, see Van Maanen and Katz (1974).

For the present analysis, only three portions of the survey instrument are pertinent: (*a*) role design features; (*b*) overall work satisfaction; and (*c*) longevity measures. The Yale Job Inventory, discussed in detail by Hackman and Oldham (1975), was used to determine the 'objective' task characteristics of the respondents' job. According to Hackman and Lawler (1971), this instrument provides a reasonably accurate—insofar as self, peer, supervisor, and outside observer ratings of a job converge—description of the following task dimensions:

(1) *Skill Variety:* The degree to which the job requires different activities calling for the use of different skills.

(2) *Task Identity:* The degree to which the job requires the completion of a 'whole' and identifiable piece of work—i.e. doing a job from beginning to end with a clear outcome.

(3) *Task Significance:* The degree to which the job has a perceivable impact on other people or their jobs, whether in the immediate organization or the community at large.

(4) *Autonomy:* The degree to which the job provides an employee with freedom, independence, and discretion in scheduling and carrying out work assignments.

(5) *Feedback-from-Job:* The degree to which an employee receives information from the job itself as to the effectiveness of his or her efforts.

Other work role factors—'feedback-from-agents' and 'promotion fairness'—were also measured in this study. These role design characteristics tap the loci of the interactional context and organizational policy, respectively. They were defined as follows:

(6) *Feedback-from-Agents:* The degree to which an employee receives clear information about his or her performance effectiveness from coworkers or supervisors.

(7) *Promotion Fairness:* The degree to which advancement procedures are standardized, i.e. apply equally to all employees.

All of the above dimensions were measured by use of seven-point, Likert-type items. Overall work satisfaction was measured by an eight-point, Likert-type scale ranging from completely dissatisfied to completely satisfied.

Finally, respondents were asked to answer a number of demographic questions including age, sex, current job longevity, and time spent in the organisation. The results that follow are based upon only the male portion of the sample ($N=2,084$).[7]

DATA ANALYSIS AND RESULTS

Table 6.1 demonstrates that each of the role design features was indeed associated with overall work satisfaction. The five task dimensions, feedback-

Table 6.1. Correlations of design features with overall work satisfaction ($N = 2,084$)

Design feature	Correlation with work satisfaction
Skill variety	0.19^a
Task identity	0.18^a
Task significance	0.21^a
Autonomy	0.23^a
Feedback from job	0.20^a
Feedback from agents	0.26^a
Promotion fairness	0.34^a

$^a p < 0.01$.

Table 6.2. Correlations with overall work satisfaction for different job longevity periods

Design feature	Correlations with work satisfaction										
Skill variety	0·03	0·22	0·12	0·22[a]	0·29[a]	0·29[a]	0·14[a]	0·17[a]	0·15	−0·01	−0·11
Task identity	0·13	0·33[a]	0·17	0·21[a]	0·29[a]	0·14	0·16[a]	0·29[a]	0·12	−0·08	0·11
Task significance	0·39[a]	0·29[a]	0·21[a]	0·38[a]	0·33[a]	0·16	0·23[a]	0·20[a]	0·23[a]	0·07	−0·04
Autonomy	−0·21	0·26[a]	0·29[a]	0·35[a]	0·37[a]	0·30[a]	0·20[a]	0·26[a]	0·17[a]	0·06	0·00
Feedback from job	0·32[a]	0·27[a]	0·33[a]	0·21[a]	0·29[a]	0·27[a]	0·24[a]	0·23[a]	0·25[a]	0·08	0·11
Feedback from agents	0·28	0·28[a]	0·39[a]	0·30[a]	0·25[a]	0·35[a]	0·25[a]	0·27[a]	0·25[a]	0·25[a]	0·25[a]
Promotion fairness	0·30	0·30[a]	0·37[a]	0·31[a]	0·41[a]	0·41[a]	0·37[a]	0·33[a]	0·40[a]	0·21[a]	0·24[a]
Job longevity period =	<3 Mos.	4–6 Mos.	7–12 Mos.	13–18 Mos.	19–24 Mos.	2–3 Yrs.	3–5 Yrs.	5–10 Yrs.	10–15 Yrs.	15–20 Yrs.	>20 Yrs.
N =	55	90	172	174	112	184	366	455	187	129	160

[a] $p < 0.01$.

from-agents, and promotion fairness were correlated positively and significantly with global satisfaction.[8]

From these correlations, overall satisfaction appears equally sensitive to each of the five task characteristics, slightly more related to feedback-from-agents, and most associated with promotion fairness.[9] Accordingly, one might conclude that the satisfaction level of a group of individuals can be enhanced if proper improvements are made in any of the role design features.

As shown in Table 6.2, however, the real world is considerably more complex. By calculating separate correlations for employees with different job longevities, it becomes clear that none of the design features are uniformly related to overall satisfaction. Specifically, the correlational results suggest that the satisfaction of employees who are just beginning work on a particular job (less than three months) is not associated with the amount of skill variety, task identity, or autonomy on the job. If anything, high autonomy may be distressing for the employee as shown by the negative correlation. At the same time, the other two task characteristics—task significance and feedback-from-job—are related positively to overall satisfaction.

Following this initial adjustment period, however, the correlations for most role design features increase in significance, peak in strength somewhere around two years, and subsequently decline in importance.[10] Correlations for those employees who have been assigned the same job for at least 15 years do not reveal any relationship between overall satisfaction and the various task characteristics. Thus, the consequences of simply having the same job for a long period of time apparently counteract the constructive effects of having high skill variety, high task identity, high task significance, high feedback-from-job, and high autonomy.[11] Figure 6.1 displays in graphic form the over time correlations between overall satisfaction and both skill variety and autonomy—the two task characteristics considered by most theorists to be the essence of job enrichment.

Employees hold new jobs either because they are new to the organization (novices) or because they have recently been promoted or transferred (veterans). For my purposes here, the term socialization will refer to the former condition, while the latter situation is labeled resocialization. Importantly, it has been suggested that the experiences associated with these two processes are not identical; thus, they need to be examined separately (Wheeler, 1966). In socialization situations, the novice must learn about and adjust to the organization from scratch. Such a process requires that the newcomer must sift and digest large amounts of sometimes vague and ambiguous information in order to discover where he fits in the overall scheme of the organization—finding a 'niche' (see Van Maanen, Chapter 1). Consequently, the novice must build social as well as task relationships in order to sustain and nourish his new existence.

The transferred or promoted employee also undergoes an initial learning phase to restore the temporary loss of the familiar. But, in contrast to the novice, employees in a resocialization situation have already acquired a sizeable

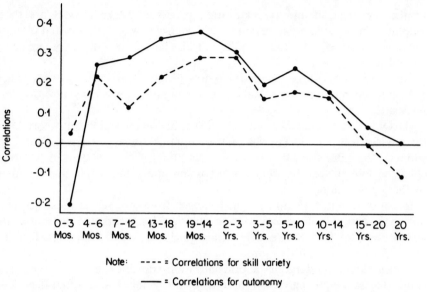

Figure 6.1 Correlations between overall work satisfaction and skill variety and autonomy for different job longevity periods

Table 6.3. Correlations with overall work satisfaction for respondents in either a socialization of resocialization setting

Design feature	Correlations with work satisfaction					
	Novices	Veterans	Novices	Veterans	Novices	Veterans
Skill variety	−0·09	0·03	0·31[a]	−0·04	0·15	0·09
Task identity	0·01	0·30	0·38[a]	0·40[a]	0·14	0·18
Task significance	0·35[a]	0·13	0·43[a]	−0·05	0·19	0·25[a]
Autonomy	−0·43[a]	−0·05	0·32[a]	0·41[a]	0·29[a]	0·24[a]
Feedback from job	0·22	0·56[a]	0·28[a]	0·26	0·23[a]	0·48[a]
Feedback from agents	0·40[a]	0·43[a]	0·29[a]	0·23	0·22[a]	0·54[a]
Promotion fairness	0·39[a]	0·33	0·22	0·29	0·38[a]	0·46[a]
Current job longevity =	(0–3 months)		(4–6 months)		(7–12 months)	
N =	22	21	40	29	64	60

[a] $P < 0.05$.

knowledge base about the organization, established contacts within the organization, and developed some sort of personal reputation. Hence, it is reasonable to assume that novices will be more responsive to the social issues ('getting on board'), while the veterans will be more sensitive to the task performance issues ('doing a good job'). Table 6.3 presents a comparative analysis of the socialization and resocialization processes where novices are those employees new to the organization and, of course, new to their job, and veterans are those employees new to their jobs, but who have been with the organization for at least five years.

Table 6.3 shows three major differences (in terms of job properties) when individual correlations are calculated to distinguish between socialization and resocialization.

(1) Only task significance and overall satisfaction are significantly correlated for novices in the early months of their organizational careers. This finding supports the contention that it is more essential for novices than for veterans changing jobs to feel that they are becoming integrated within and accepted by the organization.

In contrast, the task dimension, feedback-from-job, seems most germane during the first year of a resocialization situation. It appears that veterans might be more anxious than novices to ascertain quickly how well they are performing or can perform on their new jobs.

(3) Employees undergoing a resocialization transition are not necessarily stimulated by a high degree of autonomy on a new job. It seems that they must reestablish a sense of security in the workplace. On the other hand, neither are 'turned off' by high autonomy as are the organizational novices.

DISCUSSION

These findings suggest that there may be some serious weaknesses associated with job enrichment programs—with respect to both theory and practice. Current ideology contends that, in general, employees will respond positively (in terms of satisfaction, motivation, commitment, etc.) to appropriate increases in the various task dimensions. They survey results presented here also noted the correlational linkage between satisfaction and task characteristics, but, at the same time demonstrated the dependency of such relationships upon job longevity. Jobs featuring more autonomy, variety, identity, significance, and/or feedback do not necessarily evoke greater overall satisfaction—especially for employees with either very new or very old jobs. Consequently, to trust correlations that represent aggregations over eventful and important career periods is misleading and no longer justifiable.

The inescapable implication of these results is that job enrichment programs are potentially limited and of short-lived effectiveness. Jobs, no doubt, can be richly reconstructed along appropriate task dimensions and, hopefully, after a short period, employees will perhaps demonstrate the anticipated positive outcomes. However, there is little reason to believe that even the most enriched jobs will not eventually become routinized and boring as employees become more proficient and accustomed to their redesigned tasks. Hence, longitudinal considerations must be included when advocating a tactis of improving work satisfaction through job redesign.

Further complications arise even if one assumes, as many do, that proper job enrichment programs are not 'one-shot' occurrences—the routinization issue addressed through the periodic re-enrichment of jobs. Yet as the data suggest, greater amounts of skill variety or autonomy or identity may not have the same positive impact the second time around, particularly if the employees have the same job titles and positions. In fact, it may not have any overall constructive effects—recall that the relationships between task dimensions and overall satisfaction diminish with increasing job longevity. Hence, the enduring effectiveness of continuous job enrichment efforts may be severely restricted.[12]

To be successful, therefore, we must broaden the theories, strategies, and concepts related to work motivation and satisfaction. Often, it is more than just the immediate task that is important. It is the individual's job position, organizational role, and career path (actual, as well as potential) which must be included in the overall framework. For example, Schein (Chapter 3) isolated five distinct managerial types, each of which was 'anchored' by a different syndrome of talents, ambitions, and behavior styles. Thus, if organizations were to allow and legitimize alternative career tracks to satisfy these five very different career needs, the organization would be likely to be more attractive to more of its managerial employees. And certainly the same sort of considerations are as applicable to workers at the lower levels in organizations as they are to managers.

Certainly, neither the data nor the discussion is intended to dismiss the importance of or need for the design of jobs which include challenging and responsible tasks. The crux of the argument is simply that just having such jobs is not enough, for attention must be paid to job and career movements. Indeed, it is possible that these considerations will become even more crucial in the near future. Although empirical support is scanty, employees at all organizational levels seem to be shifting from an emphasis on the short-term, immediate rewards for their participation, to an emphasis on the long-term, career-related rewards (Lawler, 1975). Apparently, employees are thinking and planning further into the future than ever before. Increased life expectancies, society's emphasis on planning, early retirement, declining birth rates, and increased leisure time activities have all combined to enlarge the temporal perspective of today's labor force. Merely focusing on immediate tasks, therefore, does not take into account such a broadened horizon.

It is important to note also that the success of any job enrichment program depends not only on the validity of its theoretical foundation, but also on the worth of this particular implementation strategy as well. Hackman and coworkers (1974) specified recently seven types of procedural errors that ostensibly invite failure. One such problem area occurs in the 'assessment of readiness for change'. The correlational results from the foregoing analysis support this concern. The readiness of employees to accept a high degree of autonomy (or additional amounts of autonomy) is perhaps the most crucial feature. Wherever job enrichment involves the placement of individuals in new jobs, the amount of autonomy should be injected gradually, carefully, and with considerable support. Maslow's hierarchy of needs is not a 'one-way' street and employees, regardless of their organizational tenure, emphasize their safety and security needs when undertaking a new job.

Theoretical advocates of job enrichment, such as Herzberg (1966), readily acknowledge and forewarn potential users to expect an initial, although temporary, setback resulting from early confusion and learning. Such introductory declines are also likely to be aggravated by the entrance of too much change, too much autonomy, or too much variety, especially since employees are probably experiencing a brief resurgence of lower-order needs. There is nothing to suggest, however, that a job must be enriched simultaneously along each of its deficient task dimensions. On the contrary, the results here indicate that it might be more effective initially to increase task significance in the case of socialization and to increase feedback-from-job in the case of resocialization. This suggestion is consistent with the contention that when undertaking a new job, organizational veterans are more concerned with establishing and demonstrating their competence while novices are more concerned with becoming a helpful and needed part of the overall operation. In either case, the enrichment of a job along the autonomy and skill variety dimensions is not an immediate necessity and perhaps will be far more successful if introduced slowly during the first year of experience.

In situations where task dimensions are to be improved, but the job positions are to remain the same with the same personnel, employees must be assessed for receptiveness—especially with regard to job longevity. The reader will recall that the correlations for the task design features of Table 6.2 diminish with increased longevity. Therefore, if the majority of affected employees have considerable job tenure, it is unlikely that a job enrichment program *per se* will have any predictable positive influence on overall work satisfaction. Furthermore, the amount of turnover in an enriched group of jobs can cause a reverse effect. Because the redesigned jobs are supposedly characterized by high autonomy, individual's 'breaking-in' on these new jobs are likely to undergo a very stressful experience. In order to avoid this result, mitigating initiation methods would have to be developed and incorporated into the organization to help the individual during the early socialization or resocialization period.

Naturally, the greater the turnover, the more difficult and disrupting will be this continuous process of initial adjustment. Herein lies a potential contradiction, for as one strives to limit turnover for a redesigned job, one is increasing job longevity. And, as discussed, increased longevity eventually limits or inhibits the success of the program. Certainly low turnover is desirable and reducing turnover is a legitimate managerial objective, but too much stability can also be self-defeating. A job enrichment program should not discourage employees from wanting to shift jobs, nor should it be declared a failure if employees on jobs that have been enriched seek job changes. One must avoid the use of turnover as a uniform criterion of success.

SUMMARY AND CONCLUSIONS

The analysis reported in this paper represents only a peek into the dynamic world of work. A great number of questions still remain unanswered and even unexplored. In connection with this study, some of the more important problems are as follows:

(1) The findings reported here were based on cross-sectional and not panel data. Consequently, we cannot really be sure about what happens to a designated group of individuals over time. What we do know from this study is that the relationships between the assorted task dimensions and general work satisfaction become progressively weaker as we examine different respondents with more job longevity. From these results, we can only infer that the relationships between the task dimensions and overall satisfaction will dissolve as job tenure increases. Carefully planned longitudinal studies are needed to clarify the situation.

(2) The present analysis had focused exclusively on the modifying impact of job longevity. The demographic characteristic usually defined as either age, life stage, or career stage (i.e. early years, mid-years, and late years) is an additional variable that might moderate the relationships between overall satisfaction and the various design features. Investigators such as Porter (1961) and Hall and Mansfield (1975) have tried to show that the needs and interests of employees change as one ages. Job security seems, for example, to become more prominent as one gets older. The implication is that the relevance of job enrichment would also vary with age or life stage. Since job tenure and age are connected, it is possible that age is the 'true' moderator, or that age and job longevity, in some combination, both influence the investigated relationships. Preliminary inquiries into this issue reveal that the same pattern of results as shown in Table 6.2 reemerge when separately computed for respondents under 35 years of age and for respondents over 35. Hence, it presently appears that job longevity is a more powerful moderator than age, although considerably more research is needed on the possible added influence of age or life stage.

(3) Since the notion of a 'new' job was a focal concept in the analysis, it is imperative that we determine exactly what constitutes a new job. In the current study, we relied on the respondents' own interpretations. However, we need to explicate what the elements, dimensions, or rules are that determine whether one job is the same of different from another. Such knowledge is essential if we hope to improve the quality of working life in organizations through a combination of role redesign, job shifts, and career movements.

(4) In exploring the initial job longevity periods, the processes of socialization and resocialization were differentiated. This is only one of several important distinctions. Under resocialization, the transferred and promoted employees were all lumped together. They should be examined and treated separately. Similarly, novices with previous work experience may react differently from novices without prior employment. These issues have to be investigated and

understood in order to design and implement a more suitable work environment.

These are only a few of the problematic issues that have to be resolved if the quality of working life is to be significantly improved. Enriched roles, together with appropriate career paths (both horizontal and vertical), are more likely to achieve and sustain the desired level of work satisfaction. Finally, these conclusions are, as in most empirical studies, guilty of being deduced from the averaged responses of large numbers of respondents. Each individual employee has his personal mental image, his own 'road map' of the organization. Moreover, some of the road crossings, and stepover places are more attractive to him than others. In addition, the employee has some notions about when, how fast, and where he wants to travel. The ultimate challenge is the successful matching of these individual maps and travel plans within the organizational world. And, it is the dual responsibility of both the individual and the organization to try to achieve complimentary result.

NOTES

1. These reviews emphasize the current state of dysphoria by showing that the vast majority of workers would not willfully decide to reselect the same line of work. Furthermore, increases in alcoholism, drug usage, sabotage, crime, and absenteeism as well as decreases in production quality, family stability, and mental health are all purportedly linked with widespread work dissatisfaction. The dominant thesis is that ample remuneration, secure employment, and pleasant working conditions cannot by themselves dissipate the ubiquitous ailments known as blue-collar 'blues' and white-collar 'woes', for satisfaction is directly influenced by the amount of autonomy, variety, and responsibility in addition to the chances for personal growth, achievement, and contribution. Consequently, young workers tend to be the most disenchanted demographic group not because of a corrosion in their work ethic or assiduousness, but because they are less accepting of doltish and inane chores.
2. Some of the more well-known cases have been conducted at the Gaines Dog Food Plant, American Telephone and Telegraph, Texas Instruments, Procter and Gamble, TRW Systems, and Volvo. Glaser (1975) provides brief individual case histories of some twenty successful attempts at job redesign.
3. Reactions from managers typically stress the uniqueness of their own circumstances. For instance, a hypothetical but representative manager might say: 'Sure, job enrichment worked fine in Company X, but it would not work for us because our situation is not comparable. Our jobs are not as amenable to change or enrichment, our technology is intractable and precludes redesign, or simply, 'our problems are not as serious, for automation will soon eliminate the troublesome tasks'. Thus, it is the inability to build from diverse case studies that deters most managers from trying it and keeps about half of the adventuresome few from being successful with it.
4. Skill variety, task identity, and task significance span the state of experienced meaningfulness; autonomy covers experienced responsibility; while feedback from job taps the state called knowledge of results.
5. There are theoretical views of satisfaction that either do not encompass or believe in such career fluctuations. For example, Herzberg's (1966) two-factor theory of satisfation claims that the determinants of satisfaction and dissatisfaction are not only distinct but also remain constant throughout one's work life.

6. A more thorough and comprehensive discussion of career stages and the socialization process can be found in Van Maanen and Schein (1975).

7. On the supposition that there may be sex-linked differences, especially for older women returning to work, only the male respondents are used in the forthcoming analysis.

8. With a sample size as large as the one utilized in this table, statistical significance has very little meaning (i.e. virtually all correlations even slightly above or below the zero level are significant). The arguments reported throughout this paper, therefore, rest upon the patterns in which the data falls as well as upon the logic underpinning the research questions asked.

9. Basically, this is the same pattern of results reported by Van Maanen and Katz (1974) with a different measure of overall satisfaction. That report, in addition to Hackman and Lawler's (1971), however, found that autonomy and skill variety were more related to general work satisfaction than the other three task dimensions of identity, significance, and feedback from job.

10. The argument here does not rest on statistically significant differences between correlations from every adjacent job longevity period but rather on the existence of a clear and unambiguous pattern of correlational results.

11. These findings are based on the responses of employees from a wide range of occupations and careers. A study is currently underway by Van Maanen and Katz to determine the stability of these results over different career groupings.

12. A brief realistic example might serve to exemplify the problem. In a casual conversation with a vice president of personnel, a young factory worker commented that he was quite satisfied with his employment. The pay was comparatively high, working conditions were pleasant, and the supervision was good. He had no complaints about his present job. His father, uncle, and many friends had all worked at the factory, and he was perfectly content with his relative position or status. However, what was recently bothering him, or more appropriately 'scaring' him, was the thought that for the next 35 years, he would be entering the same building and going up the same stairs to the same room, to the same machinery, to do the same job! At the time, the vice president was about to start a job enrichment program. Having listened to this employee, however, he suddenly realized that his job redesign effort was seriously deficient, for it did not touch on career-related concerns.

Chapter 7

Managerial Careers in Transition: Dilemmas and Directions

Richard Beckhard

'*I came from a family and from a culture where being a millionaire was twice as good as being half a millionaire. Now I live in a culture where my kids think that being a millionaire is twice as bad as being half a millionaire.*' A Middle Manager

INTRODUCTION

Not long ago, a large, consumer-oriented company in the Midwest had two openings in its top level marketing management. Both carried a base salary of around $45,000—at least $8,000 more than the next lower level of the marketing hierarchy. Also, the man who took either of these jobs would greatly improve his chances to advance to a still higher income and a still higher level of management.

The company had a sophisticated system of career planning and management development. It kept close track of its middle management ranks to single out the people with the best potential for advancement up the corporate ladder, and it made a deliberate effort to broaden these people in knowledge and experience by rotating them through assignments, moving them across departments, sending them off to management courses, and the like.

When the two marketing jobs fell open, the company's top management felt it had three men in the 'pipeline' who were ready for these jobs. Top management approached the highest two men on the list and extended an offer which they felt could not be refused. Both turned down the offer. Since a move was necessary for the new job, one man said he did not want to live in the particular city to which he would have to move, the other man said that he did not want to leave the small town in which he now lived—at least not for several years, until his youngest child had finished high school.

Top management was stunned. Until then, neither of these two men with exemplary track records had given the slightest indication that he was anything but eager to keep moving ahead in the company. Now, suddenly, both had put personal concerns ahead of organizational ones, fully aware that they risked their company's displeasure, with all that implied for the careers to which they had given many years of their lives.

This is not an isolated instance. On the contrary, I have run into this kind of situation with increasing frequency over the past few years. For example, in each of three different companies with which I work and in which challenging and remunerative senior positions recently were being offered to men in their middle or late forties, I was given access to the so-called 'short list' of people under active consideration for these jobs—a longer list of people had originally been prepared but had been pared down considerably. I was also given data (from independent interviews) about the current retirement plans of all these people. Surprisingly, more than 70 per cent of the 'short listed' executives were thinking seriously of retiring at age 50 or so.

This percentage makes an important point. I believe that disaffection in the ranks of middle management is growing. I do not believe that it is widespread, at least not yet. But I do believe that it is most prevalent among the most effective and innovative managers in their forties—the very people on whom top management counts to carry on the business.

It would be too melodramatic to call these men rebels. Few of them want to turn their backs on the business entirely. Most merely want to shape the remainder of their careers in accordance with various personal preferences for which the traditional pattern of managerial development leaves little or no room. The company that fails to accommodate itself to these demands will not end up without managers. But it probably will not get the best managers it could have had.

SOME SOURCES OF MANAGERIAL DISCONTENT

Obviously, I think a company can and should go some way toward meeting the demands of promising prospects for its senior positions, even if these demands break the traditional patterns of the managerial employee–employer relationship. Before considering, though, what form such accommodations might take, it will be useful to consider why some middle managers are breaking out of the pattern. A company is unlikely to deal successfully with disaffection in its managerial ranks if it has no idea of the causes of the unrest.

When a man in his forties makes career decisions, he is under a variety of pressures. There are the pressures of his own personality, his own needs and aspirations. There are the pressures of his family. There are the more subtle but no less important pressures of his social and cultural environment. And there are the organizational pressures imposed on him by the company he works for.

I believe that the balance of these pressures is shifting in favor of the non-organizational pressures. These are becoming stronger in an absolute sense, but the crucial change is that the organizational pressures are becoming weaker. Not that management is less demanding today; on the contrary, it is perhaps more demanding. However, the penalties for resisting its demands have become less severe. For a manager to step off the corporate treadmill at 45, say, no longer carries the risk of near-catastrophe or at least the same form of deprivation, as it did 20 years ago. Naturally, as this risk has decreased, managers have become more willing to reevaluate the organizational demands on them in the light of conflicting nonorganizational demands. The strongest of these are likely to come from the manager's family.

Children always have broken their bonds to their parents. In well-off American families, this used to happen when the children went off to college or at the latest when they started careers of their own. It is now happening much earlier—commonly, I would say around the time the children graduate from junior high school. Physically they still live in the home their parents give them, but psychologically they have left it for the company of their peers.

The parents suddenly have only each other. A man of 40 no longer can assume that, if he devotes most of his time to his work, his wife will have her time equally taken up with the children.

I may be taking liberties with sociological terminology, but it seems to me that this, and not the couple with 2·2 children is the true 'nuclear family'. Young couples can always expand their family by having children, but the forty-year-old couple with adolescent offspring has only grandchildren to look forward to ten years or so in the future.

Divorce statistics show that a good many marriages break up under this strain. For every manager, however, who solves the problem of the nuclear family in this way there are several others who change their lifestyle so that they can spend more time with, and do more things together with their wives, even at the expense of working time.

Such a change in individual outlook of course could take place only in the context of important changes in the broader social climate. I do not think I have to document that the Horatio Alger ideal of single-mindedly amassing wealth no longer attracts many people. But in our context it is instructive to consider this development in the light of Maslow's theory of man as a needs-meeting animal, which shows that no matter how important a need is initially, it becomes much less important once it has been met. Contrary to a good deal of popular mythology, a person's needs do not remain the same through-out his or her adult life.

At one time a manager worked simply to keep the roof over his head. This probably ceased to be true at the end of the Depression, but 20 year ago a middle-aged manager still had to keep working hard to make enough money for his retirement. Now that is ceasing to be true. For many people, pension and social security payments add up to a comfortable retirement income, and this situation will become more common as pensions become portable. Eventually, national health insurance also will remove much of the financial threat of sickness in old age.

Another revealing change is that managers no longer feel a duty to leave their children a large estate. The younger people themselves do not expect it, and even if a father takes his children's antimaterialist rhetoric with several grains of salt, such rhetoric hardly inspires him to keep working harder and harder. Moreover, he knows perfectly well that in our affluent society all but the least capable children of the managerial classes will make out all right with or without silver spoons in their mouths.

Finally, retirement has lost the psychological threat it once held of letting go and, in effect, preparing for death. As we live longer and keep our health longer, while population pressure leads to earlier and earlier manadatory retirement ages, retirement becomes a normal phase of adult life that no one needs to go on working to postpone. Refusing to grow old is becoming as absurd as refusing to grow up.

Even some aspects of the manager's work setting now encourage him to pit his personal preferences against his company's. Management is more complicated than it used to be, and today's manager must weigh, and make tradeoffs among conflicting factors that his predecessors never knew about. He is therefore used to living and operating in a state of ambiguity. Faced with a conflict between personal and organizational demands, his father might well have suppressed the former, simply to avoid painful ambiguity. The son, accustomed to ambiguity, experiences the same conflict with little or no pain, and he will be that much more receptive to the demands his father shrank away from.

Then there is the confusing business of loyalty to one's company. Obviously this bond is weakening, and it is tempting to put the blame on a supposed general weakening of people's moral fiber. Tempting, but not very perceptive. Loyalty to the employer has never been a necessary condition of the employed state. In the past, the employee was tightly linked to his employer by his livelihood. By extending his loyalty and identifying his interests with his company's, the employee made this unavoidable condition of financial dependence psychologically less onerous to himself.

Now that the money link between employee and employer is becoming less important, the linchpin is being knocked out of this psychological structure. There is no reason to believe that managers have become less capable of loyalty. They merely have much less reason to extend any particular loyalty to their employer in the first place.

Aside from wanting more time with their families, the disaffected managers want something different in the way of the 'extras' in the same way that a successful executive looks for when his major economic wants have been the higher salaries, the perquisites, and the greater prestige of higher corporate rank. There will continue to be many managers who look for just these rewards and there will continue to be others who crave the greater powers of decision making and command the rewards that the most senior positions bring. But now there are also the so-called 'rebels' who want such 'extras' as the chance to devote some of their time to teaching or to public service. Or they may want to have more time for purely private pursuits like sports or hobbies.

Usually the 'rebel' is quite willing to combine continued work for his company with these other pursuits. But if his top management confronts him with an all-or-nothing choice, he may well quit and look for work somewhere else, where he will be able to spend part of his time teaching or studying or taking color pictures of hummingbirds.

It will also become more common for managers to value the intrinsic rewards of the work they have been doing over such extrinsic ones as money and 'perks'. That would not be a new attitude in business, since there have always been research executives who would rather run a laboratory than an industrial empire, but it will crop up in new and unexpected places. I know of a sales manager who turned down a promotion to a position of companywide responsibility on the grounds that he was comfortable where he was and would not be at all comfortable dealing with engineers, accountants, lawyers, and other types with whom he would be required to interact with on the new job— these types had always 'bored' or 'scared' him.

WHAT COMPANIES CAN DO?

Much of what I have said so far is projective, but not all. The pressures of deviance from the managerial norm already are strong enough to have forced some companies into notable departures from traditional operating modes. In increasing numbers (I myself have direct knowledge of three instances) companies are allowing certain key executives to take six-month or one-year sabbaticals. Usually the word 'sabbatical' itself is avoided, but even if the company calls it a paid leave of absence for purposes of study, a man who is not heard from for months and then comes back to pick up where he left off in effect is on a sabbatical.

Somewhat less unusual, though still exceptional, is the shortened work year on the academic pattern, which gives a manager two or three months at a time in which he is on his own, instead of just two or three weeks of vacation. And not at all uncommon is the joint appointment in which a company buys only half of an executive's time and he spends the other half teaching or consulting on his own. Both IBM and TRW Systems, for example, on occasion, make arrangements of this kind.

Finally, an impressive number of companies have responded to pressures from all classes of employees by going to the four-day week and/or flexible working hours. Even though such arrangements are rarely made with management in mind, such arrangements could give the executive more time of his own or more control of his time and so meet his increasingly common expectation to make his own choices instead of always accommodating himself to the company.

All these innovations are partial solutions to the new problems the disaffected manager poses for top management. Foremost among these is that a company that adheres to the traditional policies and practices of managerial manpower planning loses control if it can no longer be sure that the executives to whom it wants to offer top positions will accept these. The top management that wants to avoid this sort of embarrassment will have to stop assuming that its view of the company's interests as paramount is shared by everyone at the lower executive levels. It must realize that manpower planning these days involves more than sorting the junior talent into those who will probably perform well at or near the top of the corporate pyramid and those who will not. It will have to find out just how much the promising prospects for advancement themselves are interested in climbing ever higher on the corporate ladder and what it can do about any of them whom it wants particularly badly to keep from getting off the ladder.

Obviously, an elaborate system of manpower planning requires a great deal of information that is not easy to come by. In the typical company setting, a 39-year-old junior executive is unlikely to say to his superior, at the annual performance review, 'Incidentally, you realize, don't you, that I plan to retire at 50?' Nevertheless, it is not impossible to develop a good idea of where a manager's true interests lie. If top management genuinely respects its subordinates' right to their own career preferences, it should be able, in fact, to create an atmosphere of trust in which it becomes conceivable for a middle manager to tell his superiors, years in advance, that they cannot necessarily count on him until the day he reaches retirement age.

Realistic executive manpower planning in the future also will have to take into account that at some point some managers now become impervious to the financial inducements their companies can hold out to them. The offer of more money, in straight salary or any other form, no longer produces, as a virtually Pavlovian response, a willingness to shoulder heavier responsibilities. I believe there are certain departures from traditional compensation practices that a company can usefully make in this situation, but above all it must acknowledge that as an incentive the money it pays its managers is not what it used to be, and that it therefore had better look around for other sources of leverage. One of the most effective of these, in my opinion, is to offer middle and junior managers a variety of compensation plans and multiple tracks of career development.

Yet, even the company with the best career development and compensation systems runs the risk of finding itself in the sort of bind I described at the beginning of this article. What should management do when a person turns down an important promotion? Fire him? Put him on the shelf until he himself decides to quit? These have been the traditional responses. But if the man is really a top talent, is it so smart to let him go just to assuage a case of corporate pique? If he is not ready to give the company everything he has got, does that cancel the value of any lesser contribution he may still be able and willing to make?

In the broadest terms, it seems to me, the changes a company should make in order to cope with managerial disaffection have to do with problems of choice. One problem is that the company must reconcile itself to having less of a choice in picking people for its top positions. Another is that it has to offer its junior and middle managers a wider choice of work and pay arrangements—in part to gain the lasting loyalty of some talented managers who otherwise would become disaffected, and partly to retain the services of valuable managers whom nothing can motivate forever to keep climbing the corporate pyramid.

Such changes call for some sharp and perhaps painful attitudinal reversals on the part of top management. Not every kind of accommodation to the disaffected manager, however, needs to be painful. A company can do itself a lot of good with at least some of these managers by including them in novel work arrangements that it may have to institute anyway for entirely different reasons.

The best case in point is the four-day week, which is becoming quite common in manufacturing but has rarely been extended to the white-collar level. One of the few exceptions is the John Hancock Mutual Life Insurance Co. of Boston, which has started to experiment with the four-day week to give its clerical employees and administrative managers longer weekends and has discovered that the managers are just as grateful as the typists for the extra day off.

I know I will be told that the four-day week is out of the question for executives because they work harder than everyone else. Admittedly, many executives work 50 hours or more, but it does not follow that they have to. Some recent experimental changes in the working arrangements of the executives at a large consumer company produced some startling findings. Quite a few of the executives, it appeared, habitually stayed late out of inertia—the same inertia that makes people watch the late movie much longer than they had intended. For others, the office had become a refuge. A man who cannot stand human company first thing in the morning very sensibly may prefer his quiet office to the noise of the family breakfast table. Finally, a number of managers who did not really have that much work to do turned out to work long hours simply because their superiors did.

The case for the irreducible executive work week remains unproven. On the other hand, it can plausibly be argued that if 30 years ago it was possible to go from six working days a week to five, enough has happened since to make the thought of going from five days to four anything but preposterous.

Even easier to implement, I believe, are flexible working hours. These are already fairly common in certain segments of the communications industry, and I have yet to hear of an advertising agency that collapsed because the creative types never showed up before ten or eleven. The traditionalists' argument in this case usually is that if everyone comes and goes as they please administrative procedures and internal communications become tangled beyond repair, but actual experience does not bear this out.

A counterexample I am familiar with is a recent move by a company from a downtown location to a distant suburb. In an effort to attract its employees to the new location, the company offered everyone his choice of any eight-hour working period between 7·30 am and 5·30 pm. Moreover, every employee was given the right to change his working period at any time (so long as he kept his supervisor informed). For a while, the situation was a bit chaotic, but after about two months virtually everyone had found a routine of his own and they proceeded to observe their new patterns as religiously as they formerly had observed the common nine-to-five routine. The orderly pattern without which business indeed cannot function had been preserved. It had merely ceased to be monolithic.

Matters become much trickier, of course, when the time an executive gets off is measured in months rather than days. However, for this practice, too, some of the problems already have proved fully solvable in certain, if somewhat exceptional, situations. The nine-month academic work year, for example, is becoming more frequent in training departments (which do not have many people to train during the summer vacation months). Not surprisingly, it has also been widely adopted by nonacademic educational enterprises, and it is not unknown among several public agencies that deal mostly with universities and other schools.

That the concept of the academic work year can be extended to businesses whose work load does not drastically slacken at certain times of the year is shown by the frequency of part-time appointments at some companies in high-technology fields. In most of these cases, the part-time employee wants time off to devote to teaching or consulting, but for the company the net effect would be no different (aside from intangible prestige considerations) if one just took unusually long vacations.

If a company simply cannot cotton on to the notion that working for it does not necessarily mean working full time, perhaps it should think of part-time employees as in-house consultants. I am presuming that such a company would not hesitate to have the ordinary kind of consultant on a retainer to perform some special service, even though he would devote only some fraction of his working time to the company's concerns. If that should indeed be the company's attitude, it is hard to see why it should not also apply to the other kind of 'consultant' merely because he happens to be on the payroll.

The real problem, of course, is the sabbatical. How can a company make sure it will not be hurt badly, either operationally or financially, if it were to let key executives disappear for months on end? How can it make sure that the ones who stay behind will not be consumed with envy? There is even the problem of convincing a manager that he can go away without risking his job.

This last difficulty is in a sense the least complicated to cope with. Naturally, no manager will leave on a sabbatical unless he trusts his company to keep his job open for him. Top management should have no trouble determining if such trust exists. If the executives on the lower levels keep shying away from the idea of sabbaticals, it has to do some more convincing.

Real as they are, even the problems of the sabbatical in business can be exaggerated. To begin with, companies are not about to send off their managers in droves. For some time, the sabbatical will remain an exceptional arrangement, and that will give both top and middle management the chance to adapt to this novelty. Furthermore, I believe that the companies that give sabbaticals probably also will be the ones that offer their managers a choice of working and pay arrangements. This will accustom their people to the idea that they can get ahead without all following the same basic career pattern, and they will be less easily upset if the fellow next door is getting something they are not.

Once again, too, I am not talking about something without precedent. I am not referring to the few cases of more or less openly acknowledged managerial sabbaticals, for to date most of these have involved technical and scientific executives in fairly specialized positions. Rather, I have in mind the dozens of companies that every fall send highly paid managers, together with their families to *advanced degree programs in colleges* throughout the country. Somehow, all these companies keep going without these key people. There is also no evidence that the manager-students are harmed. On the contrary, most of them move on to higher positions in their companies.

So far I have talked mostly about specific measures that I believe companies should consider. Equally important are some changes in business practice that cannot be blueprinted so precisely, demand more complicated decisions, and take more of a wrench to carry out, since they go against the grain of long-standing traditions.

People cannot be expected to work more flexibly in the typical rigid organizational structure of business. On the shop floor this fact of life is already widely acknowledged. A process or work unit may have six people assigned to it, even though for 'maximum efficiency' only five are needed. Experiments in optimizing work performance show that when workers are given both the means and the responsibility to manage their own work, productivity tends to go up.

This approach has not, on the whole, been extended to managerial functions, but I think it should be. It need not necessarily lead to a greater number of managers. Often it may require no more than reassignments based on matching the work load to the actual capabilities of the available managers and not to their functional titles, positions, or other secondary factors. A recent work reorganization program at Imperial Chemical Industries in England, for instance, revealed that the *disciplinary* efforts exerted by part of the supervisory management could be handled by the workers themselves and that the principal contribution of part of the administrative management was to hamper communications between engineering and production groups. In such a situation, there are enough managers on hand already to handle the managerial tasks that really need doing in teams whose members can back up each other and therefore will no longer be shackled to repetitive routines every day.

The compensation of managers too, bears some thinking about. Every sophisticated top management knows that its company needs several kinds of executives—some with strong entrepreneurial leanings for example and some with a penchant for administration. It also knows that these different managers are apt to have very different preferences in the matter of rewards and will put completely disparate valuations on a solid pension plan, say, or a speculative stock option. Nevertheless, most companies reward all their managers in essentially the same fashion, striving for some median that never quite satisfies anyone.

Some companies I know of have realized that uniform compensation policies become counterproductive once managers insist that they be valued more for the individual contributions they can make than for their ability to adapt themselves to their superiors' expectations. Consequently, they are experimenting with permutations of straight salary, bonuses, pension benefits, stock options, and the like, among which each manager can choose the package that most appeals to him. Equally significant is that most of these companies give a manager the option of switching from one package to another at certain intervals, so that he will not feel locked in by a decision he took years ago, when for perfectly good reasons he was of a different mind than he is now.

As I mentioned before, I doubt that any repackaging of compensation will attract the manager who genuinely is no longer interested in increasing his income. This does not mean that money as an incentive has no place in sophisticated manpower planning. It can still do a lot to prompt some executives to pay serious attention to the development of the managers below them.

In many companies, improvement of the managerial reward system is one of the subjects to which lip service is forever being paid but about which little is done. Their executives know that if they neglect this part of their jobs they risk at most a chewing-out, but they may well be fired if they let short-term profits slide.

Just this kind of problem no long ago confronted the president of a consumer company split into four profit centers. Despite his most energetic efforts, he had found himself unable to get the heads of the four centers to collaborate, as a corporate group, on the exploration of new markets, the development of new product lines, and the improvement of the company's managerial manpower policies. He finally started getting results when he told his four top executives that henceforth, although they would still be fully accountable for short-term profits, only 60 per cent of their annual bonuses would be based on profit performance, while 20 per cent would be based on their effectiveness as corporate planners and the final 20 per cent on their contributions to the development of their subordinates.

If more managers feel disaffected toward their employers now that they can afford to, one of the reasons is that some companies in effect encourage the growth of such an attitude from the very day a future manager is hired. Often, for example, a company hires more potential management than it conceivably needs, and has college graduates going out as starting salesmen of soap or toothpaste or food. Not surprisingly, many of these salesmen quit long before the company has any chance to make up its mind if someday they would make good managers or not. The company probably might be better off with high school dropouts as salesmen, who would be more likely to derive a sense of worth from doing well in this job and would put a higher value on its financial rewards.

Such hoary traditions as always hiring in management's self-image or always on the assumption that every manager is a potential company president or that every manager stays with the same company until he retires also are becoming increasingly counterproductive. Frequently they lead to a Darwinian struggle for survival in the junior ranks, which creates great bitterness all around, mostly on the part of those who drop by the wayside. However, there will also be some, which may rankle for years, in those who stick it out. A lot of distracting rivalry and politicking could be avoided if both sides at the very beginning acknowledged the true state of affairs: that for the company as much as for most managerial trainees the first few years have to be a period of experimentation. If the new hire and the company can agree to postpone any long-term commitment for at least two years, say, and at most four or five, they will not have a play games with each other during this initial period and will find it that much easier to come to an understanding (which may lead to an amicable parting of the ways) about what each has to offer to, and expects from the other.

Management training and development programs, too, are encrusted with a lot of unnecessary pretense. Years ago, when business was done along less complicated and formalized lines, it probably was true that varied field experience taught a manager important lessons that he could not have learned any other way. Today, intimate familiarity with every aspect of any but a fairly small business requires more information than a man can keep in his mind so that much of the detail knowledge generated by intensive job rotation actually can become a burden. It may also be irrelevant in view of the diversity of business conditions—what a junior executive learns about selling in Kankakee may have little or no bearing on the sales problems of Walla Walla. Often, therefore, the principal effect of job rotation is to put the young manager under great pressure from his family and to give him a feeling of rootlessness and of never being allowed to catch his breath. From there, it is a short step to lasting disaffection.

Naturally, there are still cases in which job rotation makes sense. A multinational corporation can reasonably expect its top executives to have lived and worked in several countries. It does not follow, though, that it would be equally sensible of that company to insist on invariably rotating people across functional or divisional boundaries too.

Another reason for reexamining management development programs is that it is no longer necessary to base them exclusively or even primarily on learning by doing. As the years pass, more and more management skills can be taught with the help of game theory, computer modeling, and other forms of simulated experience. Those manager-students at MIT's Sloan School see nothing odd in gaming the acquisition and reorganization of companies. Many firms have drawn the obvious lesson and begun to apply the same principle in their in-house training programs.

Of course, formal management training, too, can miss its mark—if it is applied in a uniform pattern to all managers. The managerial-grid program, for example, has a lot to offer to production executives, for whom it was originally designed. It has been much less successful when applied to sales managers, who tend to grant it little relevance to the more individualistic job of selling. This is a misconception, but it nevertheless raises the problem of fitting the training to the trainee's perceived needs. Like all the other investments a company makes in its junior and middle managers, the training investment will be the more productive. I believe, the more closely it is tailored to each manager's needs, aspirations, and abilities.

160

SUMMARY

I have suggested in this paper that there is considerable restlessness among high-potential managers—indeed such restlessness is perhaps growing among all managers. Furthermore, I believe that this restlessness reflects a widespread concern on the part of executives today for a more integrated and fulfilling work and family life. Undoubtedly, such concern also expresses the decreasing financial dependence of people upon the company for which they work. Yet, whatever the cause, the critical issues surrounding the managerial career will not go away. They are in fact likely to become quite intense in the future. Given this situation, organizational leaders must begin examining the options to traditional personnel policies and begin laying the groundwork for some innovative changes. The areas that seem most promising are summarized below:

(1) Improving the quality of information about individual careers.
(2) Providing for the use of individualized contracts.
(3) Developing various sabbatical, extended leave, and vacation policies.
(4) Designing systems of differentiated work hours.
(5) Providing tenure for upper-management jobs.
(6) Enriching and redesigning managerial jobs.
(7) Developing a wider variety of choice for managers regarding their rewards.

In conclusion, the voice of managerial discontent may be barely audible amidst the complaints almost everybody seems to have these days about being treated unfairly by society or, in contemporary terms, 'the System'. It would be a mistake, however, to assume that they represent a passing fad, as some of the many other complaints we hear today no doubt do. When it is the best people who complain, the complaint is likely to be real and management had better not wait until its volume has become overpowering.

Chapter 8

Summary: Towards a Theory of the Career[1]

John Van Maanen

There is nothing inevitable about a person's work career.[2] If this were not true there would be little of theoretical or practical interest to the study of careers. All career positions are, in principle at least, transitory, hence, of critical importance to organizational members.[3] One need only listen to the conversations about careers which occur rather openly in and out of the workplace to be convinced of its problematic and pivotal nature in the scheme of organizational things. Indeed, observations and speculations about who is moving where, when, and why are perhaps the most frequent and engrossing topics dealt with by people when 'talking shop'.

Given this central position in the everyday concerns of people, it is not surprising that the issues addressed in each of the chapters of this book cover such a broad range. This is I believe a virtue because for an understanding of careers to emerge, complex, interrelated, and eclectic models are required. The purpose of this summary chapter is not therefore to simplify the foregoing work, but rather to call out the common themes in each of the disparate chapters and attempt to tie them together in a theoretically-relevant fashion. I approach this in several ways.

The first section 'The Practicality of Career Studies', suggests that four issues are central to each of the chapters in this book. These concerns grow from some very real dilemmas or problems associated with an organizational society. The second section 'The Analytic Properties of a Career', classifies the major theoretical contributions of each chapter. This classification is accomplished from several perspectives and provides a way of contrasting the various analytic foci of the authors. And, in the third section 'Concluding Comments', some general directions are mapped as to where career studies might go from here. Attention in this section is paid to the larger cultural context within which our career theories are constructed.

THE PRACTICALITY OF CAREER STUDIES

Virtually every area of social scientific inquiry reflects particular substantive problems of a given society. That is, all abstract or general areas of discourse such as socialization, role theory, cognitive dissonance, or deviant behavior are relevant to certain concrete issues such as professional education, mental health, race relations, or juvenile delinquency. This situation is no different for career studies as an area of general theory.[4]

Each chapter of this book mirrors the substantive base for career studies in different ways. However, each chapter speaks to four related, but conceptually distinct, issues of widespread concern in the modern industrial world. The four areas are: contemporary value shifts; alienation from work; organizational effectiveness; and adult development. These issues are discussed below not only as a means of integrating the ideas presented by the various authors, but also as a means of providing a sort of pragmatic backdrop to the formal study of careers. In other words, I am arguing that the practical worth of the study of careers resides primarily in its ability to shed light on the critical social issues identified in the various chapters of this book.

Contemporary Value Shifts

During the last decade or so, there has been a growing recognition that the values surrounding work, life, and leisure are changing. Perhaps it has been overstated at times, but, nonetheless, one would be hard pressed to suggest that traditional work-related values have remained stable. The evidence is all about us. To wit: the emergence of the women's movement from which has come a strong challenge to the institutionalized division of labor between the sexes; the continued presence of the so-called counter-culture in which some children of the middle class eschew the traditional American success syndrome of climbing the socioeconomic ladder; the tremendous interest of late in 'personal awareness' as indicated by the growth of what the popular press calls the 'mind expanding' industry.[5] And, at least insofar as men are concerned, there has been a gradual turning away from the view that work must necessarily be a source of life satisfaction.[6] All of these trends both signify and promote a change or evolution in the meaning we attach to work and career. The stern Calvinistic belief in a demanding, rigorous work career to which every thing else in a person's life must be subordinated is no longer a very persuasive point of view.

To paraphrase Lotte Bailyn's cogent arguments in Chapter 5, whether or not one holds greater affluence, increased education, or improved technology responsible, we do live in an era of rapid change and peculiar complexity. A greater variety of life styles affecting fundamental aspects of industrial life is realistically available today than has ever been available before. But, as the possibilities expand, so do the painful necessities for choosing. And, as all the authors here suggested, so also do the difficulties of meshing the sometimes conflicting social, organizational, and individual demands and aspirations. For instance, the requirements of a work career no longer are assumed to take precedence automatically in a man's life, nor are they presumed *pro forma* to be secondary in a woman's life. Thus, as individual's introduce more intricate considerations into their personal career choices, organizations are faced with new and unexpected complications in their traditional ways of mobilizing and directing human beings. Certainly the organizational problem of creating, revising, and abandoning various career paths is likely to increase in importance as contemporary values continue to change. As Beckhard suggested in Chapter 7, it would be a serious mistake to assume that the present trends in society represent a passing fad.

Alienation from work

A concern for work careers cannot help but distinguish between those careers which seem to be enriching and those which seem to be alienating.[7] All of the chapters in this book, whether or not the authors used the term alienation, addressed the problem of matching individual talents, interests, and hopes to the demands, requirements, and constraints of organizational environments. From this standpoint then enriching careers are, in general, those in which this matching of personal and organizational concerns is present. On the other hand, alienating careers are by and large those in which little or no matching is present. Several plausible explanation for this latter situation have been presented throughout the book.

Van Maanen, in Chapter 1, suggested that alienation in the workplace occurs under those circumstances in which an individual's anticipated future in the organizational looks empty or grim. In such cases, a sort of disenchantment sets in and the person figuratively, and sometimes literally, withdraws from the workplace. The remaining six chapters provided a number of alternative explanations for this phenomena. The work of Schein, Kolb, and Plovnick, and Keen located a possible cause in the incongruity between a person's career anchor, learning style, or cognitive orientation, and the sort of work the person is called upon regularly to perform. Bailyn argued persuasively that there are certain roles in organizations that over time seem to promote an alienated response among the majority of occupants. Similarly, Katz found that long tenure in any sort of role is likely to create difficulties for the role holder. And Beckhard observed that for a number of executives who were at or beyond the mid-career point, life interests change, leading to a subtle, but sometimes dramatic, shift in the person's relation to work.

What is surprising is that in the main this book has been concerned with various strains of managerial roles—roles commonly thought to be among the more lucrative, desirable, and interesting ones offered by any organization. Apparently, as Bailyn pointed out, even status, position, and remuneration provide no guarantee of personal involvement across the career.

Relatedly, the interest expressed here in alienation at work (or the lack thereof) directed attention outside the workplace in an attempt to find some sources of individual fulfillment. In other words, all authors remarked on the impossibility of viewing work in isolation from other aspects of a person's life. This is a refreshing development for it is obvious that we do not live neat, compartmentalized lives in which each of our separate concerns operate within a closed system. For too many years we have studied and made proclamations about individuals and their work as if people cared about nothing else. Such a bias in our studies leads to a glorification of what Kolb and Plovnick so aptly termed, the 'role encapsulated ego'.[8] Certainly, the career studies represented in this book have attempted to move away from such a narrow focus.

Organizational Effectiveness

If it can be said that the central problem of organizations is captured by the aphorism 'getting the right people in the right places at the right time', several new dimensions were described in this book in terms which the managers of our large organizations might consider this problem. Simply the evidence presented here testifying to the diversity of managerial careers suggests that people in organizations are not always oriented toward hierarchical rewards. In fact, most people want a good deal more from their organizational career than simply promotion upon promotion. Certainly a main theme running throughout each chapter was that mobility is not all that is at stake for an employee. Time-off, job challenge, an opportunity to learn and develop new skills may be just as important, if not more so, for many organizational participants than perpetual advancement.

Also related to the organizational effectiveness focus are the interrelated issues of company loyalty, dedication to work, and the importance of the work career to people. As all authors pointed out, commitment to the organization or to a particular work role cannot be assumed as a sort of *fait accompli* among any employee category. Even among the upper-echelon members of an organization, multiple sources of attachment are common. Whether it is to one's family, one's leisure pursuits, or to one's residential, political, or intellectual community, work cannot be expected to control a person's life interests. Thus, individuals will not always respond as expected to preordained career paths. People do not behave as if they were iron filings attracted to the magnet of upward mobility. Indeed, we have seen that unless organizations can construct career paths which accurately reflect and reward the changing interests and abilities of their members, they are likely to run into problems when it comes to getting the right people in the right places at the right time.

Finally, several of the chapters hinted at perhaps the major difficulty encountered by organizations when an integration of effort is required. In brief, such integration is made problematic because of the differing cognitive orientations of organizational participants. For example, Keen in Chapter 4 documented the contrast between the cognitive styles of generalists and specialists. Each to the other is viewed with suspicion and distrust—'they are not like us'—thus valid communication is all but impossible. And, if one takes the accentuation process postulated by Kolb and Plovnick seriously, the difficulties associated with varying cognitive orientations are likely to be amplified over time.[9]

In summary, each chapter was concerned in various ways with issues of direct importance to the effectiveness of organizations. Indeed, organizations themselves are little more than interlocking sets of career paths.[10] Hence, if these paths are seen as inappropriate to the people passing through them, it is a foregone conclusion that the overall performance of the organization will suffer.

Adult Development

In many ways, this book in its entirety gives evidence to what could be called the 'coming of age of developmental psychology'. No longer is the image of adult functioning dominated by a set of invariant personality traits which are established for all time in early childhood. Following the insights of Erickson (1950, 1959), all the authors represented here devoted substantial attention to the view that identity is not fixed once and for all, but rather grows continually from life long experience and activities.[11]

Each chapter suggested also that individual's at various points in the life cycle critically reassess their total life situation. Such reassessments sometimes lead to personal changes of deep and lasting significance. And, as was pointed out at various junctures in the book, the individual's successful resolution of such personal crises often alters the role of work in the person's life. To see how central this idea of the changing needs of the person was to the authors, note the numerous references to such issues as mid-career shifts, second careers, career reappraisals, career crises, and so on.

Career studies, by their very nature, entail a full consideration of adult identity. One way of developing a more accurate account of personality or identity is by the study of the role work plays in a person's self-image across the life time. Certainly the interest expressed by several authors in the career *cul de sac* (i.e. plateau) directs attention to the study of those situations in which an individual must revise his or her self-image, leading perhaps to an entirely new sort of attachment to a work role. As suggested, the study of such crisis periods cannot help but increase our understanding of the sociology and psychology underlying all career processes as well as increase out ability to perhaps ease and improve the organizational handling of such personally traumatic periods.[12]

To conclude this section, the four themes discussed here seem to cover much of the commonality found across all chapters. This is not to say that each theme was emphasized equally for clearly this is not the case. But given the task of finding the unifying or shared problems which were examined in this book, the list serves remarkably well. Let us now turn to consider some of the contrasts.

THE ANALYTIC PROPERTIES OF A CAREER

In the Introduction, I noted that there were three conceptual notions running across all seven chapters. The first was the explicit acknowledgement on the part of the authors that a career must be viewed from two basic perspectives—the internal perspective, which refers to an individual's subjective apprehension and evaluation of his or her career; and the external perspective, which delineates the more or less tangible indicators of a career (e.g. occupation, task attributes, accommodation, job level, and the like). The second notion referred to a shared perspective regarding the requirement that careers be viewed within the total life space of a person. That is, any career variable must be seen in light of its position within the entirety of a particular career history. The third conceptual notion concerned the necessity to view career outcomes as a result of interaction among a fairly large set of variables within a complex career domain. In other words, contingency theories, emphasizing patterns and relationships among many variables, were thought by the authors to be more appropriate and fruitful explanations for career outcomes than deterministic, cause–effect ones.

These three central ideas are used below to compare and contrast the main interests of the chapters of this book. I begin by constructing a simple paradigm of the career with special attention placed upon the differences between internal and external perspectives. Each chapter is then compared in terms of the attention paid to particular elements of the paradigm.

The Shape of the Career : The Internal and External Perspectives

The shape of any career can be described by combining two principal variables—direction and time (Strauss and Martin, 1956). The term shape refers simply to a line that results when one graphs a career using these two dimensions. Figure 8.1 depicts a hypothetical illustration of a career shape by using a regularized career in a police organization.[13]

As can be inferred from the example, the shape of a career is the combination of ups, downs, and plateaus. Hence, over the history of a career there is a notion of total distance that a person covers, as well as how far an individual moves during a specific period of time. And, for those persons who move from organization to organization, several career shapes are possible—each corresponding to particular organizational experiences. Many such career shapes are readily apparent. Most professionals, for example, have flat career shapes, regardless of how well or poorly they fare in their occupations. The downwardly mobile career described by Gouldner (1965) would have a shape marked by an early rise followed by several dips and plateaus. And, the successful, upwardly mobile career of the stereotypic man-in-the-grey-flannel-suit would be represented by a steep, stairlike ascending line.[14]

This model of the obvious descriptive attributes of a career corresponds to what we have been calling the external career. But, since people are concerned with shaping their own careers, they have, at any given time, an internal conception of their past and prospective career shape. For instance, individuals are aware (or at least guess) whether they are moving up, down, or standing-still. They also have an idea of the timing associated with such movement.

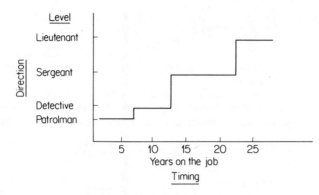

Figure 8.1 Hypothetical police career

Thus, the internal career—one's aspirations, expectations, and evaluations—can also be described by direction and timing components. Indeed, people can be thought of as orienting their efforts in order to achieve whatever shape they desire at the moment and in the future. This then is the internal counterpart to the external career shape.

Let us now examine in greater detail this simple model by tying an illustrative set of variables to the three concepts. As Figure 8.2 denotes, there is a prescriptive and descriptive side to a concern for career shapes. Both sides contain internal and external elements. Considering the prescriptive side, externally, the relevant characteristics covered in this book include the tasks a person has performed, the roles and/or levels occupied, and the various settings in which the individual has worked. Internally, the major prescriptive characteristics were the person's cognitive orientation toward the career, and the person's handling of conflicting demands arising from work and nonwork sources. On the descriptive side, the external variables examined were the mobility and performance patterns exhibited by an individual. In addition, internal factors were the desirability or satisfaction felt by the individual in relation to work and career, the degree to which the person was involved in his or her work career and the degree to which the person was accommodating to family demands. These paradigmatic elements are discussed below in relation to the central interests of each chapter.

Direction

For the most part, the three chapters in Part II were concerned solely with the internal causes and consequences of an individual's career direction. Each of these chapters examined the biases associated with given careers which arise from individual interests and competences. Thus, Schein postulated the evolution of a career anchor which guides and stabilizes a person's career. Similarly, Kolb and Plovnick, and Keen suggested that individual's favor certain sorts of careers over others on the basis of the implicit match between

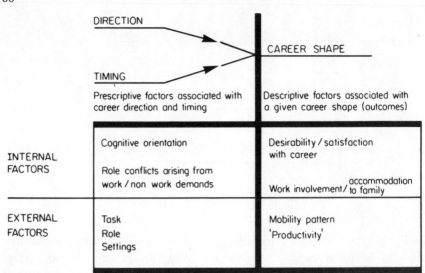

Figure 8.2 Elements of a career shape (as studied in chapters 1–7)

the perceived characteristics of the occupational role and a person's cognitive or learning style. Consequently, if we take, for example, the technical-functional career anchor, this anchor presumably constrains a person's choice of career direction and is buttressed, perhaps accentuated, by a learning style of the convergent or assimilative mode, and a related cognitive style that is both receptive and systematic. Directionality, therefore, flows toward a specialist career.

Taking a slightly different approach, Van Maanen, in Chapter 1, was also concerned with career directions. However, the interest in that chapter was primarily with the external side of the issue. That is, given a person's general lack of directional clarity and awareness associated with the onset of a career, how do organizational recruitment, socialization, and reward processes induce various career orientations among people. In other words, Van Maanen was concerned with how people come to define their career direction ('the career map') and attach certain feelings to a given direction on the basis of structural properties and processes associated with organizational life.

Timing

Three chapters focused upon career timing. First, Van Maanen discussed the kinds of questions individuals need to answer if they are to build a useful internal career schedule ('timetables'). The emphasis in Chapter 1 was, however, upon the way in which external clues are made available and used by a person to confirm or discount an expected or idealized internal career shape.

Katz, in Chapter 6, also focused on issues related to career timing. Katz's concern was upon the way in which external task characteristics influence an individual's satisfaction with work at different periods in the career. And

Katz was able to demonstrate rather convincingly that the effects of the structure of particular jobs were directly contingent upon the stages individuals were at in their respective careers.

Finally, Backhard's concluding essay stressed the overall and general importance of the timing variable for career studies. Through illustration, Beckhard argued that for some managers past the mid-career stage, advancement up the hierarchical ladder is perhaps less important than certain other options unrelated to an upward climbing career shape. Sabbaticals, flexible work schedules, the chance to act as a mentor to others in the organization become more critical desires for some mid-career managers than climbing up the hierarchy.

Career Outcomes (Shape)

Although all chapters touched, at least inferentially, upon both internal and external career outcomes, Bailyn's work was the most direct and pertinent. In Chapter 5, she discussed the accommodation and involvement patterns associated with technically-based careers. The analysis suggested that certain career paths (e.g. staff specialist) were more likely to create difficulties in adjustment (both organizational and individual) than others. Katz was also concerned with the affect of certain careers upon internal responses. Although the career shapes in Katz's study were less explicit, differential outcomes in terms of satisfaction were clearly related to particular career stages. The remaining chapters were less concerned with career outcomes, although they implicitly dealt with the individual's response to the career shape by emphasizing the normative concept of internal–external matching of personal desires and styles and organizational constraints and opportunities.

Finally, several chapters (particularly those by Van Maanen and Keen) alluded to certain individual and organizational outcomes associated with novel or first-of-a-kind careers. Keen, for example, noted the difficulties computer specialists and management scientists may experience mid-way or late in their specialty careers. Since these careers are relatively new, individuals passing through them have no role models or formal guidelines to inform them as to how their careers will unfold. Furthermore, organizational decision makers perceive few ways to continue to 'develop' such personnel in ways commensurate with the technical expertise of the people. Such specialists therefore are either promoted to jobs for which their preparation has been less than adequate,[15] or they are left in a 'technical rut' in which they perhaps have little desire to continue.

Career Phases: The Temporal Perspective

Recalling that a major theme of this book was the necessity to view career variables in terms of their relationship to an individual's life span, Figure 8.3 depicts in very rough chronological order the dominant interests of each chapter.

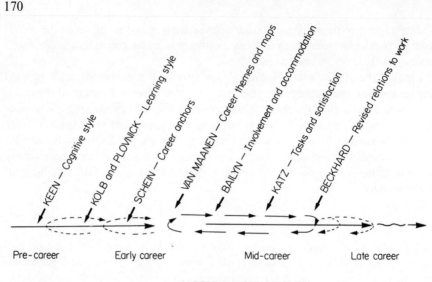

CAREER PHASES / CYCLES

Figure 8.3 Selected variables and career phases/cycles

In terms of precareer phases, both Chapters 3 and 4 presented evidence that individuals develop characteristic styles of relating cognitively to the world of their experience. Keen's theory on the formation of distinct problem-solving strategies can perhaps best be thought of as preceding Kolb's notion of learning styles in time since the latter was considered to be more dependent upon an experiential base—although the two cognitive theories are, in most respects, analogous.

Given a particular cognitive orientation, Schein's conception of a career anchor seems logical as the next major chronological category. But career anchors can be constructed only after a person has had at least some direct knowledge of and experience with the occupation of choice and preparation. Anchors then can be discovered or formulated fully only after the person has entered the work world. Furthermore, it seems apparent that anchors are required if people are to truely make sense of their work situations. Such understanding is accomplished, as Van Maanen points out, through the building of both a temporal theme and social frame-of-reference. However, this interpreted location in time and space may be viewed by a person with a situationally inappropriate career anchor as unsuitable and/or discouraging, thus promoting a desire for a career shift. And, of course, each time an individual undergoes a career change, the person must revise or discover new temporal and spatial properties to associate with a new organizational role.

Bailyn's concerns for the patterns of involvement and accommodation are, to a degree, based upon a person's anchor, organizational location, and, most importantly, position in the life cycle. For example, accommodative patterns of career adjustment become far more significant (and problematic) if a person has a young and growing family than if the person does not. It seems likely therefore that characteristic patterns of involvement and accommodation follow, rather than precede, the person's interpretation of where they are and where they might go in the workplace.

Katz's study suggests the existence of several contingencies or preconditions involved in the influence task factors have on employee satisfaction. First, task attributes were relatively unimportant during the initial period of learning a particular job. This would suggest that people must first locate themselves within a work world in terms of their own particular styles and anchors. Second, a certain amount of work involvement would appear to be a prerequisite if task characteristics were to be related significantly to satisfaction. That is, people are oriented primarily to seeking satisfaction in non-work spheres of life, (e.g. if they were highly accommodative) it seems improbable that altering one's work role would make much difference to that person—though this certainly is an open empirical question upon which we can only speculate here.

Finally, Beckhard's work speaks of possible alternating patterns of personal interest in work across the career. Beckhard notes that some managers undergo significant changes in their work orientation as career shapes flatten out, life situations change and/or new demands are made on the person. This phenomena probably does not represent a change of anchor or cognitive orientation (although it may represent a thematic change) within the person, but rather reflects: (a) a response to facing the same problems year after year at work which eventually begin to lose their ability to generate personal interest and involvement—in the same way that Katz suggests certain tasks, no matter how challenging or significant, tend, over time, to lose their potential for individual satisfaction; (b) the Jungian notion discussed by Kolb and Plovnick that as people pass through the middle to late phases of the life cycle they have an increasing tendency to express nondominant needs and abilities in their life's activities; and (c) a change in the family structure as a person moves beyond the mid-career phase thus enabling the individual to consider alternative uses of time.

This chronological ordering should not be thought of as fixed. Perhaps, as Figure 8.3 suggests, the activities that follow the development of a career anchor can best be thought of as cyclical in nature. That is, for many reasons, people frequently revise their notions of organizational location and, by so doing, may also alter their patterns of involvement, accommodation, task performance, and role perceptions. These sorts of career adjustments are no doubt both significant and systematic to the person even though they are unlikely to disturb the deeper adjustments represented by the individual's cognitive orientation and career anchor.[16] Although, as Figure 8.3 also notes, a change of learning style, cognitive style, or career anchor is not to be totally disregarded as a possibility. At any rate my purpose here was merely to show how the main interests of each chapter could be tied together in a temporal fashion. It does seem, however, that this discussion points toward the utility of building career theories in terms of a developmental foundation.

The Career Cube: The Interactive Perspective

The third theme running throughout this book dealt with the interactive nature of a career. Concerns about work and career were not viewed in isolation, but were discussed in terms of the totality of life roles in which a person operates. The scheme presented below in Figure 8.4 is a way of conceptualizing the interactive nature of career issues. For pictorial reasons it is called the career cube.[17] It is presented here as a heuristic device useful for analyzing the sorts of issues raised by career studies. There are three graphic dimensions associated with the cube which must be conceived of as in continual interaction. Such interaction then leads to many kinds of outcomes which can be located conceptually in the cells of the cube. Underlying the three main dimensions is a fourth which represents the temporal plane upon which the cube must rest. Hence, at any given time during a career, the interaction among the three generic dimensions of the cube result in a set of characteristic outcomes. The dimensions are discussed very briefly below.

Roles, Tasks, and Settings

The diagonal dimension represents the major categories for classifying occupational and organizational positions associated with a given career. In this book, the work of Katz and Van Maanen focused most upon certain properties of roles, tasks, and/or settings as external factors having implications for various sorts of outcomes.[18]

Individual Characteristics

The vertical dimension represents the internal variables related to the career. In particular, Schein, Kolb, and Plovnick, and Keen drew attention to anchors,

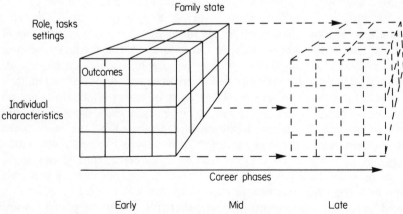

Figure 8.4 The career cube

learning styles, and cognitive styles respectively as variables which are appropriate to this dimension.

Family State

The horizontal dimension of the cube represents the features of a person's family life at a particular point in time. Variables of interest along this dimension would be, for example, marital status, whether or not the spouse is working, the presence or absence of children, the ages of the children, and so on.[19] This dimension was only of tangential interest in this book, although the work of Bailyn and Beckhard point clearly to its importance in understanding career dynamics.

Outcomes

As a result of the interaction among the factors associated with each dimension, certain sorts of career outcomes can be better understood. And they can be examined at any particular time in a variety of ways. To illustrate, outcomes can be seen as 'cells' in the career cube—reflecting specific family states, individual characteristics, and external roles, tasks and settings, all of which are viewed at a particular period of time. Beckhard's case materials come closest to this sort of 'cellular' analysis. Outcomes can also be viewed as 'prisms'— where the relationship between two dimensions on the cube is of central interest. Van Maanen, Katz, and Bailyn exemplify this sort of analysis. Finally, outcomes can be looked at in terms of 'strips'—where only one dimension of the cube is of primary interest. The concern with individual factors expressed by Schein, Kolb, and Plovnick, and Keen is representative of this type of analysis.

Certainly there are internal and external outcomes and all the chapters of this book were concerned with both—although perhaps most discussion was dominated by a manifest interest in the internal side of career outcomes. But the central point here is not the specific operational definition of an outcome, but rather the more general point illustrated by the cube—the interactive nature of the career.[20]

CONCLUDING COMMENTS

It is instructive to note that Studs Terkel, after interviewing hundreds of working Americans, ranging from housewives to corporate presidents, concluded that the one person who was most satisfied with his or her work career was a 57 year old stonemason.[21] Thus, a flat career, characterized by hard physical work, performed in relative isolation, and operating under conditions of reasonably high economic insecurity provided, from Terkel's perspective, the most personal fulfillment. Things are not always what they seem.

If there is a lesson to be drawn here for the future of career studies it resides primarily in the necessity to always attempt to understand the actor's perspective. Indeed, careers that on the surface appear to be enriching, may turn out upon inspection, as many examples in this book demonstrate, to be viewed by the people in them as devoid of challenge, frustrating, and all too constraining.[22] A career is, first and foremost, an individual accomplishment. And, regardless of its shape, must be considered through the eyes of the beholder.

What is needed, albeit demanded, is the careful, sensitive study of a variety of careers. In this way, the differing perspectives which arise both between and within careers can be contrasted to features of work environments, family situations, and individual variables. However, to call for the comparative study of careers is, however grand, a sort of ambivalent mandate. Surely there are some substantive issues that can guide our research efforts. Without repeating the research priorities suggested at the end of each of the chapters, let me suggest here that there are indeed a number of important substantive concerns around which we can perhaps direct future study. I will organize my brief and somewhat allegorical discussion around the three main career variables discussed in this summary—work, family, and self.

Work

In contemporary American fiction there seem to be only two recognizable human types that provide examples of the work oriented. One is the Budd Schulberg sort of character who, in a ruthless drive to the top, never ceases to be concerned with work interests. Everything this character does is geared toward the Machiavellian climb to financial reward and external success. It is an all-consuming, around-the-clock, almost maniacal activity that knows no social or principled limitation. The other extreme is the impoverished, down and out, John Steinbeck type whose every efforts are continually aimed at work, lest the impoverished soul slip irrevocably below the survival level. Virtually every waking hour of this literary type is occupied with either finding work or doing work of the dull, dehumanizing variety.

Fortunately, the vast majority of work careers are considerably more complex and mysterious than these two overdrawn types. People are most often vaguely unsure of the purposefulness of their activities. While it is unlikely that they will either starve or achieve riches, they must still make meaningful their work efforts. Given this middle ground, what kinds of question should we be asking? Several substantive concerns can serve as useful illustrations. Flat or unstaged careers, for instance, are interesting. A great number of work careers entail little or no upward mobility. How do people define these careers and what effect do such definitions have upon the person? Investigations here would include both professional and nonprofessional occupations. Or, take, for example, the downwardly mobile careers. These career shapes imply some sort of rejection. How do people adjust to such rejection and what effect does this have on their work performance? Also, multiple organization careers are of considerable interest. Many people jump from organization to organization for a number of different, yet largely unknown, reasons. What are these reasons and what are the factors that facilitate, promote or retard such career switching?[23]

Again, these areas are merely suggestive of a very few substantive bases for research. Many more are easily discoverable as the various chapters of the book denote. At the theoretical level, an interest in work and career involves building an understanding of what people in different occupations do, how they form a perspective on what it is they do, how their work is patterned over time into a set of stages which can be thought of as a career, and how their cognitive styles, needs, motives, and values influence initial choices and later adjustments within the career? In other words, the formal question is simply what is the underlying order of a particular work career and how does it operate?

Family

Hollywood movies are unusually good when it comes to overstating the work versus family tradeoff. Quite often, the typical male hero is trapped in a romantic dilemma wherein he has a maddening choice to make between a career of considerable reward and a woman of considerable charm. Thus, the hero must settle for either something less than success is the work world and get the adorable, loving woman, or get the job and lose romantically. Most interesting to those of us concerned with work, our typical cultural hero most often chooses the former—although, in many a final reel, the hero turns out to get both, once his priorities have unequivocally been straightened out.

Again the point is that for most of us, the choice is rarely so cut and dried. We are usually caught in a crossfire of motivations in which we must juggle the many objects of our concern. Certainly, a number of crucial substantive issues can be raised here. For example, consider the so-called dual career families. Since the number of such families is likely to grow in coming years, what are the patterns of involvement and accommodation for both parties and how do these patterns develop and change during the course of each career? Also, consider the impact of geographic mobility upon a career holder and the family. How do families deal with the rootlessness and continual detachment processes associated with such careers? Or, what are the effects of children on the career patterns of their parents? The educational aspirations that parents have for children may, for example, affect the economic requirements of the family and thereby determine some career decisions. Clearly, there are many such substantive issues to be raised regarding the family and the career.

Theoretically, the family issues spring from an interest in the effects that role demands in the family have on a person's career (and vice-versa). For instance, the age at which one marries, the characteristics of the spouse, the ages, number, and characteristics of children will all influence the way the career unfolds. To date, very little work has been done in this area.

Self

Durkheim (1933) in a most perceptive statement suggested that 'there are as many morals as there are callings'. Career studies of necessity must be concerned with the manner and degree to which one's perspectives, self-images, and rules of everyday conduct are shaped by a person's work career. Work in contemporary society, without doubt, provides a way for people to stabilize and give direction to their lives. It may provide, as I remarked in the Preface of this book, the single most important source of identity for individuals living in modern industrial societies. Yet, it is also clear that there are many careers that do not appear to offer much aid insofar as the construction of a positive self-image is concerned (and the number of these careers may well be growing). This suggests a matter of considerable substantive and theoretical importance that can and should guide our research activities. Namely, to what degree do people build their identity and organize their lives around the work career? Essentially, it is to this last question that all career studies must ultimately be oriented. For careers are, in the final analysis, human artifacts and it is therefore toward greater human understanding that their study must be aimed.

NOTES

1. Although the main concern in this book has been with organizational or occupational careers, to concentrate exclusively on careers defined solely in terms of the labor market would be misleading and inappropriate. Indeed, the so-called nonmarket careers—housewives (and the growing number of 'househusbands'), welfare recipients, the unemployed, criminals, volunteer workers, recreational enthusiasts, and so on—constitute distinctive ways of life organization and are therefore proper and worthy areas for career research. Certainly our theoretical work must allow for all kinds of careers. Importantly, some interesting work is going on in these areas. See, for example, Lopata (1971), Oakley (1975), Seidenberg (1975), Waldorf (1973), and Bernard (1974).

2. It is true that the notion of individual self-determination is rooted deeply in the Western ethos, but it is also interesting to note that 'good fortune' is not entirely ignored in our cultural success stories. The role of luck, serendipity, chance, happenstance and circumstance is captured well by the cliche, 'being in the right place at the right time'. Career studies can ill afford to ignore the fortuitous occasion as an event deserving of study. Perhaps it is well worth remembering that our deified bootstrapping hero, Horatio Alger, was not able to begin his legendary climb on the ladder of success until after he had found himself in the enviable position of being able to stop the rich man's runaway horse.

3. All career positions are simply resting places, for no matter how long a person remains in a particular office, there is an implicit, perhaps explicit, date at which the individual must vacate the position. Strauss (1959) noted that always there is a clause which is either hidden or openly acknowledged whereby a man may be desposed from his present status. For research purposes, therefore, we can look to individuals and ask 'what transition is the person going through today?' For a sound introduction to the general characteristics of all transition processes, see Glaser and Strauss (1971).

4. For a good discussion on the differences between substantive and formal theory, see Glaser and Strauss (1967). In brief, substantive theory develops around a concrete, empirical, and problematic concern, whereas formal theory develops around an analytic, conceptual, and general area of inquiry. The difference is not unlike those thought to characterize the basic and applied pursuits of the natural and physical scientist.

5. This 'mind-expanding' industry includes the various wings or cults associated with the so-called human potential movement such as Scientology, est, Silva Mind Control, Transcendental Meditation, ESP, Arica, and so on. Whether such movements acheive their objectives in terms of the 'total development of the human being' or in terms of a narcissistic 'worship of self' seems beside the point. Simply the fact that it is a growth industry in more ways than one should alert us to the apparent instability of traditional values and the apparent lure of new ones at this point in our cultural history.

6. Support for this perspective can be seen in some American universities where the study of leisure, play, and other nonwork activities of adult life has been legitimized through the recognition of new academic areas of concentration. Thus we see the emergence of new subdisciplines in psychology and sociology and, in certain cases, the invention of new disciplines (e.g. the Department of Leisure Studies at the University of Illinois).

7. Within this context, it is important to distinguish work and career. Many managers, for example, are quite careful to separate the two in the sense that their careers may involve a great variety of different kinds of work (Bailyn and Schein, 1975, 1976). In other careers, such as perhaps law or medicine, the distinction may be less crucial. Thus, the possibility arises that a person could be alienated in response to the work performed, but still engaged in a enriching or fulfilling career.

8. There is a noticeable similarity here with Merton's (1945) 'bureaucratic personality', Mill's (1959) 'cheerful robot', Whyte's (1956) 'organization man' and Howton's (1969) 'functionary'. In all of these cases, a strong critique of the slavish devotion to work pursuits was mustered, in part, on the basis of what certain careers can be seen to do to the people that follow them.

9. Several writers have remarked upon other sorts of cognitive orientations that apparently provoke tension among participants in organizations. For instance, Merton (1957) coined the twin concepts of locals and cosmopolitans to refer to two types of people distinguished by their attachment to the employing organization. Consider also Riesman's (1950) inner-directed and other-directed types which represent another possible base for distrust and misunderstanding between people. What is interesting here, however, is that each of these classifications, including Keen's, seem to operate within organizations in much the same manner and with very similar results.

10. If we take seriously the requirement to ground our organizational theories in terms of what organization's actually do, it is clear that one of the things they do is provide careers for the people that populate them. From this standpoint, it is unlikely that without the direct study of careers we will ever explain much about organizational functioning *per se*. For example, consider the difficulties involved in changing an organization without changing various career paths within the organization. In many respects, careers provide the mortar which cements our organizations together.

11. Developmental theorists stress the notion that persons undergo fixed stages of growth and maturation which span the life cycle. These stages of development are tied to biological and/or cultural universals and are related to the key psychological problems all individuals face at certain times in their lives—crisis points. Thus, passing through any particular stage requires the individual to face and cope with a new set of emotional problems. See, for example, the recent work of Levinson and coworkers (1974), Gould (1975) and the recent, altogether fascinating, work by Sheehy (1976).

12. In terms of helping organizations discover ways of improving the quality of work life, Bailyn and Schein (1976) make use of a developmental perspective. For example, they argue that during the early career phases, organizations must find ways of providing employees with meaningful opportunities to learn, whereas, during the late phases of a career, organizations need to find ways to allow employees to teach or contribute the wisdom they have gained through experience to others. In other words, Bailyn

and Schein argue that work careers must be handled in ways that respect and compliment the stages of general identity development. See also Schein (1971).

13. For a discussion of the material upon which this hypothetical police career shape was derived, see Van Maanen (1974a).

14. For many workers, the entry level job taken by an individual represents a terminal career node as well. Coal workers, garbage collectors, secretaries, janitors, and, to a somewhat lesser degree, schoolteachers, policemen, and social workers enter jobs from which hierarchical advancement is not the norm. To a degree, then, these jobs represent very flat careers. Yet, from the individual's standpoint, there almost always exists the possibility of achieving a better assignment, freedom from close supervision, higher pay with seniority, job tenure, and perhaps increasing recognition for a job well done. There is also a recognition of a sort of 'collective career' on the part of people holding these jobs. That is, the career-related hopes and aspirations of workers tend to be pinned to the outcomes of collective bargaining. While for some occupations this is a recent phenomena, the notion of a 'collective career' has roots planted deeply in the history of the labor movement.

15. One is reminded here of Veblen's (1953) notion of 'trained incapacity' as well as the less serious, but perhaps all too accurate, idea embodied in the 'Peter Principle' [(i.e. people in organizations tend to rise to their level of incompetence—Peter (1972)].

16. This conception of career cycles suggests that individual energies and interests flow back and forth between work and family demands in discernible, regular rhythms. Of course, those who marry, for example, follow different patterns from those who do not. But the point here is simply that each time a change occurs in a person's work or family situation, revisions of the individual's internal and external career perhaps follow.

17. The career cube presented here is a simplified version of the one developed by Van Maanen and Schein (1975).

18. This dimension of the cube involves perhaps the most intricate considerations. In this paper, I have included only the categories which were discussed in this book. Certainly, finer-grained distinctions are possible. For instance, roles, tasks, and settings can themselves be thought to vary according to observable differences in the time it takes a person to qualify, the arduousness of the preparation, the complexity of the skills required, the knowledge necessary to maintain performance, the stages of socialization associated with entrance and confirmation, and so on.

19. I am aware that I am talking only about the nuclear family in industrialized societies— and then only of the high economic strata of such societies. A full exposition would have to include the role of other famial institutions—whether they be families of origin, precreation, and/or habitat.

20. This point is deserving of emphasis. I am not arguing that the career cube represents the sort of theoretical construction that can be filled eventually with data. Indeed not. The cube is merely an abstraction—a heuristic—useful for conceptualizing and classifying the various interactive concerns raised by the study of careers.

21. See Terkel (1974). An argument regarding the career satisfactions associated with what might be seen as modern equivalents of the so-called 'free-trades' is made in LeMasters' (1975) sensitive portrait of 'blue-collar aristocrats'. In brief, LeMasters' attributes the attractiveness of such occupations as the contraction trades, certain public services (particularly police and fire), and many transportation jobs to reside primarily in the following properties: outside work, loose supervision, immediate comprehensible results, male peer group, responsibility for expensive equipment, unlikely probability of obsolescence, strong union, and, with overtime pay, earnings that are approximately twice as much as even the best paid schoolteacher.

22. Several examples are useful here. Take the tenured science professor at a famous university who, externally, has all the trappings of success. But, upon inspection, this professor may well feel quite unsuccessful if he has failed to attract the attention

and respect of academic peers with a novel and significant discovery. Or, consider the standards of success utilized by public defenders, who, according to Platt and Pollack (1974), do not think themselves as successful (regardless of courtroom record or position in the office hierarchy) unless they have had at least one offer from a prestigious private law firm.

23. In this regard, it is interesting to note the sorts of ghoulish terms employed in this society to describe the institutions that specialize in assisting people to change jobs — 'meat markets', 'body snatchers', 'head hunters', 'flesh peddlers', 'warm body shops', and so on. Simply the pervasiveness of these terms suggests that the profit motive is not necessarily an optimal guide when it comes to people processing. A most interesting discussion of job switching is presented from this perspective by Granovetter (1974).

Bibliography

Albrow, M., 'The study of organizations—Objectivity or bias?' In J. Gould (Ed.) *Penguin Social Sciences Survey*, Penguin, London, 1968, pp. 146–167.

Altemeyer, L., Education in the Arts and Sciences, Unpublished doctoral dissertation, Carnegie-Mellon University, 1966.

Bailyn, L., 'Career and family orientations of husbands and wives in relation to marital happiness,' *Human Relations*, **23**, 97–113 (1970).

Bailyn, L., 'Family constraints on women's work', *Annals of the New York Academy of Sciences*, **208**, 82–90 (1973).

Bailyn, L., and Schein, E. H., 'Where are they now and how are they doing?' *Technology Review*, **74**, 7–11 (1972).

Bailyn, L., and Schein, E. H., 'Work involvement in technically based careers: A study of M.I.T. alumni at mid-career,' Unpublished manuscript, 1975.

Bailyn, L., and Schein, E. H., 'Life/Career considerations as indicators of quality of employment,' in A. D. Biderman and T. F. Drury (Eds.), *Measuring Work Quality for Social Reporting*, Sage, Beverls Hills, Calif., 1976, pp. 151–168.

Becker, H. S., and Strauss, A., 'Careers, personality and adult socialization,' *American Journal of Sociology*, **62**, 253–263 (1956).

Becker, H. S., Greer, B., Hughes, E. C., and Strauss, A., *Boys in White: Student Culture in Medical School*, University of Chicago Press, Chicago, 1961.

Becker, H. S., 'Personal change in adult life,' *Sociometry*, **27**, 40–53 (1964).

Berger, P., 'Some general observations on the problem of work,' in P. Berger (Ed.) *The Human Shape of Work*, Henry Regnery, Chicago, 1964, pp. 211–291.

Berlew, D. E., and Hall, D. T., 'The socialization of managers: Effects of expectations on performance,' *Administrative Science Quarterly*, **11**, 207–223 (1966).

Bernard, J., 'The housewife: Between two worlds,' in P. L. Stewart and M. G. Cantor (Eds.), *Varieties of Work Experience*, Halstead, New York, 1974, pp. 49–66.

Bittner, E., 'The concept of organization,' *Social Research*, **32**, 239–255 (1965).

Blau, P. M., *The Dynamics of Bureaucracy*, University of Chicago Press, Chicago, 1955.

Blau, P. and Schoenherr, R. A., *The Structure of Organizations*, Basic, New York, 1971.

Blauner, R., *Alienation and Freedom*, University of Chicago Press, Chicago, 1964.

Brim, O. G., 'Socialization through the life cycle', in O. G. Brim and S. Wheeler (Eds.), *Socialization after Childhood*, Wiley, New York, 1966, pp. 1–52.

Bruner, J. A., Goodnow, J. J., and Austin, G. A., *A Study of Thinking*, Wiley, New York, 1956.

Bruner, J. A., *The Process of Education*, Vintage, New York, 1960.

Bruner, J. A., *Essays for the Left Hand*, Antheneum, New York, 1966.

Chinoy, E., *Automobile Workers and the American Dream*, Random House, New York, 1955.

Cicourel, A., *The Social Organization of Juvenile Justice*, Wiley, New York, 1968.

Cicourel, A., 'Basic and normative rules in the negotiation of status and role,' in H. P. Dreitzel (Ed.) *Recent Sociology # 2*, MacMillan, New York, 1970, pp. 4–45.

Clas, P. N., 'The relationship of psychological differentiation to client behavior in vocational choice counselling,' Unpublished doctoral dissertation, University of Michigan, 1971.

182

Cohen, S., and Taylor, L., *Psychological Survival: The Experience of Long-term Imprisonment*, Penguin, Harmondsworth, 1972.

Cooley, C. H., *Human Nature and the Social Order*, Scribner and Sons, New York, 1922.

Crozier, M., *The Bureaucratic Phenomenon*, University of Chicago Press, Chicago, 1964.

Cullen, J. F., Tharpes, C. R., and Kidera, G. J., 'Perceptual style differences between airline pilots and engineers,' *Aerospace Medicine*, **4**, 407–408 (1969).

Dalton, M., *Men who Manage: Fusions of Feelings and Theory in Administration*, Wiley, New York, 1959.

Davis, J. A., *Undergraduate Career Decisions*, Aldine, Chicago, 1965.

Department of Health, Education and Welfare Task Force, *Work in America*, M.I.T. Press, Cambridge, Ma., 1973.

Doob, L., *Patterning of Time*, Yale University Press, New Haven, Conn., 1971.

Dubin, R., 'Industrial workers' worlds: A study of the 'central life interests' of industrial workers,' *Social Problems*, **3**, 131–142 (1956).

Durkheim, E., *The Division of Labor in Society* (Trans. by G. Simpson), MacMillan, New York, 1933.

Durkheim, E., *Rules of the Sociological Method* (Trans. by S. Solovay and J. Mueller), Free Press, New York, 1964.

Emerson, J., 'Behavior in private places: Sustaining definitions of reality in gynaecological examinations', in H. Dreitzel (Ed.), *Recent Sociology* 2, MacMillan, New York, 1970a, pp. 73–100.

Emerson, J., 'Nothing unusual is happening', in T. Shibutani (Ed.), *Human Nature and Collective Behavior*, Transaction Books, New Brunswick, New Jersey, 1970b, pp. 208–222.

Erickson, E. H., *Childhood and Society*, Norton, New York, 1950.

Erickson, E. H., 'Identity and the life cycle,' *Psychological Issues*, **1**, 1–171 (1959).

Evans, P. A. L., 'The price of success: Accommodation to conflicting needs in managerial careers,' Unpublished doctoral dissertation, M.I.T., 1974.

Faulkner, R. R., 'Coming of age in organizations: A comparative study of career contingencies and adult socialization,' *Sociology of Work and Occupations*, **1**, 131–173 (1974).

Feldman, K., and Newcombe, T., *The Impact of College on Students*, Vols. I and II, Jossey-Bass, New York, 1969.

Filmer, P., Phillipson, M., and Silverman, D., *New Directions in Sociological Theory*, M.I.T. Press, Cambridge, Ma., 1972.

Flavell, J., *The Developmental Psychology of Jean Piaget*, Van Nostrand, New York, 1963.

Fogarty, M. P., Rapoport, R., and Rapoport, R. N., *Sex, Career and Family*, Allen and Unwin, London, 1970.

Ford, R. N., *Motivation through Work Itself*, American Management Association, New York, 1969.

Fox, A., *A Sociology of Work in Industry*, Collier-MacMillan, New York, 1971.

Frazier, R., *Work*, Penguin, Middlesex, England, 1968.

Garfinkel, H., 'Conditions of successful degradation ceremonies,' *American Journal of Sociology*, **61**, 420–424 (1956).

Garfinkel, H., *Studies in Ethnomethodology*, Prentice-Hall, New York, 1967.

Gerstl, J. E., and Hutton, S. P., *Engineers: The Anatomy of a Profession*, Tavistock Institute, London, 1966.

Getchell, E., 'Factors affecting employee loyalty,' Unpublished Master's thesis, M.I.T., 1975.

Ginzberg, E., Ginsburg, S. W., Axelard, S., and Herma, J. L., *Occupational Choice: An Approach to a General Theory*, Columbia University Press, New York, 1951.

Glaser, B. G., *Organizational Scientists: Their Professional Careers*, Bobbs-Merrill, New York, 1964.

Glaser, B. G. (Ed.), *Organizational Careers: A Sourcebook for Theory*, Aldine, Chicago, 1968.

Glaser, B. G., *Work, Careers, and Professionalization*, Aldine, Chicago, 1975.

Glaser, B. G., and Strauss, A., 'Awareness contexts and social interaction,' *American Sociological Review*, **29**, 669–679 (1964).

Glaser, B. G., and Strauss, A., *The Discovery of Grounded Theory*, Aldine, Chicago, 1967.

Glaser, B. G., and Strauss, A., *Status Passage: A Formal Theory*, Aldine, Chicago, 1971.

Glaser, E. M., *Improving the Quality of Worklife . . . And in the Process Improving Productivity*, Human Interaction Research Institute, Los Angeles, 1975.

Goffman, E., *The Presentation of Self in Everyday Life*, Doubleday, New York, 1959.

Goffman, E., *Encounters*, Bobbs-Merrill, Indianapolis, 1961.

Goffman, E., *Interaction Ritual*, Aldine, Chicago, 1967.

Goldstein, K., and Scheerer, M., 'Abstract and concrete behavior: An experimental study with special tests,' *Psychological Monographs*, **53**, 239 (1941).

Goode, W. J., 'Community within a community: The professions,' *American Sociological Review*, **22**, 194–200 (1957).

Goode, W. J., 'The theoretical limits of professionalism,' in A. Etzioni (Ed.), *The Semi-professions and their Organization*, Free Press, New York, 1969, pp. 226–314.

Gould, P., and White, R., *Mental Maps*, Penguin, Harmondsworth, 1974.

Gould, R., 'Adult life stages: Growth toward self-tolerance,' *Psychology Today*, February, 1975, 35–38.

Gouldner, A., 'Cosmopolitans and locals: Toward an analysis of latent social roles I,' *Administrative Science Quarterly*, **2**, 281–306 (1957).

Gouldner, F. H., 'Demotion in industrial management,' *American Sociological Review*, **30**, 714–724 (1965).

Granovetter, M. S., *Getting a Job: A Study of Contacts and Careers*, Harvard University Press, Cambridge, Ma., 1974.

Grayson, C. J., 'Management science and business practice,' *Harvard Business Review*, **51**, 4, 41–53 (1973).

Growchow, J., 'Cognitive style as a factor in the design of interactive decision-support systems,' Unpublished doctoral dissertation, M.I.T., 1973.

Hackman, J. R., and Lawler, E. E., 'Employee reactions to job characteristics,' *Journal of Applied Psychology*, **55**, 259–286 (1971).

Hackman, J. R., and Oldham, G. R., 'Development of the job diagnostic survey,' *Journal of Applied Psychology*, **60**, 159–170 (1975).

Hackman, J. R., Weiss, J. A., and Brousseau, K. R., 'On the coming demise of job enrichment (Technical Report No. 5),' New Haven, Conn. Yale University, Department of Administrative Sciences, 1974.

Hall, D. T., and Mansfield, R., 'Relationships of age and seniority with career variables of engineers and scientists,' *Journal of Applied Psychology*, **60**, 201–210 (1975).

Hall, D. T., and Nougaim, K. E., 'An examination of Maslow's need hierarchy in an organizational setting,' *Organizational Behavior and Human Performance*, **3**, 12–35 (1968).

Harvey, O. J., Hunt, D., and Schroder, H., *Conceptual Systems and Personality Organization*, Wiley, New York, 1961.

Heller, J., *Something Happened*, Knopf, New York, 1974.

Henry, J., *Culture Against Man*, Random House, New York, 1963.

Herzberg, F., *Work and the Nature of Man*, World, Cleveland, 1966.

Hewitt, J. W., and Stokes, R., 'Disclaimers,' *American Sociological Review*, **40**, 1, 1–11 (1975).

Holland, J. L., *The Psychology of Vocational Choice: A Theory of Personality Types and Environmental Models*, Ginn, London, 1966.

Holland, J. L., *Making Vocational Choices: A Theory of Careers*, Prentice-Hall, Englewood Cliffs, New Jersey, 1973.

Homans, G. C., *The Human Group*, Brace and World, New York, Harcourt, 1950.

Howton, F. W., *Functionaries*, Quadrangle, Chicago, 1969.

Hudson, L., *Contrary Imaginations*, Penguin, Harmondsworth, 1966.

Hughes, E. C., *Men and their Work*, Free Press, Glencoe, Ill., 1958.

Hunt, D. E., *Matching Models in Education: The Coordination of Teaching Methods with Students Characteristics*, Ontario Institute for studies in education, Toronto, 1971.

Husserl, E., 'Phenomenology,' in *Encyclopedia Britannica*, 14th ed., Vol. 17, Chicago, 1946, pp. 699–702.

Ichheiser, G., 'Misunderstandings in human relations,' *American Journal of Sociology*, **54**, 634–637 (1949).

Institute of Electrical and Electronics Engineers Manpower Report, R. W. Bolz (Ed.), *The E/E at Mid-career: Prospects and Problems*, Institute of Electrical and Electronics Engineers, New York, 1975.

Irwin, J., *The Felon*, Prentice-Hall, Englewood Cliffs, New Jersey, 1970.

Jaffe, A. J., *The Middle Years: Neither too Young nor Old*, National Council on Aging, Washington D. C., 1971.

James, W., *Psychology: The Briefer Course*, Holt, Rinehart and Winston, New York, 1892.

James, W., *The Principles of Psychology*, Dover, New York, 1950.

Jacques, E., 'Death and the mid-life crisis,' *International Journal of Psychoanalysis*, **46**, 502–514 (1965).

Jenkins, D., *Job Power*, Penguin Books, Baltimore, 1974.

Jung, C. G., *Psychological Types*, Pantheon, London, 1923.

Kagan, J., Rosman, B. L., Day, D., Alpert, J., and Hillips, W., 'Information processing in the child: Significance of analytic and reflective attitudes,' *Psychological Monographs*, **78**, 1 (1964).

Kaplan, S., 'Cognitive maps in perception and thought,' in R. M. Downs and D. Stea (Eds.), *Cognitive Mapping: Images of Spatial Environment*, Aldine, Chicago, 1972, pp. 131–154.

Katz, E., and Lazardsfeld, P. F., *Personal Influence*, Free Press, Glencoe, Ill., 1955.

Katz, R., and Van Maanen, J., 'The loci of satisfaction: Job, interaction and policy,' Sloan School of Management Working Paper, 741–774, M.I.T., 1974.

Keen, P. G. W., 'The implications of cognitive style for individual decision-making,' Unpublished doctoral dissertation, Harvard University, 1973.

Keen, P. G. W., 'Cognitive style and the problem-solving process: An experiment,' Sloan School of Management Working Paper, 700–74, M.I.T., 1974.

Keen, P. G. W., 'A clinical approach to implementation,' Sloan School of Management Working Paper, 780–75, M.I.T., 1975.

Kelley, G., *The Psychology of Personal Constructs*, Vol. I, Norton, New York, 1963.

Kelley, H. H., 'Two functions of reference groups,' in G. F. Swanson, T. M. Newcombe, and E. L. Hartley (Eds.), *Readings in Social Psychology*, Holt, Rinehart and Winston, New York, 1952, pp. 410–414.

Klineberg, S., and Cottle, T. J., *The Present of Things Past*, Little-Brown, Boston, 1973.

Kolb, D. A., 'Individual learning styles and the learning process,' Sloan School of Management Working Paper, 535–71, M.I.T., 1971.

Kolb, D. A., 'On management add the learning process,' Sloan School of Management Working Paper, 652–73, M.I.T., 1973a.

Kolb, D. A., 'Toward a typology of learning styles and learning environments: An investigation of the impact of learning styles and discipline demands on the academic performance, social adaptation and career choices of M.I.T. Seniors,' Sloan School of Management Working Paper, 688–73, M.I.T., 1973b.

Kolb, D. A., and Fry, R., 'Toward an applied theory of experiential learning,' in C. Cooper (Ed.), *Theories of Group Processes*, Wiley International, London, 1975, pp. 33–57.

185

Kolb, D. A., Rubin, I., and McIntyre, J., *Organizational Psychology: An Experiential Approach*, Prentice-Hall, Englewood Cliffs, New Jersey, 1971.
Kolb, D. A., Rubin, I., and Schein, E. H., 'The M.I.T. Freshmen Integration Research Project: A summary report,' Unpublished paper, M.I.T., 1972.
Kopelman, R., Dalton, G., and Thompson, P., 'The distinguishing characteristics of high, middle and low performing engineers: A study of four age groups. Unpublished manuscript,' Graduate School of Business, Harvard University, August, 1971.
Kris, E., *Selected papers of Ernst Kris*, Yale University Press, New Haven, Conn., 1975.
Kuhn, T. S., 'The essential tension: Tradition and innovation in scientific research,' in C. W. Taylor and F. Barron (Eds.), *Scientific Creativity: Its Recognition and Development*, Wiley, New York, pp. 235–261, 1963.
Lancashire, R. D., 'Occupational choice theory and occupational guidance practice,' in P. Warr (Ed.), *Psychology at Work*, Penguin, Harmondsworth, 1971, pp. 162–181.
Larson, K., *The Workers*, Bantam, New York, 1971.
Lawler, E. E., 'Improving the quality of work life: Reward systems,' in J. R. Hackman and L. Suttle (Eds.), *Improving Life at Work: Behavioral Science Perspectives*, Department of Labor Monograph Series # 4, Washington D. C., 1975.
Leavitt, H. J., *Managerial Psychology*, 3rd University of Chicago Press, Chicago, 1972.
LeJunne, P., 'Career paths: A study of Sloan School of Management Alumni Sample,' Unpublished doctoral dissertation, M.I.T., 1973.
LeMasters, E. E., *Blue-collar Aristocrats*, University of Wisconsin Press, Modison, Wisconsin, 1975.
Levinson, D. J., Darrow, C. M., Klein, E. B., Levinson, M. H., and McKee, B., 'The psychological development of men in early adulthood and the mid-life transition,' in D. F. Ricks, A. Thomas and N. Roff (Eds.), *Life History Research in Psychopathology*, Vol. 3, University of Minnesota Press, Minneapollis, Minn., 1974.
Levy, S., 'Field-independence, field-dependence and occupational interests,' Unpublished Master's thesis, Cornell University, 1969.
Lewin, K., *The Conceptual Representation and Measurement of Psychological Force*, Duke University Press, Durham, North Carolina, 1938.
Likert, R., *New Patterns of Management*, McGraw-Hill, New York, 1961.
Locke, E. A., 'The relationship of task success to task liking and satisfaction,' *Journal of Applied Psychology*, **41**, 141–148 (1965).
Lopata, H. Z., *Occupation: Housewife*, Oxford University Press, New York, 1971.
Luthans, F., and Rief, W. E., 'Job enrichment: Long on theory, short on practice,' *Organizational Dynamics*, **2**, 30–43 (1974).
Lyman, L. M., and Scott, M. B., *A Sociology of the Absurd*, Meredith, New York, 1970.
Lynch, K., *The Image of the City*, M.I.T. Press, Cambridge, Ma., 1960.
Madrazo, A., 'Personal and environmental factors affecting engineer career development,' Unpublished Master's thesis, M.I.T., 1974.
Mannerick, L. A., 'Client typologies: A method for coping with conflict in the service worker–client relationship.' *Sociology of Work and Occupations*, **1**, 396–418 (1974).
Mannheim, K., 'On the interpretation of *Weltanschauung*.' in P. Keeskemeti (trans. and Ed.), *Essays on the Sociology of Knowledge*, Oxford University Press, New York, 1952, pp. 53–63.
Manning, P. K., 'Talking and becoming: A view of organizational socialization,' in J. D. Douglas (Ed.), *Understanding Everyday Life*, Aldine, Chicago, 1970, 239–256.
Maslow, A. H., *Motivation and personality*, Harper, New York, 1954.
Mayer, M., *The Bankers*, Weybright and Talley, New York, 1974.
McClelland, D. C., 'On the psychodynamics of creative physical scientists,' in H. E. Gruber, G. Terreu, and M. Wertheimer (Eds.), *Contemporary Approaches to Creative Thinking*, Atherton, New York, 1962, pp. 142–158.
McHugh, P., *Defining the Situation: The Organization of Meaning in Social Interaction*, Bobbs-Merrill, Indianapolis, 1968.

McKenney, J. L., and Keen, P. G. W., 'How managers minds work,' *Harvard Business Review*, **52**, 3, 79–90 (1974).

Mead, G. H., 'The social self,' *Journal of Philosophy, Psychology and Scientific Methods*, **10**, 375–380 (1913).

Mead, G. H., *Mind, Self and Society*, C. W. Morris (Ed.), University of Chicago Press, Chicago, 1930.

Mead, G. H., *The Philosophy of the Present*, Open Court, Chicago, 1932.

Merton, R. K., 'Bureaucratic structure and personality,' *Social Forces*, **23**, 405–415 (1945).

Merton, R. K., *Social Theory and Social Structure*, Free Press, New York, 1957.

Messinger, S. L., Sampson, H., and Towne, R. D., 'Life as theatre: Some notes on the dramaturgic approach to social reality,' *Sociometry*, **25**, 98–110 (1962).

Mills, C. W., *The Sociological Imagination*, Grove Press, New York, 1959.

Mitchell, T. R., and Biglan, A., 'Instrumentality theories: Current uses in psychology,' *Psychological Bulletin*, **76**, 147–173 (1971).

Mitroff, I. J., *The Subjective Side of Science: A Philosophical Inquiry into the Psychology of the Apollo Moon Scientists*, Elsevier, New York, 1975.

Mouzelis, N. P., *Organization and Bureaucracy*, Routledge and Kegan Paul, London, 1967.

Myers, I. B., *The Myers–Briggs Type Indicator*, Educational Testing Service, Princeton, New Jersey, 1962.

Nisbet, R., *The Sociological Tradition*, Heinemann, London, 1967.

Oakley, A., *The Sociology of Housework*, Pantheon, New York, 1975.

Olson, J., *The Girls in the Office*, Simon and Schuster, New York, 1972.

Olson, J., *Sweet Street*, Simon and Schuster, New York, 1974.

Parsons, T., *The Social System*, Free Press, New York, 1951.

Perrow, C., *Complex Organizations: A Critical Essay*, Scott, Foreman and Co., New York, 1972.

Perucci, R., and Gerstl, J. E., *Profession without Community: Engineers in American Society*, Random House, New York, 1969.

Peter, L. J., *The Peter Principle*, Morrow, New York, 1972.

Piaget, J., *The Child's Conception of Time* (trans. by A. J. Pomerans), Routledge and Kegan Paul, London, 1969.

Platt, A., and Pollock, R., 'Channeling lawyers: The careers of public defenders,' in H. Jacob (Ed.), *The Potential for Reform of Criminal Justice*, Sage, Beverly Hills, Calif., 1974, pp. 235–262.

Plovnick, M. S., 'A cognitive theory of occupational role,' Sloan School of Management Working Paper, 604–72, M.I.T., 1971.

Plovnick, M. S., 'Social awareness and role innovation in engineers,' Sloan School of Management Working Paper, 604–72, M.I.T., 1972.

Plovnick, M. S., 'Individual learning styles and the process of career choices in medical students,' Unpublished doctoral dissertation, M.I.T., 1974.

Plovnick, M. S., 'Primary care career choices and medical student learning styles,' *Journal of Medical Education*, **50**, 849–855 (1975).

Polsky, N., *Hustlers, Beats and Others*, Aldine, Chicago, 1967.

Porter, L. W., 'A study of perceived need satisfaction in bottom and middle management jobs,' *Journal of Applied Psychology*, **45**, 1–10 (1961).

Porter, L. W., and Lawler, E. E., *Managerial Attitudes and Performance*, Richard D. Irwin, Homewood, Ill., 1968.

Porter, L. W., Lawler, E. E., and Hackman, J. R., *Behavior in Organizations*, McGraw-Hill, New York, 1974.

Rapoport, R., and Rapoport, R. N., 'The dual career family: A variant pattern and social change,' *Human Relations*, **22**, 3–30 (1969).

Riesman, D., *The Lonely Crowd*, University Press, New Haven, Conn., 1950.

Ritti, R. R., *The Engineer in the Industrial Corporation*, Columbia University Press, New York, 1971.

Roe, A., 'Early determinants of vocational choice,' *Journal of Couseling Psychology*, **4**, 212–217 (1957).

Roe, A., *The Psychology of Occupations*, Wiley, New York, 1956.

Rosenthal, R., *Experimental Effects in Behavioral Research*, Appleton-Century-Crofts, New York, 1967.

Roth, J. A., *Timetables: Structuring the Passage of Time in Hospital Treatment and other Careers*, Bobbs-Merrill, Indianapolis, 1963.

Roy, D., 'Banana time: Job satisfaction and informal interaction,' *Human Organizations*, **18**, 158–169 (1960).

Rubin, I., 'Managing the learning Process,' Sloan School of Management Working Paper, 460–70, M.I.T., 1970.

Salaman, G., *Community and Occupation: An Exploration of Work/Leisure Relationships*, Cambridge University Press, Cambridge, England, 1974.

Salaman, G., and Thompson, K., *People and Organizations*, Longman, London, 1973.

Scheff, T. J., 'Toward a sociological model of consensus,' *American Sociological Review*, **32**, 32–46 (1967).

Schein, E. H., 'Management development as a process of influence,' *Industrial Management Review*, **2**, 59–77 (1961).

Schein, E. H., 'Problems of the first year at work,' Report of the first career panel reunion. Sloan School of Management Working Paper, 03–36, M.I.T., 1962.

Schein, E. H., 'Organizational socialization in the early career of industrial managers,' Sloan School of Management Working Paper, 39–63, M.I.T., 1963.

Schein, E. H., 'How to break in the college graduate,' *Harvard Business Review*, **42**, 68–76 (1964).

Schein, E. H., 'Organizational socialization,' *Industrial Management Review*, **2**, 37–45 (1968).

Schein, E. H., *Organizational Psychology*, (2nd ed.), Prentice Hall, Englewood Cliffs, New Jersey, 1970.

Schein, E. H., 'The individual, the organization and the career: A conceptual scheme,' *Journal of Applied Behavioral Science*, **7**, 401–426 (1971).

Schein, E. H., 'How career anchors hold executives to their career paths,' *Personnel*, **52**, May–June, 11–24 (1975).

Schutz, A., *On Phenomenology and Social Relations*, University of Chicago Press, Chicago, 1970.

Schutz, A., *Collected Papers I: The Problem of Social Reality*, Nijhoff, The Hague, 1962.

Seeman, M., 'On the meaning of alienation,' *American Sociological Review*, **24**, 783–791 (1959).

Seidenberg, R., *Corporate Wives—Corporate Casualties?* Doubleday, New York, 1975.

Sheehy, G., *Hustling*, Dell, New York, 1974a.

Sheehy, G., 'Catch 30 and other predictable crises of growing up adult,' *New York*, February, 1974b, pp. 30–44.

Sheehy, G., *Passages: Predictable Crises of Adult Life*, E. P. Dutton, New York, 1976.

Sheppard, H. L., and Herrick, N., *Where Have all the Robots Gone?* Free Press, New York, 1972.

Shibutani, T., 'Reference groups and social control,' in A. M. Rose (Ed.), *Human Behavior and Social Processes*, Houghton Nifflin, Boston, 1962, pp. 127–139.

Silverman, D., 'Some neglected questions about social reality,' in P. Filmer, M. Phillipson and D. Silverman (Eds.), *New Directions in Sociological Research*, M.I.T., Press, Cambridge, Ma., 1972, pp. 165–182.

Silverman, D., *The Theory of Organizations*, Basic, New York, 1971.

Simmel, G., *The Sociology of Georg Simmel* (trans. by K. H. Wolff), Free Press, New York, 1950.

Singer, J., 'The importance of daydreaming,' *Psychology Today*, **1**, 11, 18–26 (1968).

Slater, P., *The Pursuit of Loneliness: American Culture at the Breaking Point*, Beacon, Boston, 1970.

Sofer, C., *Men in Mid-career*, Cambridge University Press, Cambridge, England, 1970.

Sorokin, P., and Merton, R. K., 'Social time: A methodology and functional analysis,' *American Journal of Sociology*, **43**, 614–629 (1937).

Stabell, C., The impact of a conversational computer system on human problem solving behavior, Unpublished paper, M.I.T., 1973.

Strasmore, M., 'The strategic function re-evaluated from the organizational development perspective,' Unpublished Master's thesis, M.I.T., 1973.

Strauss, A., *Mirrors and Masks: The Search for Identity*, Free Press, Glencoe, Ill., 1959.

Strauss, A., and Martin, N. H., 'Patterns of mobility within industrial organizations,' *Journal of Business*, **29**, 101–110 (1956).

Sudnow, D., 'Normal crimes: Sociological features of the penal code in a public defender office,' *Social Problems*, **12**, 255–272 (1965).

Super, D. E., *The Psychology of Careers*, and Row, New York, 1957.

Super, D. E., Starishevsky, R., Matlin, N., and Jordan, J. P., *Career Development: Self-concept Theory*, Princeton College Entrance Examination Board, Princeton, New Jersey, 1963.

Sykes, G., *The Society of Captives: A Study of a Maximum Security Prison*, Princeton University Press, Princeton, New Jersey, 1958.

Tarnowieski, D., *The Changing Success Ethic: An AMA Survey Report*, Anacom, New York, 1973.

Terkel, S., *Working*, Pantheon, New York, 1974.

Terkel, S., *Division Street: America*, Random House, New York, 1968.

The status of women in Sweden: Report to the United Nations. Reprinted in E. Dahlstrom (Ed.), *The Changing Roles of Men and Women*, Beacon Press, Boston, 1971, pp. 209–302.

Thomas, W. I., *The Unadjusted Girl*, Little Brown, Boston, 1931.

Tiedman, D. V., and O'Hara, R. P., *Career Development: Choice and Adjustment*, Princeton College Entrance Examination Board, Princeton, New Jersey, 1963.

Tolman, E. C., 'Cognitive maps in rats and men,' *Psychological Review*, **55**, 183–208 (1948).

Tönnies, F., *Community and Association*, Routledge and Kegan Paul, London 1955.

Torrealba, D., 'Convergent and divergent learning styles,' Unpublished Master's thesis, M.I.T., 1972.

Turner, R., 'Some formal properties of therapy talk,' in D. Sudnow (Ed.), *Studies in Social Interaction*, Free Press, New York, 1972, pp. 367–396.

Vaillant, G. B., and McArthur, C. C., 'Natural history of male psychological health: The adult life cycle from 18–50,' *Seminars in Psychiatry*, **4**, 417–429 (1972).

Van Maanen, J., 'Observations on the making of policemen,' *Human Organizations*, **32**, 407–418 (1973).

Van Maanen, J., 'Working the streets: A developmental view of police behavior,' in H. Jacob (Ed.), *The Potential for Reform of Criminal Justice*, Sage, Beverly Hills, Calif., 1974a, pp. 53–130.

Van Maanen, J., 'The asshole: Notes on the police typification of moral character', Unpublished paper, Massachusetts Institute of Technology, December, 1974b.

Van Maanen, J., 'Police socialization,' *Administrative Science Quarterly*, **20**, 207–228 (1975).

Van Maanen, J., 'Breaking-In: Socialization to work,' in R. Dubin (Ed.), *Handbook of Work, Organization and Society*, Rand McNalley, Chicago, 1976, pp. 67–130.

Van Maanen, J., and Katz, R., *Work in the Public Sector*, Washington D. C.: National Training in Development Service Technical Report, Washington D. C., 1974.

Van Maanen, J., and Schein, E. H., 'Improving the quality of work life: Career Development,' in J. R. Hackman and L. Suttle (Eds.), *Improving Life at Work: Behavioral*

Science Perspectives, Washington D. C., Department of Labor Monograph Series # 2, 1975.

Veblan, T., *The Theory of the Leisure Class: An Economic Study of Institutions*, New American Library, New York, 1953 (first published in 1899).

Vollmer, H. M., and Mills, D. J. (Eds.), *Professionalization*, Prentice Hall, Englewood Cliffs, New Jersey, 1966.

Vroom, V. H., *Work and Motivation*, Wiley, New York, 1964.

Waldorf, D., *Careers in Dope*, Spectrum, New York, 1973.

Walker, C. R., and Guest, R. A., *Man on the Assembly Line*, Harvard University Press, Cambridge, Mass., 1952.

Walsh, J. L., Police career styles and counting coups on the beat: Sources of police incivity. Paper presented at the American Sociological Association, San Francisco, Fall, 1975.

Walton, R. D., 'How to counter alienation in the plant,' *Harvard Business Review*, **50**, 70–81 (1972).

Weber, M., *The Theory of Social and Economic Organization* (trans. by A. D. Henderson and T. Parsons), Free Press, New York, 1947.

Weinberg, M., 'Becoming a nudist,' in E. Rubington and M. Weinberg (Eds.), *Deviance: The Interactionist Perspective*, MacMillan, New York, 1968, pp. 240–251.

Wheeler, S., 'The structure of formally organized socialization settings,' in O. G. Brim and S. Wheeler (Eds.), *Socialization through the Life Cycle*, Wiley, New York, 1966, pp. 53–116.

Whyte, W. H., *The Organization Man*, Simon and Schuster, New York, 1956.

Whyte, W. H., 'The wife problem,' in R. F. Winch and L. W. Goodman (Eds.), *Selected Studies in Marriage and the Family*, Holt, Rinehart and Winston, New York, 1968, pp. 175–191.

Wilensky, H. L., 'The professionalization of everyone?' *American Journal of Sociology*, **70**, 137–158 (1964).

Witkin, H. A., Dyk, R., Patterson, H., Goodenough, D., and Karp, S., *Psychological Differentiation*, Wiley, New York, 1962.

Witkin, H. A., 'The role of cognitive style in academic performance and in teacher–student relationships,' *Research Bulletin* 73–11, Educational Testing Service, Princeton, New Jersey, 1973.

Witkin, H. A., Lewis, H. B., Hertzman, M., Machover, K., Meissner, P. B., and Wagner, S., *Personality through Perception*, Wiley, New York, 1956.

Wittgenstein, L., *The Blue and Brown Books*, New York: Harper and Row, New York, 1965.

Yankelovich, D., *The Changing Values on Campus: Political and Personal Attitudes of Today's College Students*, Pocket Books, New York, 1972.

Zangwill, O. L., 'The consequences of brain damage,' in L. Hudson (Ed.), *The Ecology of Human Intelligence*, Penguin, Harmondsworth, 1970, pp. 142–157.

Author Index

Subject Index